P9-CAR-974

The Complete Runner

By

The Editors of Runner's World

WORLD PUBLICATIONS
Post Office Box 366
Mountain View, Calif. 94040

© 1974 by
Runner's World Magazine
P.O. Box 366
Mountain View, CA 94040

No information in this book may be reprinted in
any form without permission from the publisher.

Library of Congress Catalog Card Number 74-83666

ISBN   0-89037-041-9

Second Printing, February, 1975

Published in the United States of America

CONTENTS

FOREWORD

The good times started with the "aerobics revolution" of the late 1960s. Other factors contributed to the growth spurt that was to come to running, but none so much as the work of Dr. Kenneth Cooper. Cooper, author of the *Aerobics* books, brought running to the common man and woman.

Aerobics, *New Aerobics* and *Aerobics for Women* preach the gospel of endurance fitness to a receptive congregation. Several million books have sold. And even if a tenth of the buyers practiced what Cooper preaches, they had the numbers to give running a new shape.

Most of those in the aerobics generation were non-athletes. They originally ran not for sport but to shake off the decay of age and neglect. Formerly, almost everyone who ran did it with competition as an end. And few runners competed unless they could do well at it, meaning few raced unless they were fast by nature and were at an age when speed was highest. Running was an elite sport.

Aerobics changed that. Men and women who started by running once around the block found that they progressed rather quickly to the top of Dr. Cooper's fitness standards. Many looked beyond fitness. They looked to low-key road races. They, not the elite from the schools, turned road racing into a thriving sport that supports 150 marathons a year in the United States and turns out almost 2000 runners a year at Boston.

The aerobics generation spawned the over-40 program, which opened up the sprints and hurdles as well as the distances to older competitors of both sexes. They wrote a new definition of competition, which is, "We're doing as well as we can within our physical limitations. If we do that, we're winners." They created a new atmosphere of acceptance for all runners, simply by becoming an everyday sight on the tracks and streets.

Running is more open now and more fun than it was just a few years ago when competition in its narrowest definition was the only reason to be in it. It has a diversity of people and opportunity which few sports can match. Anyone can run now—whether it be for fitness, for speed or simply for the primitive joy of it.

Men and women run, children under 10 and their grandparents over 60. They run 50 yards and 50 miles. They run miles in 3:50 and 10 minutes. They make running their whole life, and they spend less than an hour a week at it. It isn't possible to give a single definition of a runner, and we don't want to try.

Runners have differences. Never have there been so many different types of them. They run, act and think differently—and this is good for the sport. It was small and somewhat dull when everyone in it was about the same. Running, as it has grown up since aerobics, prides itself in having room for everyone.

Runner's World magazine has tried its best to further running in this spirit. The magazine was born and grew up in the early aerobics era. Most of the current subscribers, not to mention the editorial contributors, are aerobics graduates. Aerobics got them started in running, and *RW* and the *Runner's Monthly Booklets* kept feeding their interest as it matured.

Half of each magazine and most of the booklets concentrate on practical material. The articles tell how to run and how to promote running. Unfortunately, many of the runners who need these articles most never see them. They don't subscribe to the publications or started subscribing too late to read what they need. They lose or throw away old magazines and don't have them when a question comes up. They try to reorder and find the issues are out of print.

In 1971, we solved some of these problems by bringing out *Guide to Distance Running*. It was, and is, a popular volume, but has two limitations: (1) It covers only distance running and (2) much of the sport's growth—both in terms of numbers and knowledge—has happened since 1971.

The Complete Runner fills in the gaps of distance and time. It was at the time of publication in mid-1974 the biggest project this company had ever undertaken. It had to be this way because running had grown so much. The book is "complete' in the sense that it covers all running distances, shortest to longest, and all kinds of runners. It also crosses the spectrum of ideas and opinions.

RW always has been a forum for varying ideas from the varied people in the sport. This book has a similar forum-like organization presenting various viewpoints on 14 different running topics ranging from "Philosophy" to "Promotion."

Joe Henderson, September 1974

1

PHILOSOPHY

THE NEW FRONTIER

Dr. George Sheehan is author of the medical advice column in Runner's World. Dr. Howard Mickel is an associate professor of religion at Wichita State University. Garrett Tomczak is a runner and philosophy student. This series of articles orginally appeared in Runner's World, April 1973.

Going Beyond Fitness

BY DR. GEORGE SHEEHAN

Most recreational directors, physical education instructors, and promoters of exercise-for-your-health programs feel much the same as the fellow who finds it difficult to give away five-dollar bills down Main Street. People just won't believe it's for real.

The programs they prescribe seem so sensible and so in keeping with our nature it is incredible that people don't accept them. But facts are facts and there is no use railing against them. If the plane won't fly, there's no use appealing that the blueprints said it would. A bridge that insists on collapsing in defiance to all engineering theory will not respond to oaths and imprecations. Nor will our neighbors bestir themselves to physical activity unless we find the proper approach to the problem.

This approach will have go to back to basics. Where did we go wrong and how can we fight it? How can men be motivated to do what's good for them? Motivation is the main factor in the continuation of any activity, and especially in adult athletics where there is no longer the need to continue in compulsory school exercise and sports activity. Indeed it is just that transition period from school to work and marriage which carries with it the critical choice to continue in sport and exercise or not.

This would seem to suggest that exercise and sport and the maximum use of the body is not part of our nature, and that students have not been given (a) adequate instruction in the totality of the body and the role of physical fitness in our mental and psychological development, or (b) sports and activities tailored to their person and personality.

It seems self-evident that the quality of one's life is determined by the state of one's health. From time's beginnings health has been considered the sine qua non of the good life. "When health is absent," wrote Herophilus, the physician to Alexander the Great, "wisdom cannot reveal itself, art cannot become manifest, strength cannot fight, wealth becomes useless, and intelligence cannot be applied."

A run above Golden Gate Bridge, with the skyline of San Francisco as a backdrop. (Bill Reynolds photo)

Strong words, but this seems a poor argument in the current ineffectual campaigns against cigarettes and booze and drugs, lack of exercise.

Threats fail. Horror stories of future heart attacks, diabetes and strokes have predictably fallen on deaf ears. People are not inclined to do something just because it is good for them. Athletics in schools should be chosen on the basis of what the teachers would like to do themselves. This is the rule followed by James Herndon, author of *How to Survive in Your Native Land*. What you don't do, the students won't do, was what Herndon found out.

"Why should we assume that the kids would want to do a lot of stuff that we didn't want to do, and wouldn't ever do of our own free will?" he asks. "Does the math teacher go home at night and do a few magic squares? Does the English teacher go home at night and diagram sentences?"

What about the physical education teacher? What about the other teachers? Can't they bring to the student the vitality of the drama, the esthetics that they themselves get out of the sport? Can we find coaches who can make lifelong athletes out of their students?

We have forgotten that we are talking about play. We are dealing with one of the primary categories of life, one which resists all logical interpretation. Play has a deeper basis than utility. It exists of and for itself.

When we expose play to the function of promoting fitness and preventing heart attacks, we change its gold to dross. As countless fairy tales have told us, the choice of treasure over truth will always fail. What we need then is to conserve those mysterious and elusive elements of play which make it its own reward. We must remove anything that suggests practicality and usefulness. What we do must be fun and impractical and useless, or else we won't do it. If we become fit and impervious to heart attacks and all those other dread diseases, it will be because we don't care if we drop dead doing what we like to do.

We should be in sports not because they are practical but because they're not, not because we feel better but because we don't care how we feel, not because our fitness is increased but because we are so interested we don't even notice.

Play is the key. We all love to play. We like only the jobs that have a play element for us. Anything as practical as physical education or physical fitness is not going to get to first base with most of us.

Going Beyond Competition

BY DR. HOWARD MICKEL

Through the years, it has gradually dawned on me that I am a "humanistic" athlete. I run to get more out of life, to increase the human potential. This discovery has been very important to me. In fact, it is one of the best things that has happened to me in the last 12 years.

I used to be primarily a competitive athlete. But by the time I reached 20, I was training very little and sporadically. I gained weight, felt loggy, thought my lack of zest for life was just normal "old age." I felt that a regular exercise program might help. After all kinds of trials and errors, I finally began running longer and longer distances with less fatigue and more enjoyment.

More important, I discovered a new way of looking at and appreciating running. I found myself getting a great kick out of bettering my own earlier performances, transcending my own potential rather than beating opponents. I enjoyed the very feel of my body and its rhythms, the production of sweat, the love affair that developed between myself and Kansas skies, country roads, grass, ponds and wind. I regained the vital thrust I thought I had lost because of "old age." I can body-surf for hours and enjoy it. Roll down a hill with my kids and laugh. Run a mile faster than I did in my high school gym class. I feel physically alive to a degree that I didn't think possible 12 years ago. (However, one of my wise-guy college-age friends claims it is "fey"—the artificial euphoria that precedes death.) While running, I have met others who have a new lease on life through "humanistic" training. Because of the high promise for individuals as well as athletics as a whole, it seems highly important to carefully assess the ideal of the "humanistic athlete" as compared with the more familiar type, the competitive athlete.

Competitive athlete: He is primarily concerned with the highest possible athletic success within a competitive social system. His tradition is a long and venerable one—going back to ancient Greece and Rome when the word "athlete" emerged as "one who contends for a prize." The competitor is concerned with winning—rank, records, fame, awards—all types of recognition for accomplishment within the competitive social system. By focusing on athletic success, the competitive athlete must subordinate other areas of his life such as study, work, family and social responsibilities in order to fulfill his dominant goal.

"The values he receives from sport do not depend ultimately on the competitive system." (John Cooper photo)

The competitive athlete cannot be described simply as an alienated man striving for empty, extrinsic rewards, like a donkey following a carrot tied to a stick on his neck. Rather, his training and discipline directly contribute to athletic success and some intrinsic rewards, involving the thrill of participation, the joy of triumph, the glamor of success. There are, in addition, many other human and highly educational values in the life of the competitive athlete: meeting interesting competitors, building a strong body, enriching travel experience, etc.

What distinguishes the competitive athlete from others is that the goal of athletic success within a competitive system and its rewards is dominant in his thinking. He is most as home in the values of Reich's Consciousness II: status, power, success and—perhaps most important of all—the drive for excellence. The American competitive system has been remarkably effective at stimulating enormous improvements in athletic performance. If you look at world records in such sports as track and field, weight lifting and swimming since World War II, it is clear that most current performances were beyond the imagination of athletes a generation ago.

Humanistic athlete: However great the potential value of the competitive athlete as an ideal type, there are a growing number of well-rehearsed defects in the American competitive system that have helped stimulate the growth of what I call the humanistic athlete. The humanistic athlete, like his competitive counterpart, has developed skill in a sport, exercise or game requiring physical strength, agility or stamina.

What distinguishes the humanistic athlete is that he feels the major purpose of athletics is to fulfill the human potential and produce the playful enjoyment and sense of achievement that comes from self-actualizing activity. The values he receives from sport do not depend ultimately on the competitive system. He may, for example, run all of his life without entering a race.

The humanistic athlete is most at home in many of the values of Consciousness III: wonder, honesty, growth, non-competitiveness, brotherhood, play. The point of competition—if indeed he does compete—is not to vanquish another but, by facing worthy opponents, to force oneself to new levels of performance.

Second, the humanistic emphasis upon human values may provide a much needed alternative to unrestrained "winning-at-all-costs" that frequently results in the loss of human values and potential. Some of these human losses include unnecessary athletic injuries, the creation of burned-out athletes, the moral scandals and deceits that permeate college athletics. Most serious is the production of many athletes living, eating and studying in "athletic ghettos," who appear largely untouched by the college experience because of the demands that drain them of motivation, time and attention.

Third, the humanistic athlete can remind the competitor that college athletics, for example, is but one stage in a life-long involvement in sports that can become increasingly beneficial and enjoyable. All too frequently, the day after the competitive season is over, athletic fields are deserted. Was the college athlete running for his school, medals?

The humanistic athlete, by his example and influence, can challenge the college athlete to re-evaluate athletics in terms of its contribution to his own life and others as a human being, rather than a member of a team or school whose value is assumed.

Practical suggestions: A whole spectrum of new possibilities might emerge if we began looking at sport from a new humanistic-competitive perspective. Among these new possibilities might be:

1. The creation of local "total" amateur athletic organizations

that would include all ages, sexes and types of athletes and activities within its flexible structure.

2. More physical education courses designed along humanistic lines that would utilize every activity from yoga to interval running to increase the human potential of the student.

3. The entrance of more humanistic teachers and alumni onto our school and college athletic boards to promote an increased humanistic orientation in competitive sports.

The final vision: The steady, breath-taking improvement in world records in all sports, and the amazing conditioning of runners in their 40s, 50s and 60s, is giving a new, exciting vision of what human potential can be. But I am convinced that if we are to achieve the full-orbed completion of this vision, the competitive and humanistic athlete must move toward it together.

This typology does not attempt to cover all types of athletes; merely two kinds—the competitive and the humanistic athlete. It is not my purpose to force everyone into one of two cubbyholes, but to clarify dominant concerns in athletics. One competitive athlete may be so humanistic in his approach to sports that he is hardly distinguishable from a humanistic athlete who is highly competitive. For example, when Ron Daws says, "You run because you want to see if you can make yourself do it." I am not sure if he is a competitive or humanistic athlete. However, the purpose here is not to be 100% effective in typing athletes, but to provide conceptual tools that can be helpful in bringing the motive and behavior of most athletes into sharper focus.

Stages of athletics: Despite some current conflicts between the humanistic and competitive athletes, I believe the two types can complement and enrich one another. In fact, these two types of athletes may be largely related to different stages in the life cycle of man. The years of maximum physiological strength and speed may be the "competitive years," while the age of childhood and advanced years are the "humanistic years" (though there are college athletes who are humanists and over-40 runners who are definitely competitors in their orientation to sport).

At the psychological level, the competitive athlete may be fulfilling what Abraham Maslow calls "basic needs"—the need for respect, self-esteem, worth—while the humanistic athlete, typically in the midst of a successful career, may be making headway toward the higher needs of self-actualization, the fulfillment of potential.

Both/and: The humanistic and the competitive athlete need one another and can enrich the lives of one another. Since the competitive value system has a dominance in our society, its values are so well-known and strong that I will cite just two.

The humanist needs the competitor, first of all, as an inspiring instance of the drive for excellence (Consciousness II). A great part of the ability to extend one's capacities is mental, a confident belief that training will allow you to surpass previous frontiers of strength and performance. Seeing Frank Shorter run the Olympic marathon in a little over five minutes a mile somehow stimulates my belief in my own middle-aged potentialities.

Second, the humanist needs the new knowledge regarding training techniques, diet, physiology, etc., that is largely being developed by the competitive athlete and coach.

At the same time, the humanist can make important but less recognized contributions to the life of the competitor. For one thing, the humanist can be a gentle reminder to the competitor that there are important values outside of the competitive social system and its rewards. The way to measure "success" is not only by the standards of the competitive social system, but how athletics contributes to the unfolding of human capacity, growth, joy. Recognition of this fact liberates the competitor from looking at himself as valuable only in terms of the competitive social system's definition of success, and can free him for the task of developing himself to the full extent of his powers *in his own terms.*

Big Sport, Little Sport

It happens every Saturday night during the winter. Large crowds fill smoky arenas to see runners on tight little tracks. Indoor track is big business. It isn't set up for the athlete, but is packaged for the excitement of the spectator and the profit of the promoter.

It happens every Sunday morning during the winter. A couple of hundred runners gather in the corner of a parking lot for a road run. There are no lines for registration because there is no registration. They don't wait around at the end for results because no results are tabulated. They simply run and the single official calls out times from a watch at the end. The promoters themselves run and there are no spectators except other runners.

Some of the people from both these areas perfect their running, not for the sake of profit but for the sake of the art.

Bil Gilbert, who coaches a girls' track team in Pennsylvania, put labels on these three levels of sport in a brilliant article at the end of 1972 for *Sports Illustrated* called "Gleanings from a Troubled Time."

"There is first True Sport," he says, "the manifestation of man's seemingly innate urge to play. True Sport is organized for and often by participants, and is essentially a private matter like eating or making love.

"High Sport is True Sport raised to the level of art by the talent, even genius, of its participants. It is public in the sense that all art is public. (Great music, painting, literature or sport is incomplete until that time when it is displayed, judged and acclaimed.)

"Finally, there is Big Sport in which elements of True and High Sport are present but are modified by other considerations, notably commerce and politics."

In running terms, True Sport is the Sunday morning runs, where no results are recorded or reported. The run itself is the thing.

The big marathons, like Boston or the Olympic Trials, are the next step up to High Sport. The runners there have perfected their form to the point where it attracts some attention and criticism, but not to where it is a paying or political proposition.

The pay and politics are part of the Big Sport circuit, notably in indoor track, at the Olympic Games, and on the new pro track tour.

Political groups and businesses, Gilbert says, start with good intentions but grow rigid and defensive with time.

"Human organizations are created as instruments for achieving some practical end. They are purposeful... But as instruments age and increase in power, they devote less and less of their energies to satisfying the needs for which they were created. They become concerned with perpetuating themselves. In short, they become institutions.

"Instruments are aggressive, flexible, innovative, often both efficient and ruthless. Institutions tend to react slowly and be wasteful, needing more resources to accomplish less. They are characterized by bureaucracies that are fearful of change, and thus enamored with consistency as an operating principle since consistency greatly reduces both the necessity for being ingenious and the element of risk. As time passes, institutions devote increasing energy to

"True Sport is the play of children, or of adults who for a moment want to be like children again." (Paul Sutton photo)

self-inflating projects of a public relations nature."

Gilbert thinks Big Sport inevitably takes on this institutional
philosophy. As a result, "the quality of sport almost inevitably de-
clines. Each year play becomes more regimented, conservative and
less playful."

True Sport is the play of children or of adults who for a moment want to be like children again. There is no special preparation needed to play.

Graduating to High Sport means putting the element of work,
training, preparation into it.

"High Sport," Gilbert says, "is the creation of geniuses, the
exceptionally talented and passionate. It satisfies the same needs
as other arts. It provides a medium and method of expression by
which the talented can comment on themselves and their world.
High Sport artists also serve their audiences by stimulating them to
consider the nature of man and the world."

Gilbert says True Sport is to High Sport as a craft is to an art, and that Big Sport is to the other two as a "plastic angel (is) to sculpture and pottery."

He doesn't see much future in Big Sport.

"Given the tenacity with which all institutions seek to preserve themselves, and the considerable resources of many of our institutions, the professional and pseudo-amateur circuits may linger for some time. As they struggle to maintain themselves, it seems probable that they will be decreasingly concerned with sport and become increasingly show-biz operations."

Gilbert seems to welcome the predicted decline and fall of show-biz sports. He sees no serious consequences in it "since even now they serve little purpose other than perpetuating themselves."

As for the future of True Sport (and by implication High Sport as well), it "seems to be in as good or better shape than ever. Because True Sport is necessary and useful, it would appear to have about the same survival prospects as those of man himself."

Is the Pain Necessary?

BY GARRETT TOMCZAK

"How did philosophers ever come to think that man is an animal which seeks pleasure and avoids pain?"

This is not the introduction to an abstract philosophical essay, but a question from one runner to another at the completion of a staggeringly hot and hilly marathon as an ambulance, siren screaming, drove to the aid of a collapsed runner. In such circumstances, one is inclined to doubt that the search for pleasure and the avoidance of pain are universal characteristics of mankind.

One might ask if there can be any pleasure so laboriously won and so dangerously indistinguishable from pain as is the marathon experience. Although the majority of runners do not, thank God, suffer the extreme of complete physical incapacitation, the gamut of bodily discomfort (blisters, aches, dispossessed toenails and all manner of fatigue) make long distance running a highly questionable activity for one who makes pleasure his primary aim.

Marathoning can be extremely demanding, onerous and sometimes physically dangerous. It cannot be taken as a self-evident source of pleasure (except, of course, by those whose philosophical disposition or physical makeup does not allow pain to be a factor in the marathoning encounter). A marathon demands hours of relatively painful effort, in sometimes very uncomfortable circumstances, when the day might well be spent watching television or sleeping as an air conditioner softly hums away the heat.

We are generally taught in our society that the healthy man is the normal man, and that the healthy man is free from pain. The problem of pain is usually limited to the question of how to combat it. To be told of someone who welcomes pain is to receive a shock. This is not the way we are accustomed to thinking about ourselves.

The non-runner, convinced that we are masochistic and misguided madmen, watches our efforts in bewilderment and incredulity, as though we were teetering, *en masse*, on a ledge high over a busy intersection rather than merely lining up for the start of a race.

There would be little need to discuss the question of pain at all if marathoners actually were masochists. One could simply dismiss the activity as perverse and emotionally unhealthy and be done with it. Public opinion to the contrary, it doesn't appear to be as easy as all that.

If marathoning is sometimes painful, and a runner accepts that pain as part of the total experience—whether for a best time, a coveted award, or simply because dropping out could cause more distress than the worst physical pain—does it necessarily follow that he is a masochist? Probably not.

A masochist is one who is confused about what is painful and what is pleasurable. If nothing else, a marathon makes a very clear distinction between the two states. If an individual fails to catch that distinction, perhaps he is a masochist. For the most part, though, those who have experienced pain while running are more than aware of the fact and are unlikely to mistake it for enjoyment.

The danger is not so much that runners may be masochists. It is that, in striving to deny that label, they risk the danger of believing that pain is somehow of no value. While pain is hardly fun, it should not lead one to think that it is necessarily without significance or importance.

Pain can have relevance in two rather distinct areas: physical health and spiritual awareness.

In the most elementary way, pain is nature's warning, letting the body know something is wrong. It is extremely difficult for an individual to live without pain sensitivity. The congenitally insensitive are known to damage and injure themselves repeatedly and without realization. In some cases, a person unequipped to feel pain can literally chew off his own tongue, choking and bleeding to death in the process. Few congentially insensitive persons live to adulthood.

There are many cases, though, of adult coaches and runners who can feel pain but try to act as if it doesn't exist. This myth of the unreality of pain is perpetuated every time an athlete persists in running on a bum leg or a coach dismisses an injury with, "It's all in your head."

Pain is not something which is strictly "in a person's head." Excluding the deliberate faker, all pain is real and should always be treated as such. Silent and absurdly stoic suffering can frequently lead to much more complicated injuries and the possibility of permanent physical damage (such as ending up at 40 years of age with traumatic arthritis—not an uncommon ex-athlete malady).

In addition to the importance of pain in warning an individual of impending injury, there are other values to pain which can significantly contribute to a person's growth in humanity and awareness. If an individual is rational and intelligent, he will soon recognize and understand his pains—and know which ones are warning lights and which are challenges.

These challenges, or "growing pains," can be seen as the birth-pangs of transition to better things—to a more fully potentiated level of individual existence. We don't grow through fun or pleasure; we grow through pain. Pain is the transition between different and ever higher levels of consciousness. It can open up profound depths whose existence is not even suspected by the man who goes gaily on his way, untried by pain. As Dostoyevski has said, "Suffering is the sole origin of consciousness."

A person may "lose" himself in fun, but can only truly find himself through suffering. A marathon, for example, is a way for a man to seek out his limits. It would be difficult to imagine that pursuit taking place without a confrontation with pain. A runner (or anyone else for that matter) who never pushes himself to the point of physical discomfort is obviously learning little about the range of his potential.

The pain of racing is undeniable, and perhaps even essential to giving the race meaning. (John Marconi photo)

If a man wants to know if he is awake or dreaming, he pinches himself. No other sensation demonstrates as clearly that he is "there." The marathon is a 26.2-mile pinch. It is not a stroll, a leisurely ride in the country, or a picnic on the grass. It is an experience and a revelation. One discovers things never discovered before.

The complete eradication of pain could result in one-sidedness uniformity, and consequently human indifference. The mastery of pain has to be learned, and civilized man is rapidly losing the art. Because he is accustomed to the elimination of pain, he is all the more helpless in those cases where it cannot be eliminated.

Pain impels a human being to make a personal decision, an act of will. The individual must decide whether to surrender to it, to suffer it or to fight it. A man cannot be truly free or have viable options if he is forever a slave to the fear of physical discomfort. The man who drinks beer and watches television all day is not free. He lives a very narrow and cautious existence.

To totally reject pain is to reject life itself. Those runners we suspect of not feeling pain, we refer to as "animals" or "machines." Man's grandeur, in a sense, stems from his knowledge of his own misery. An animal or a machine does not consciously understand itself to be miserable.

Pain is real and it is necessary—both physically and spiritually. Those who don't heed pain's warnings are doing a disservice to their bodies. Those who can't recognize its ability to increase awareness and expand humanity are doing a much greater injustice to their souls.

The marathon is one possible way in which a man can maintain contact with pain, and consequently with the glory which only comes from being a fully aware human being. It is suffering and then glory.

Perhaps, after reading my arguments in justification of pain and suffering, you would like to know how I behave when I am experiencing it.

I am a great coward.

Although I have run many marathons, and plan more in the future, the decision to run yet another is never lightly taken. I fear the pain of a marathon and this, in great part, is what gives it significance. Finishing the race conquers that fear of pain, and facing the formidable gives self-esteem.

And self-esteem is what can make a person a hero—if only to

himself. Heroism simply doesn't apply to those who are too cold to know apprehension, too confident to know fear, and too un-intelligent to understand pain or danger. I may not have the oppor-tunity to fly to the moon, rescue dragon-besieged damsels (beauti-ful or otherwise) or hold the Pass at Thermopylae. But I can run the marathon.

I am not arguing that pain is not painful. By definition, pain hurts. I am only saying that a man can choose to explore his capa-bilities and raise his level of consciousness through the vehicle of suffering.

TRANSCENDENTAL RUNNER

BY CRISPIN CUSACK

The writer of this article, which appears for the first time here,
is a distance runner and philosophy graduate from New Jersey.

"But I have promises to keep,
And miles to go before I sleep..."

He descends the stairway backwards, one step at a time, ignoring the glances of his neighbors. When he crosses the street, he
mounts the curb with a wrenching pain in his thighs. For the rest
of the day, he must seek support for himself when he rises or sits
down. That night, he rolls carefully into the bed from which he rose
so happily in the morning, in the hours before the marathon.

Running without grace, beauty or elegant style, the marathoner confronts distance, weather, terrain and endless time in an intense struggle to discover how well-tempered is the gentle fiber of
his flesh, how stern is the tinsel thread of his will.

Sawyer: *"You have been running well. You haven't been cautious—you've been laying it on from the very start... You are proud
of your run. You have run in front of the wind of fear..."*

Soon, the marathoner confronts himself in the reflections of
fatigue, images deeper and duller and more dragging than any pain.
The ugly hills hover over him, manifold. The first amoeboid clutch-
es of exhaustion grasp his innards. The leadened layers of burden
thicken into an immense crusted shell, leaving but one narrow, slender cord of residual energy to claim.

Sawyer: *"You are down to it now; the agony reaches deeper
and deeper, to the depth where it almost becomes abstract; the sur-
roundings become more and more vague, almost disappear... Your
overpowering desire: to be released from this—but on your own
terms... You desperately want to (stop), simultaneously to (continue). The two tides of impulse surge against each other within
you..."*

All sensibility and purpose recede into a viscous quagmire

of doubt. The last sediments of volition fade away and the marathoner enters a hair-width corridor of resolve in which survival looms as the only discernible end. His companions in pain cry and cough and curse and wobble and (some) walk to the last half-mile. Inspired by the gusts of hope latent in the imminent release of so many fathoms of fatigue, a last heartbreak of will gets the runner to recall the correct procedures of running. There is no other reality...

Athletics historian George Gretton has written in *Out in Front* that "the immense strain imposed by the marathon...is not comparable with anything else in athletics."

Roger Bannister, the first sub-four-minute miler, has called it "the acme of athletic heroism."

Veteran marathoner Hal Higdon has admitted that "immediately after almost every marathon, I have sworn that it would be my last."

A doctor, Fred Blanton, said after finishing the Boston maraton, "I learned how much the body can stand. You don't know what pain is until you get up around 21 or 22 miles. You just hurt like hell. You'd give anything to quit, but you just keep going."

Former world record holder Buddy Edelen wrote of his first marathon: "The last six miles can seem an eternity, the last three miles can seem longer than the first 23 miles... I didn't ever want to go through as much pain, torture and hell again. I was actually crying."

Sheehan: *"It is a pain that is sometimes forgotten like the pains of childbirth, so that a runner...reaches the 21-mile mark and suddenly the pain is there. And for the first time he remembers how terrible it was the last time, and how terrible it is going to be now in the forever that is this race..."*

Moore: *"The pain in a marathon's closing stages can be so great as to force meaning upon the run... Men submit to the ordeal not in spite of the pain but because of it...The distance and discomfort already endured scream that this must not be for nothing, so you go on. Afterward, in the dressing room, men hang stiffly on one another, too exhausted to untie their shoes...*

Yet in the dull reflections immediately following the race, somewhere within the first comforts of physical release, lies cradled the infant idea of all who challenge the marathon:

Sheehan: *"Sooner or later he will think about running the*

marathon again... not, perhaps, slumped in the locker room, or on his hands and knees taking a shower... But sooner or later. Because the perfect marathon is like the perfect wave, and every marathoner keeps looking for it."

The power of an almost fanatic devotion seems to possess the marathoner's enthusiasm. "It is, after all," warns British running coach Brian Mitchell, "one activity among many and a fast (race) is not as valuable as a Beethoven Symphony. The (race) takes in part of what the symphony totally covers." Yet the aura of a unique essence contained in the pursuit of the marathon forces one to question: why do they do it?

Runners begin an answer by way of analogy:

Sheehan: *" 'Why climb mountains?' is a question, which, it turns out, cannot be satisfactorily answered even by mountain climbers. Every one, of course, attempts an answer. But all freely admit that the whole truth is not there. The whole truth, they imply, cannot be captured."*

Moore: *"It's like trying to explain pretty colors to someone blind from birth."*

Fifty-five-year-old age record holder Paul Reese has added, "Someone who asks, 'What is love?' has never been in love; someone who asks, 'why do you run?' has never run. Only lovers and runners know."

A successful young champion, Bob Deines, says, "We can talk about it, but we shouldn't transfer the reality of the race to the talk."

Frank Shorter, American Olympic marathon winner in 1972, states flatly, "To tell you the truth, I hate to talk about it." The muteness of those who run the marathon suggests something of a presence, something to be revealed only from behind the physical curtain...

Thoreau: *Perhaps the facts most astounding and most real are never communicated by man to man."*

This dilemma finds partial settlement in what Dylan Thomas called "...the soul and the spinning head."

Neil Cusack en route to his victory in the 1974 Boston marathon. (Jeff Johnson photo)

Sawyer: *"For whatever value such classification has, I see it (running) as an art. It is a creative art, demanding discipline and shrouded in unfathomable mystery... The runner is an artist. There is a creative energy within, surging to manifest itself, burning to manifest itself, even in a strange way disconnected from the person— the run flowing through the person... He must do it... When he is in the midst of it, the work of art must be produced."*

Joe Henderson, editor of *Runner's World* quotes George Leonard in *Education and Ecstasy:* "Primitive man did not see art apart from life. He seems to have been indifferent toward his cave painting or scultpure once it was completed. We find the same cave wall painted over and over again. The important thing was not the finished work but the act of making it."

Sawyer: *"Running* is. *The ultimate reality is the* doing *of the running."*

If running is a primitive or formless art, it is nevertheless an authentic one—the beautiful lyric of an unspoken langauge. For the athlete with one foot in the locker room and one foot in the library, running is demonstrably poetic. Said Robert Frost: "A poem is a reaching out toward expression, an effort to find fulfillment." To shift the analogy, the blended oils of flesh, the internal canvases of mind, fleeting self-portraits painted in pain, these are the interior furnishings of an athlete's studio.

Thoreau: *Every man is the builder of a temple, called his body... We are all sculptors and painters, and our material is our flesh and blood and bones."*

The athlete entering his studio may enter the shadow-enclosed, hushed and secret world of upcoming hills. Frost: "Two roads diverged in a wood, and I—I took the one less-traveled by." Urged by the beckoning of the past, the haunt of the future, the runner can travel in rhyme "the life of muscles rocking soft/and smooth and moist in vernal heat." He can run miles of new wonder, miles of purely smooth flowing, all with an ease, all with a magical and persistant strength, all without need for explanation or logic.

Sheehan: *"All is suddenly as easy as a bird in flight."*

Sawyer: *"Your clarity of self-awareness is heightened to almost overwhelming levels... There is an energy exchange, nature to runner, runner to nature... It is the rare world of direct experience."*
Moore: *"It is common, once a person becomes well-condi-*

tioned, to run 20 miles through the hills and literally not feel tired."

At the close of such a session, the runner has no quarrel with his soul. Frost: "Drink and be whole again beyond confusion."

Thoreau: *All nature is your congratulations and you have cause momentarily to bless yourself... Of all ebriosity, who does not prefer to be intoxicated by the air he breathes?*

In the moments afterward, the runner contemplates his sense of good feeling balanced precisely upon the merit of his effort, an equilibrium of satisfaction, a dual respect for what he has done and what he has yet to do. He reflects...

Thoreau: *I never found the companion that was as companionable as solitude.*"

All that day and all that night, a long arm of exuberance extends through him, lifting him above the ground. Power thrusts beneath it all, contained, returned to itself after the unleashing, gathering itself again. Pride is here under the skin like muscle gained, solid and material within him. Something significant has happened internally, a gift, a birth, a mysterious contribution to inner space.

A serious young runner named Jim Colvin has formulated it for himself: "To run to me means to practice a religion that reflects life in a microcosm, that cleanses the entire man—mind and body— and that allows an almost mystical communication with nature and meditation on existence... Running allows me to communicate with an inner being."

Thoreau: *Direct your eye right inward and you'll find a thousand regions in your mind yet undiscovered.*"

The successful runner achieves something of the transcendentalist's solitary status in which observation and imagination blend to span the schism between mind and matter. He extends himself toward something beyond common scrutiny, something almost indecipherable, something at once natural and cultivated.

A contemporary psychiatrist, Alan McGlashin, has noted in *The Savage and Beautiful Country*: "For the profoundest questions the seeker himself is the essential instrument of the seeker." The runner, in the sensual euphoria of his inner soliloquy, discovers McGlashin's "central point within oneself: the secret threshhold where the world of the senses and the world of the psyche meet in mutual simultaneous recognition." For such a moment of illumination—the eternal *now* of the transcendentalist—dichotomies such as mental-physical, inner-outer and pain-pleasure are suspended while "a man for a timeless moment discovers his own Center." The runner often wonders whether or not he has brushed against, however momentarily, the shadow of a fourth dimension.

When such a fragile moment is discovered, it represents not the end but only the beginning. "All discovery," McGlashin asserts, "is at the deepest level rediscovery." The runner returns to training with yet another inward turn of the heart. Midway between hope and calculation, he plans. He plans and dreams and works for mastery. Flashes of new and old accomplishments dance before him, each finding in the other an odd reflection. His hopes glimmer, shine, dazzle his ego. The intangibility of success, of failure, startles him. He begins to build flimsy visions of attainment beyond him. He runs...

The day of the marathon, the runner returns to a restless gathering of enthusiasts. Says runner Norman Harris: "You live richly on the prospect of the approaching marathon... You feel someone special, with a special mission. You feel that you've got something no one else has."

At the same time, each runner bundles about him 1952 Olympic marathon champion Emil Zatopek's strong tone of soberness in the undertaking: "We are different in essence from normal men. Whoever wants to win something runs 100 meters. Whoever wants to experience something runs the marathon."

At the starting line the runner steels himself for a journey, an investigation. Sawyer, Sheehan, Moore and the rest meet in a shared vulnerability born of singular responsibility...

Thoreau: *I went to the woods because I wished to live deliberately, to front only the essential facts of life, and see if I could not learn what it has to teach... "*

Each envisions a great and powerful run, paced to perfection, confronted through every pain to the perfect end... At the finish line, two and a half, three, three and a half, four, four and a half hours later, each runner arrives at a resolution and conclusion: "I felt how great and how small I was," wrote the philosopher Kierkegaard in his *Journals,* "then did those two mighty forces, pride and humility happily unite in friendship."

"And that has made all the difference," Frost might add. Each runner who momentarily rides the crest of a personal wave one day, on a day when he is approaching yet another starting line at yet another starting time, *may* delve within himself and retrace his *Walden* and his Concord and regain the moment when, in the words of Thoreau:

"All that he could think was to... let his mind descend into his body and redeem it and treat himself with increasing respect."

Afterword: A distance runner desires, in Sheehan's words, "to possess experience rather than be possessed by it." Thoreau's aim at Walden Pond was to simplify his existence, clarify his senses, drive life into a corner and reduce it to its lowest terms. Thus, we see the marathoner as a modern day transcendentalist. His discoveries are not new, but recurrent. It is the same in writing. In this essay, I quote others freely. Reading them, I was, in Thoreau's terms, "distinctly made aware of a presence of something kindred to me." Benjamin Sawyer is a Santa Cruz educator who first competed in 1951 and has since run in over 200 races. George Sheehan is a New Jersey internist who writes medical and other columns for *Runner's World*. Ken Moore set an American record for the marathon in 1969.

YOU NEVER NEED TO LOSE

BY RAY WILL

Ray Will, a native of England who now lives in Canada, runs long distances and writes humor and fiction.

Sometimes I think the purists of our sport lose sight of what it's all about. To listen to them talk, you'd think that running is the passport to eternal bliss on earth. But one look at any runner's reddened face and unsteady post-race knees tells a different story.

Running is work, and hard work at that, and there are few of us who do it for the lofty motives of self-discovery and environmental awareness which have recently crept into our athletic vocabulary. And certainly some of us do it so that we may brag to our friends that we ran 20 miles today, though any self-respecting individual keeps quiet about a quirk like that.

No! Our motives are simple and untainted with idealistic mysticism. Plain, simple old greed and desire for glory keep most of us at it. A mention on the sports page, your name on the local radio station, even a photo in the church magazine. All this can be had simply by taking part and using the telephone afterwards.

And then there is winning, the supreme goal of all athletes. Winning brings with it more tangible rewards: prizes, medals and trophies. Trophies, of course, are the mainstay of every man's conversation. And one of the great advantages of running trophies is that they are rare (unless you're in the habit of mixing with other runners). Anyone who hasn't won a bowling trophy these days just hasn't been bowling. But what a conversation stopper a well-placed trophy can be!

I have a favorite that I always put out when we have visitors. "Aha!" they say, "What's this?" picking up the rusty statuette from its discreet hiding place in the center of the card table and reading the inscription out loud, "B.A.A. Road Race, Third Place, 1959."

"The initials B.A.A. stand for Boston Athletic Association," I say, modestly. "They have a marathon down there every year. You may have heard of it." And that's it. Only the Ron Hills of the world can top that, and I haven't actually lied.

The initials in my case stand for Bolterville Anglers Association and the road race was a 1½-mile downhill effort we organized as part of the mayor's fitness campaign. Of course, we had to let the mayor win, and one of the other three runners was sick half-way down the hill and had to drop out.

All of which goes to show that you don't have to wear your-self out to get recognition. The rewards are there for very little effort, provided you are prepared to use a little bit of imagination and ingneuity. In the words of the immortal C.J. (Crafty) Phitz-boyle, "You may not always be able to win, but you never need to lose."

In these fiercely competitive days, it isn't always easy for an individual to live up to this ideal. Even Bolterville now invites internationals to their annual road race. But at the interclub level, it isn't hard to make sure that your team never finishes behind any other team.

The number one rule here is "hospitality," and I can do no better than quote Phitzboyle again. In his book *Sports Injuries and How to Inflict Them* he writes, "...always insist on using your home ground. Demand that your team supply the refreshments, the first aid staff and the bulk of the officials. Above all be kind, kind, kind..."

And in that word "kind" lies the whole key to your success. I once saw an opponent reduced to tears by great kindness. It was a 100-yard race, and the visitors had each been guilty of a false start. The gun was up for the third time and the starter had called "set" when Crafty turned to the crouched figure on his left and said, "Excuse me, but isn't that a snake near your left foot?" At that moment the gun sounded and the man leaped into the air. He came down sobbing and kicking away hysterically at the skipping rope which had been carelessly dropped onto his blocks by Crafty's daughter on her way to the ice cream stand.

Of course, the effect on the man's teammate was disastrous. After all, you can't ignore your friends when they are going berserk. He led his companion away to the ambulance.

Crafty said afterwards, "It was unfortunate, but what if it had been a snake? I would never have forgiven myself." Noble words indeed.

It is in the sprints that some of the finest opportunities exist for demoralizing and even disqualifying the opposition. Even starting blocks provide enormous scope, particularly with young and

inexperienced competitors. One ploy that comes to mind is to take a look at their blocks while they are hammering them in, then walk out with a set of different style.

A typical approach goes like this: "Oh, I see you guys are still using the illegal blocks. Well, I don't mind personally, of course, but some of the others might object, particularly after that scandal at the Olympics. I'll tell you what, though, our guys are a decent bunch. I'll make sure that they don't protest unless the match result is at stake. So we'll see how it goes. Okay?"

Few men can run an uninhibited sprint after that sort of thing. Naturally, you offer to lend them a legal set, but these will be fixed permanently with rusted bolts in a position suitable for a dwarf with one leg nine inches longer than the other.

While on the subject of the shorter distances, some mention should be made of the importance of the starter. We have been lucky with Old Bill but few clubs are as fortunate. Old Bill is a veteran of World War I. He's past 80 now, and the war left him with infirmities that have not greatly affected his life but have made him invaluable as a starter. His greatest attribute is his reaction to the sound of the gun. Immediately after the shot, his eyes close and his index finger twitches violently, causing a second shot to be fired. Of course, our men know what is going to happen and never move out of their blocks. The opponents walk back, unnerved, each blaming the other for the false start. It is normally on the third try that Old Bill gets the finger under control.

In recent years, Old Bill's finger has been getting less reliable and our runners have sometimes been caught on the starting line waiting for the second shot that never comes. To overcome this, we enlist the help of a supporter's Great Dane, a terrible beast with the body of a moose, the head of a lion, the voice of a tiger and a playful habit of nipping at running ankles. If he is released at the halfway mark, the race will degenerate and have to be re-run.

If you do have to resort to deception, the local drama group may come in handy. We have used two charming old ladies from time to time in the "False Finish Line' ploy. This consists of placing the actors 10 yards in front of the finish line. If all else has failed, and the opposition are coming in first and second, one of the ladies walks across the track holding the end of a ball of string

"In recent years, Old Bill's finger has been getting less reliable and our runners have sometimes been caught..." (Doug Schwab)

while her companion holds the other end. Then, with our support-
ers screaming as if we are only inches behind, the two front runners
make a desperate lunge for the "tape." Often they fall over, or at
least slow down enough for us to pass them and carry on to the true
finish line.

The ladies are always terribly sorry. They were only getting
the knots out of their wool and didn't know there was a race on.
Once, one of them offered a fallen sprinter five dollars to make up
for it, and we disqualified him as a professional when he accepted.
What's more, it took him the rest of the season to get himself rein-
stated.

I can think of no better conclusion to this article than the definition of the word "sprint" from C. J. Phitzboyle's great work
The Art and Craft of Craft: "... let us not forget then that the sprint
is the race in which nothing is more certain than that he of the quick
body and slow mind will be overcome by he who is endowed the
other way around." Indeed, the race will not always go to the swift-
est.

The following is a list of recommended further reading that
should be of help: *The Training of Sporting Dogs*, by Maj. Gen. S.
Smythington-Smyth-Smith; *Mental Cruelty, Theory and Practice*,
by deSade deSade; *How to Sublimate Your Conscience*, by Cecil
Wiggins (19th century doctor who murdered eight wives).

2

PSYCHOLOGY

WHAT MAKES THEM RUN?

BY JIM McFADDEN

Jim McFadden, a high school coach from Iowa, is a frequent contributor to Runner's World and to various coaching journals.

Much has been written in the last several decades about the *how* and *why* of training distance runners. Generally this information has taken the form of listing *how much* of *what distance* the champion athlete runs in his workouts, and the physiological explanation of what this work does to the body's ability to perform in competition. This approach of examining championship performance may be oversimplified and can be misused to condition some runners for failure rather than for success.

These studies have been valuable research and can be an asset to both the athlete and the coach. But workout schedules should not be looked on as the "secret" way to run the four-minute mile and followed religiously. These schedules should first be looked at as outlines of the principles of successful training and then be adapted to suit the individual's own needs and the local situation. By comparing different successful schedules, it will become clear that *many and varied* forms of physical training can lead to racing success.

Another point to be considered when looking at the champion's workouts is that the physical work may be only half or a third of the elements that combined to make his success possible. Seldom touched upon is the sensitive psychological buildup that goes into a championship performance.

Preliminary investigations into why some runners are faster than others was first carried out along the lines of work, the theory being that the best runners do the *most* or *best* training. It was often seen that this is not true. The investigation then turned toward physiological differences in successful runners, but again results could not be strictly correlated to physical differences or advantages. Some of the world's top runners have been found to have rather average pulse rates and lung capacities. In fact, some great champions have even overcome physical *handicaps* and become record setters.

All these studies are important and are not to be ignored by the aspiring distance runner and his coach. However, knowledge alone is not the final answer. Records have been set and championships won by athletes who knew little or nothing about all the studies that have been done.

Marcello Fiasconaro, the world 800-meter record breaker, has been quoted as saying, "My ignorance is my strength. I know neither the history or tactics of the 800 meters, so fast times do not worry me."

The African mile star, Filbert Bayi, has said "I have found that the Europeans train twice as much as I do." Did this bother Bayi, who beat all the best Europe had to offer? Not at all! He continued, "150 miles a week is good conditioning, I guess, but I doubt if it would help *me* run faster."

More work may not be the answer for many other runners, either, nor the tutelage of a famous coach, unless the athlete makes the more important mental change that results in his visualization of success. If the runner does not achieve this proper "mental set," he may change coaches, training schedules and diets endlessly without achieving the desired results. Scientific evidence has shown that the human brain and nervous system is a complex "goal-striving mechanism" that operates to accomplish the *aims* of the individual. These facts cannot be ignored.

The limited approach of discussing training and racing merely in terms of necessary work often may do as much harm as good. A coach may unintentionally be training the athlete's body and at the same time be "blocking" his mind. By taking the attitude, "If you can't run 12 x 440 in 59 seconds, you'll never run a four-minute mile," a coach may be limiting performance.

The runner can develop harmful identifications about success and failure, resulting in his becoming *mentally tired* when he reaches his *expected limits*, thus suffering anxiety and failure. Coaches often give up on a runner because, "He just doesn't have it," while there is still only a vague idea, at this time, exactly what *it* is.

It may be a problem of "self-image" that makes the athlete tired when he goes faster than his expected limits. A coach must be very careful not to transfer the limitations of his own thinking to his athletes.

A runner does not train in a vacuum. His environmental circumstances must certainly play an important role in his success or failure. Olympic champion, Dave Wottle, told *Sports Illustrated* that at Bowling Green University, "We all train in a group and we all draw *strength* from the group." This group has produced Wottle, steeplechase record holder Sid Sink and a record setting four-mile relay team. Isn't it significant that often when a new record breaker appears, he is part of a group or "school" of runners from one nation, one team or club, or one coach?

It is very likely that the group dynamics plays an important part in each of the individual's success. The runners receive a "positive charge" from one another. Their expectations are high. This effect could well be related to Finland's emergence, with Vaatainen, Vasala, Viren and Paivarinta all winning major titles in a two-year span. It is just as likely that a runner can receive a "negative charge" from a group or coach whose expectations are low.

Some of the success that individual runners have had with the "long steady distance" type of racing preparation may well be that it unclutters the mind of the athlete. He simply runs and thinks about his goals and his success. His mind is not blocked with demanding schedules, the anxiety of "pass or fail" type interval workouts. He does not have to psych-up or bear with workouts. Instead, he runs free and stores up his psychic energy for the race. Each of us has only limited effective energy with which to pursue our goals, running and otherwise. If this energy is wasted on failure anxieties, it cannot be used for dynamic pursuit of improved performance.

As new limits are visualized, new records are achieved—as can be observed in the progress of the world records. This idea also holds true with each individual. The runner must visualize himself capable of a high-level performance before he can unlock the effort necessary to achieve these goals. Most runners *wish* they could do well, but only a few *will*.

Percy Cerutty of Australia tried to express some of these ideas in his writings more than a decade ago, but many overlooked his real message and got lost in the sand dunes and barbells. A runner must set personal records, school records, club records, conference records, etc., before he is ready to visualize greater records. The athlete's mind must go through stages of evolution, leaping from one *realization* to the next.

Miler Jim Ryun once said, "Once I've made it up in my mind, it just sort of comes out." In the pre-Olympic season of 1972, Ryun was a classic example of an athlete in great shape who could not perform at his maximum level because "mental brakes" had tied up his physical power. Ryun, a sub-four-minute miler, found him-

self struggling to run miles in 4:19. Who knows how many other
4:19 milers could run four minute miles, if they could release their
"mental brakes" and really visualize themselves as capable of such
efforts!

Of course runners and coaches spend a lot of time talking about
work, and not enough time talking and thinking about what they
are trying to accomplish. What are the specific goals? What times
are being tried for. Which races are the most important? There
should be clearly defined objectives, not just aimless working out
to get in shape.

Reread the books written by outstanding coaches and read between the lines, hunt for clues, understand that physical work is
just one piece of the "training puzzle." Remember that the champion's training environment, morale, mental approach and interaction with others around him may be as important as the amount or
kind of work that he does. Don't just copy schedules. Think, challenge, motivate and have real goals, to go after with *mind* and *body!*

"It is very likely that the group dynamics plays an important
part in each individual's success..." This group at Boston, 1974,
is made up of 1705 individuals. (Jeff Johnson photo)

MARATHONERS' THINKING

BY NORMAN LUMIAN

Norman Lumian, a veteran southern California runner, conducted the following study of marathoners a number of years ago, but this is the first time his conclusions have appeared in print.

"I was psyched out!"

"I was psyched up!"

These phrases regularly emerge from the mouths of all athletes. Those of us who have taken part in any sport on the competitve level can empathize as we, too, recall many instances when we were "psyched" one way or another.

Although one might be hard-pressed to prove it, it is possible that distance runners suffer more psychological stress than other sportsmen. Marathoning, in particular, is an almost entirely individualistic sport, and the duration of the competition seems endless at times.

With these basic assumptions about the psychological aspects of long distance runners in mind, Victor Krumdick and I conducted a two-part survey on 50 marathoners who competed in the United States Pan-American Games Trials of 1962. Many years have passed, yet the data we collected is still applicable to the psychology of marathon running.

The psychological aspects of the survey's results which seem most pertinent were (1) the reasons why they decided to become distance runners; (2) the goals that continued to interest them in the sport, and impelled them to enter marathon races, and (3) the one major incident or event during this particular marathon which made it a personal success or a failure.

Why become a distance runner? "Please discuss the one event in your life which had the greatest effect upon your becoming a distance runner," was one of the items in the pre-race questionnaire. Most of the reactions could be included in one of the following categories: (1) the influence of coaches, families and friends; (2) the first exposure to distance running success in a physical education class (after usually having been frustrated in other sports), and (3) the examples provided by the performances of former great distance runners.

The encouragement and influence of coaches, friends and families was not only instrumental in creating the initial interest in distance running, but in maintaining it as well. Nineteen (nearly 40%) of those questioned referred to this psychological aspect.

The following quotation typifies those found in the pre-race survey: "My meeting with Coach X has had the greatest influence on my becoming a distance runner. He has made me *want* to run. He has shown me it *is* possible to attain goals I set for myself each year."

Another spoke glowingly of a former high school coach: "Having X as my coach in high school for three years definitely has had the most influence on me. I sincerely mean this; a young kid starting out couldn't have a better coach."

Sometimes, discouraging remarks can fuel an athletic fire, too, as this atypical comment reveals:

"As a freshman in high school, when I first went out for cross-country, some of the runners on the varsity tried to discourage me. They said I would never make the team or be able to beat them. So I had to prove I could beat them."

On the other hand, no fewer than four entrants in this race singled out one other competitor's positive influence as the "one event" which had turned them to distance running.

Although physical education students usually complain bitterly when they are forced to complete a timed distance run, the results of the effort can be quite dramatic—in a positive way. Seven of the respondents indicated that success in this type of test was the "one event" which led them to distance running.

Most of these seven, plus 10 others, indicated that the success they had experienced in their initial contact with distance running fulfilled a formerly frustrated desire to find a sport in which they could excel. Only 26 runners in the entire survey had competed in a sport other than track or cross-country on an organized basis in either high school or college. Many told of lack of achievement in football, baseball or basketball.

The following quotations are typical of those who either came to distance running through a physical education test and/or turned to it out of athletic frustration:

"In the B-12 semester of high school, I was in a P.E. class, and one day the coach decided to run everyone in the mile for time. I ran 5:40 and finished second. I therefore concluded it would be more fun to do something at which I might have some skill than remain in an ordinary P.E. class where I seemed to rank low in athletic ability."

The fifth-place finisher told much the same story regarding a "high school P.E. requirement that we complete a 1.8-mile cross-country course each week. I jogged with a good friend each time and we decided it was fun... Glory of being able to finish (without stopping to walk) within our P.E. group spurred me on."

The examples of great distance runners had very positive effects upon the lives of 15 of the survey's respondents. Performances of former champions like Paavo Nurmi, Willie Ritola, Gunder Hagg and "Old" John Kelley were prominently mentioned as the "one event in your life which had the greatest influence upon your becoming a distance runner." Also recalled were such contests as the Bannister-Landy mile in 1954, the 1932 Olympic Games and the Boston marathon. The influences upon youth of the actions of a leader in any sport are not to be taken lightly, according to this survey.

Why continue in distance running? Personal satisfaction seemed to be the motivation for most runners continuing in distance running. Of six answers which they were asked to preferentially rank, 20 chose "improve my personal best time in the marathon" as their first (seven runners) or second choice. Eighteen indicated that, primarily or secondarily, they were going to " prove I can run a full marathon," a response which elicited 13 first-place votes. "Because I like to run" was selected by eight as their first choice and by 13 as their second.

Winning a trophy or medal was one aspect of distance running that seemed to have little influence upon these distance runners. Only three indicated that response as their primary reason for running in the Pan-American Games Trials, while three more chose it as their second most important reason. Moreover, to another pre-race question, "What do you think makes a great runner?" none took "Desire for awards" as either their first or second choice.

Possibly the runners were inhibited in their responses regarding the matter of rewards by the fact that their names appeared in the survey, and few wished to admit to being "medal-hungry."

The one major incident in the race which made the effort a

success or a failure: The importance of psychological aspects in distance running was made very obvious in the runners' replies to the question "What do you think makes a great runner?" Twenty-five (50%) chose "mental approach to the sport" as their first of five choices, 16 indicated it as their second, while none gave it a fifth-place ranking.

Moreover, when asked, "What do you think about when you're running?" 16 indicated "race tactics" as their first choice, while 15 chose it as their second in the pre-meet survey. (There were a total of six choices to this question.)

Did their performances in the race bear out this mental approach? There can be no questioning of this if one weighs the replies to the after-race survey. Within a week after the race, follow-up questionnaires were sent to those 50 who had completed the initial survey; 33 responded.

The questions asked, among others, were, "If you ran your best race, what factors (list in order, please) do you feel contributed the most to your success (name specific instances if you can)," or, "If you failed to run your best race...what factors..." etc. The runners were also asked, "What single incident in the race was the turning point for you?" From the replies to the questions, certain truths became obvious.

First, most distance men have a built-in mental gauge, and according to this pre-set standard will run well or poorly. This gauge may be attuned to another runner (be he a good or a poor one) or to a known, established time for a given distance.

Second, the lack of a knowledge of pace can be deadly, in most cases, to a runner's psychological condition during the race. This is a part of the "time gauge" factor.

Third, it is essential that the runner be well prepared in advance —physically and equipment-wise—or he usually will suffer mentally during the race.

Time after time, runners reported that the turning point in the race for them came when they passed, or were passed by, a competitor of known quality. If the respondent was passed, he lost heart and interest in the race. If the respondent did the passing, he was filled with renewed hope and vigor.

A good example of the above point came from a young but experienced road runner of 20 who finished 20th. "The one thing which I felt helped me most was passing X right after the 15-mile point. I knew he had run 2:36 the year before, and it gave me confidence when I passed him."

Ron Hill (26), one of the greatest marathoners ever, is among the leaders of this British race. (Mark Shearman photo)

A man who had never run a marathon before (but who finished 33rd) stated: "When I saw how many runners I was catching on this 'kick,' it made me feel *terrific*. My legs had bothered me between four and 24 miles. But on the last two miles I felt *no pain* whatsoever in my legs."

On the other hand, an experienced and well-known Eastern runner (who finished 11th) depicted graphically what happened when men of known ability pulled away from or passed him: "I could not stay with the leading group at seven miles, and my running form deteriorated at this early stage of the race. From that point on, it was a struggle just to keep running at any speed and I felt that I slowed up from there. About 16½ miles, a large group passed me easily. I think it consisted of (four named runners) and perhaps a couple of others. They appeared to be running easily, and my legs were dragging."

The man who had won this race the year before, but who had

to settle for ninth in the Trial, said: "Within the race, the turning point was at the start. (I believe in most races, no matter what the distance, the important part is the start.) Another turning point occurred at the 12-mile mark when the legs began going dead and I was only in the 11th or 12th position. (The year before, the legs didn't deaden until 18 miles out and I was in front then.)"

On the other hand, knowing that one has paced himself properly and is running well can be most elevating to the spirits and the performance. The 17th place finisher, running his first marathon, said, "The best mental lift I had was when I passed the 10-mile mark and posted my best time."

Even if a time or place is erroneously announced as being better than it is, it may "lift" the runner in some instances. The 10th place finisher commented: "To be honest with you, at 20 miles I was told by error that I was in seventh place. Actually, I was in 10th. But this did help me a great deal and I knew, even being sick, that if I just maintained the even pace I was running I would finish in a good place and in fairly good time."

As far as having body and equipment properly prepared before the race, many men wrote of recent colds, pulled muscles (prior to the race), lack of sleep (although one said he had too much sleep), excess weight and lack of sufficient training as being one or more of the factors that prevented them from doing well, many others told of blisters, muscle cramps and poorly fitting shoes that hounded them during the race.

One point stood out very clearly as we examined these "physical" reasons. Almost all of the men who had complained of physical problems stated that they first felt that discomfort or pain, or that they actually dropped out of the race, between the 15- and 20-mile marks. This distance span is spoken of time and again.

On the other hand, the psychological approach by those who succeeded in the race can be best summarized by quoting a young (22) man who came out of nowhere to take fifth place. He was self-trained (and expressed some worries about this fact), but he trained 44 weeks a year, six days a week and average 1½ hours of running each day. At the 15-mile mark, he was bothered by blisters, but he removed his shoes and finished barefooted. He told of running a steadily-paced race throughout the marathon and concluded with the statement, "Light heart—light feet!"

Training methods and "staleness": A fear often expressed by

many marathon runners is that too much training will lead to staleness, but relatively little such concern was revealed in the response
of most of those surveyed.

Twenty-eight of the 50 runners pinpointed some feature of
what might be termed "consistency in training" when asked, "What
aspect of your daily routine has been of greatest value in preparing
you for the marathon?" Thirty indicated that they trained 45-52
weeks per year, 31 trained at least six days per week and 41 trained
a minimum of 1½ hours per day.

The old bugaboo of staleness did not seem to exist as a factor
for these men who covered 65-100+ miles per week (and who, it
will be recalled, ranked "mental preparation" so highly in another
section of the questionnaire). The conclusion which may be
drawn is that being "stale" is not a physical but a psychological
condition.

The marathon runner is often pictured as a lonely athlete,
and in many respects this may be so. He is also an introspective
sportsman who, in a constant effort to judge his progress, views
himself not only in his own mirror but also in those of his competitors.

He willing to train consistently with the goal of self-im-
provement uppermost in mind, but he does not seem to be able to
recognize his attainment of that goal without reference to either
the performances of his competitors and/or his own past achievements. His physical stresses during a race and/or the unyield-
ing stopwatch are accepted as the other measurements of his
progress in the current race as contrasted with those in the past.

Finally, with respect to all of these aforementioned indicators,
he may be "psyched up" to new heights or "psyched out" to un-
satisfactory results.

RUNNING FROM WORRIES

This series of articles appeared in Runner's World, October 1973.

"Years ago," Aaron Sussman and Ruth Goode began their book *The Magic of Walking*, "scientists were predicting the evolution of a race of men without legs, thanks to the automobile. Nowadays, we know they were wrong. It is not our legs we are losing. It is our minds."

Movement, self-propelled movement, is strong medicine. With it, the body stays healthy. Without it, we deteriorate. We know that. Less obvious is the effect movement has on the mind. The head apparently reacts to this kind of exercise the same way the heart does.

We really can run away from our problems—the everyday ones that cause pressure, tension, anxiety to knot up our insides and put us in black moods.

Early in 1973, Associated Press carried a story on Eileen Waters of San Diego. Eileen, 27, is one of the few American women ever to finish a 50-mile run.

Several years ago, Eileen's younger sister committed suicide. Eileen herself was understandably despondent over this family tragedy. To compensate, she ate compulsively. She started running to lose the weight she'd gained. She found that she lost her despair as well.

"Running just keeps me going," Eileen says, "gets me out of my bad moods. It makes me feel good to be alive. I want to reach out to the world now, to touch it. I'm smiling a lot now."

Running can have a measurable effect on draining away self-destructive tension and conflicts. Frank Greenberg wrote in the September 1970 *RW* about using running in the rehabilitation of mental patients. Paul de Bruhl has written how running made prison more tolerable for him. Nearly a hundred members of Synanon, most of them trying to shake hard-drug habits, ran the Bay-to-Breakers race in San Francisco in May 1973.

Movement is strong medicine. Two doctors from the University of Southern California reported in the *Medical Tribune* (May 9, 1973) that a simple 15-minute walk was more relaxing than a tranquilizer.

Herbert de Vries and Gene Adams studied 10 patients, ages 52-70. All showed above average anxiety tension. During one test, the patients took the drug meprobamate in a 400-milligram dose. Another day, they took a walk vigorous enough to raise their heart rates above 100 beats a minute.

The walk had the greater calming effect, as measured by reduction of muscle action and heart rate. Fifteen minutes of exercise soothed the patients for an hour after they'd stopped walking. And there were no harmful side-effects.

Tests with more vigorous running movement have shown even better results. Doctors from Purdue and Stanford University tell of their work later.

Running's calming quality is rooted in our heredity. Our ancestors reacted to threats in one of two ways: by preparing to stand their ground and fight, or preparing to set sail out of the danger area. Either way, the body's chemicals were marshalled for heavy work.

Man still faces threats. In a crowded, fast-paced world, he faces more than his ancestors did. But instead of fighting or fleeing, he goes home and has a martini, or worse. His chemicals have still prepared him for action. But there hasn't been any. The tensions, the urges to fight or flee, may be dulled temporarily by drugs. But the urges stay bottled up inside.

Since modern life offers so much in the way of tension and so little in the way of release, we have to work hard at relaxing. Running is one way. This sounds contradictory—running and tensing muscles to reduce tension. Yet a number of physiological investigations have shown that relaxation is most pronounced after muscular work.

Drs. Paul Insel and Walton Roth of Stanford say, "The most profound muscular and mental relaxation cannot be achieved by just trying to relax. The deepest relaxation, as measured by electrodes inserted in the muscles, follows a period of voluntarily increased muscular tension."

While the body is working, the knot inside is loosening.

Like many other strong medicines, though, running can build a dependence amounting almost to addiction.

One woman distance runner facing a divorce writes, "As the

mental pressures grew, I was running compulsively for the first time, really running hard, twice a day. It was helping me keep my head together."

A man threatened by a career-ending injury kept hobbling on. He says, "I have done a complete about-face on running—from a non-necessity to a must."

When a runner is hooked in this way, sudden withdrawal can be devastating. Tracy Smith, world indoor record holder for three miles, hurt an achilles tendon in 1969 and was out of heavy running for two years.

He says he was "deeply depressed. I had been training for three hours a day, and to go from that to nothing was terrible. I would wake up shaking, and the doctor said it was actually a physical withdrawal. I had so much mental and physical energy and nothing to use it up."

Smith joined the Los Angeles Police Department "because I needed something demanding and exciting." When he started running again, Tracy resigned from the force.

For those who have developed a craving for it and those who are temperamentally suited to start, running is good and healthy medicine. If they're already relaxed when they begin, they can feel even better.

Running offers one of the few chances left to get our feet on the ground—for the sake of our heads.

Working Hard at Relaxing

At a certain age, which carries with it a certain level of inactivity, fitness begins eroding like plowed soil under spring rains. The age is about 25, a Canadian study has concluded (see *Runner's World,* Sept. 73). This is the age when physical activity has tailed off drastically and pressures have mounted, creating a most unhealthy combination.

The body deteriorates more quickly between ages 25 and 35 than at any other time in a person's life, according to the Fitness Institute of Toronto. The doctors there didn't study their subject's minds, but most likely tensions increased proportionally during this "dangerous decade."

"Chronic tension states," says Drs. Paul Insel and Walton Roth of the Stanford University Medical Center, "are known to be associated with numerous bodily malfunctions such as ulcers, migraine headaches, asthma, skin eruptions, high blood pressure and even heart disease."

The symptoms on the psychological side are no prettier. "Irritability, touchiness, moodiness and depression." Running, the doctors say, "has been shown to relieve some of these symptoms." Running does this by pulling the plug on pent-up tension.

The relief is familiar to anyone who runs. After most runs, there's a feeling of relaxation, even euphoria. But how real is the relief? Has the tense state really been changed, or does the runner simply feel good because he thinks he should? Is he really relaxed, or does he just feel the kind of relief one gets when he quits hitting himself on the head with a hammer? If the effects are real, are they fleeting or lasting?

Conventional opinion among those who deal with the hardcore disturbed is that exercise at best does nothing positive to relieve symptoms, and that it may cause setbacks.

"Until recently," *Executive Fitness Newsletter* reports, "most authorities accepted the theory that exercise increased anxiety and that persons suffering with anxiety neurosis should avoid physical activity. The theory is based on the fact that an injection of lactate (a form of the fatigue product lactic acid) into the bloodstream results in anxiety symptoms.

"Inasmuch as it is common knowledge that exercise caused the release of lactate into the bloodstream, the obvious conclusion was that exercise caused an increase in anxiety." So exercise was ruled out for these patients.

Medical literature contains the results of another study on the mental benefits of running, or lack of same. The authors (W. P. Morgan, J. A. Roberts and A. D. Feinerman, "Psychologic Effects of Acute Physical Activity," *Arch. Phys. Med.*, 52:422-425, 1971) attempted to measure the benefits, if any.

They tried two experiments. In the first, subjects exercised at heart rates up to 180 beats per minute—at least 90% of maximum. Immediately afterwards, they completed a "depression adjective checklist." Exercise had no bearing on the scores.

In the second list, subjects divided into exercising and non-exercising groups. The exercisers ran for 17 minutes on a treadmill. The others rested. Afterwards, they were no differences in the anxiety and depression scores.

Could the good feeling after running be all in our heads? Perhaps. But read on.

Dr. William P. Morgan of the University of Wisconsin tested the lactate theory—the idea that exercise negatively alters the body's chemical balance, making it more tense. He found that the lactate released by exercise differed significantly from the chemical substance that had been injected into anxious patients, and that exercise-induced chemical changes led to a "definite decrease in anxiety levels in normal and neurotic individuals of both sexes." (*Medical Tribune*, March 21, 1973).

And regardless of the objective findings in the other set of tests, the individuals insisted they did "feel better" after their runs.

Walton Roth, a Stanford psychiatrist, found the same thing when he observed other men who run with him. "Of the group of 30 regular exercise participants," Dr. Roth says, "about three-quarters describe a feeling of increased well-being that follows exercising. Often this is described as relief from tension, or a feeling of calmness.

"One person felt no need for his scotch and water if he had exercised in the afternoon. Another claimed that he was able to think more clearly and felt less tired than when he missed his exercise."

Dr. Roth added, "Probably the fact that the majority had extremely sedentary occupations enhanced the effect of exercise. The extreme lack of physical activity during the working day seemed to

---

PERSONALITY CHANGES FROM EXERCISE

Results of the Purdue University tests by Drs. Ismail and Trachtman, as reported in the March 1973 Psychology Today. Scores are from the Cattell 16 Personality Factor Questionnaire, completed at the start and finish of the four-month test.

	High-Fitness Group		Low-Fitness Group	
	Before	After	Before	After
Emotional Stability	6.4	6.1	4.6	5.4
Imagination	7.3	7.2	5.3	6.1
Self-Sufficiency	6.5	6.6	6.4	8.0
Guilt-Proneness*	4.2	4.1	5.4	6.1

*Lower scores on "guilt-proneness" indicate increased self-assurance.

result in a motoric restlessness and tension."

Note two key points in what Dr. Roth says. These are *regular* runners observed, and they are otherwise *inactive* men in fairly high-stress occupations. They are medical professionals. Since they do prolonged, moderate running most work days, Dr. Roth has been able to see long-term results in them. The results with this kind of running and this kind of individual seem to have been good.

Drs. A. H. Ismail and L. E. Trachtman of Purdue University

"Instead of getting the greatest satisfaction from beating others, a man would try to better his own performances..." (Beinhorn)

had similar suspicions as they watched faculty members puff their
way into shape.

"We were fairly sure," they write in the March 1973 *Psychology Today*, "that our paunchy, sedentary, middle-aged academics
were undergoing personality changes, subtly but definitely... By
the time they reached the end of the (conditioning) program, they
seemed to be interacting more freely and to be more relaxed. Their
whole demeanor seemed to us to be more even, stable and self-con-
fident."

Ismail and Trachtman checked their "off-the-cuff impressions"
over a four-month period, using refined physiological and psychological methods. At the beginning, some of the men could run no
more than a quarter-mile. At the end of the test, though, they
were averaging two to three miles, a day, with some going five.

First finding: the runners progressed through easily-identified
states as they gained fitness.

● **Timid**—Feared heart attacks and ran cautiously, though all
had been cleared medically.

● **Sadistic**—"After a while, their fears subsided, and several
turned into mildly sadistic types and took great pleasure in defeating others in foot races."

● **Masochistic**—"Instead of getting the greatest satisfaction
from beating others, a man would try to better his own performances, by driving himself hard and subjecting himself to greater
stress."

Next, Drs. Ismail and Trachtman tried to test personality
changes, using the Cattell 16 Personality Factor Questionnaire.
They separated the subjects into two groups: high-fitness (at the
start) and low-fitness.

The Cattell Questionnaire rates 16 traits on a 10-point scale.
(Above six is "high," below four is "low.") The doctors chose four
traits as most important to this study: (1) emotional stability;
(2) imagination; (3) self-sufficiency; (4) guilt-proneness. Runners, they figured, should score well in the first three, and have a
low score in the fourth (which is an indication of self-assurance, or
a lack of guilt-proneness).

The high-fitness group scored as expected, and was consistent
from start to finish. "Imagination"was their best feature. The
low-fitness group's ratings soared in the first three categories—particularly in "self-sufficiency," where they shot past the more sea-

soned runners. The beginners' emotional stability "increased so markedly that there no longer was a significant difference between the groups," the authors said after the four-month test.

One thing puzzled them, though. The doctors thought guilt-proneness would drop during exercise. "Persons with very high scores on (this factor) tend to be worried, anxious, depressed, easily overcome by moods, prone to depressions," they say.

This score should be low, as it is in the fit men. It wasn't. It actually increased as the test went on. Why? Isn't this one of the things running should cure?

Ismail and Trachtmann explain that this may have been a temporary effect. The beginners may have realized the extent of their unfitness for the first time, and they felt guilty about not being able to get in shape immediately. At any rate, the scores of the regular runners show what can happen once they're settled.

The Trauma of Stopping

"It should come out," the doctor said after looking at the ugly bump on the runner's foot. "If we don't operate, it'll never get any better. And it could get worse."

The runner gave a resigned shrug, indicating it was okay with him. But he was of two minds about it.

It would be minor surgery, he told himself. The doctor would go in and scrape away a little extra bone. That's all. The procedure is almost as simple as pulling a tooth.

But "minor" surgery is someone else's surgery, he answered. If he's going to take a piece of me, that's major enough, thank you. And I don't walk and run on my teeth.

"A month from now," the doctor said, "you'll be running again." Only a month, the runner said. What's a month beside the years I've already run, and at least that many more I will run if I can get healthy?

What a month is, he answered, is the longest runless period I've had since 1958. And I get withdrawal symptoms after even a day away. Physically, I know I can bounce back quickly from the layoff. But the addiction isn't purely physical.

The doctor didn't trust the runner. And with good reason.

"Normally," he said, "casts are optional in cases like this. But

The greatest accomplishment a runner can have can often be simply keeping going day after day. To stop is the only way he can fail. (Beinhorn)

I know runners. I know if I didn't put a cast on you, you'd be trying to run in two days." You'd mess up all the good we've done."

The doctor slapped on extra strips of plaster "just to be sure you don't do anything funny."

Do I get a walking cast, the runner asked.

"No!"

That night the runner was alone with his thoughts for the first time. A formless terror crept up on him. He tried to move his leg and couldn't.

My God, he thought, I'm trapped. I can't move, and I won't be able to move for weeks. He panicked. He imagined the cast was tightening and shutting off his blood supply.

The runner called the doctor and pleaded, loosen it, please.

The doctor said, "It's not the cast that needs loosening. It's your head." He prescribed sleeping pills.

In the days that followed, the runner didn't feel much better. He recalled what he'd seen and read of other runners in the same situation and how they'd built up a dependence on running and had been shaken mentally when it was taken away.

He remembered Tracy Smith, who'd felt "deeply depressed" when he hurt his achilles and couldn't run. He thought of Vince Matthews. Matthews had quit running after the 1968 Olympics but found, "I had a lot of excess energy. I would play basketball and handball in the parks, but it wasn't enough to burn up the energy I had."

The runner thought of his friend, an American record holder, who was now in a mental hospital partly as the result of a sudden stop.

He thought of a letter to Dr. Sheehan at *Runner's World.* "I stopped running in March 1972," the writer said. "The next thing I knew, I was in the hospital suffering from nervous tension and anxiety. What happens to a person mentally and physically when he stops running altogether?"

Sheehan answered, "Your primary problem is the loss of your positive addiction. We distance runners are usually ectomorphs who react to stress with withdrawal. We are ambivalent, moody and unpredictable. Running provides solitude, contemplation and a physical activity we do well."

Sheehan advised, "If you can find another sport with these same features, you may be able to cope. We can keep fit physically with cross-country skiing, biking, back-packing, etc., but this may not be sufficient psychologically."

The runner with the cast tried substitutes. A day after the operation, he crutched around the block. Another week after that, he was bicycling at least 10 miles a day.

But he said there was no life in any of these. He did them out of a feeling of obligation, and to keep from going out of his bloody mind. They weren't the same as running, and they weren't enough. They were like an alcoholic drinking coffee, or a junkie taking tranquilizers. He was used to stronger medicine.

There were physical symptoms: Appetite so low he lost eight pounds, even without burning up much food. An all-day drowsiness and listlessness that left him more tired than when he was running. Waking up at four in the morning, twitching and not able to get back to sleep. Chronic headaches and stomach aches.

All these disappeared as quickly as they'd come, as soon as the non-running month was up. Looking back, the runner sees that his reactions were fairly normal ones.

He remembered the study by Dr. Frederick Baekeland quoted in *Practical Running Psychology* (original source, *Arch. Gen. Psychiatry,* Vol. 22, 1970). Baekeland tested the effects of exercise deprivation. The first thing he found was that it was hard to recruit subjects.

"It proved very hard," he said, "to find subjects who exercised regularly and yet were able to deprive themselves of exercise for a month. Notwithstanding the fact that they were offered higher pay than usual, these prospective subjects (especially those who exercised daily) asserted that they would not stop exercising for any amount of money."

He settled for three-day-a-week athletes, who weren't so deeply addicted. Even they showed withdrawal symptoms. The 14 volunteers had "impaired sleep (a symptom of anxiety), increased sexual tension and an increased need to be with others" during the exerciseless month.

"Among other things," Baekeland said, "exercise is a discharge mechanism for aggressive drive, while it also contributes to feelings of mastery and self-esteem in individuals who regularly seek it out. Hence, with prohibition of exercise it seems reasonable to expect compensatory increases in the expression of other drives, whose gratification would reduce general levels of drive pressure."

The feelings the runner feels when he can't run are normal, maybe even natural. But that makes them no easier to handle when they're happening to him.

PROBLEMS OF A WOMAN

BY KATHRINE SWITZER

Kathrine Switzer will be remembered as "the woman who broke the sex barrier at Boston." She entered that marathon in 1967, was almost physically ejected, and then got to see the race add an official woman's division five years later.

I hailed a cab on the corner of Central Park and got in. I had just finished a 20-mile run and, somehow, the 30-odd blocks back to my apartment seemed an all-afternoon project that I couldn't face. I lean my head on the back seat and close my eyes. I haven't felt pooped like this for a long time, I think– about seven years, actually–and it is both a haunting feeling and a revelation.

It was seven years earlier–in 1967–that I first ran the Boston marathon. And before I ran that (in)famous '67 race, I was tired all the time–just as I feel now. In '67, I was going all-out, sailing my body over uncharted seas. Now, I'm training that way again, this time just to keep my head above water. It's another uncharted sea for me, however; enough so, in fact, that the revelation part of this feeling that I want to describe–which is about the incredible evolution of women in running–hits me more than academically. It hits me square in the guts.

With every "coming of age," as I put it, there is a tremendous upheaval in personal feeling, understanding and discovery. In the 1967 era, I was the only woman I knew who ran distance. And even though I had a coach/advisor/running partner in Arnie Briggs, neither of us knew what I was doing or supposed to do. I simply ran a little bit longer every day, and every workout had a question mark at the finish line. I kept wondering at which point the legs stop moving... how many hours can one run in the cold... how much hurting is too much... how much feeling good is not good...

And on and on it went until one day I ran 29 miles and decided I should run the Boston marathon. I hate to admit it, but I didn't do it to prove a thing. I simply wanted to run it and I understood it to be an open race, which–as far as naive I was concerned–included me. I felt if no other women were running it,

it was because they hadn't yet discovered what fun long running
can be. And I didn't like short distance, which at the time I felt
all other women must. It's funny how our perceptions change.

However, I might have liked short running if there had been
an opportunity to do that. But then again, maybe I'd have been a gym-
nast or an ice skater, particularly if my parents had me take lessons
when I was 10. I don't know. I just knew I liked running because
I could do it by myself and I could create my own little running
world.

But it was no longer my own goldfish bowl after the Boston
incident. I was forced to think about the situation of women in

**(L-R) Dr. Joan Ullyot, Christa Kofferschlager, Nina Kuscsik and
Miki Gorman at the 1974 Boston marathon. (Dawn Bressie)**

athletics and the opportunities that they had, particularly in running. The more I thought, the more I fumed. Arising from it all
was a central question, and despite all the progress that has been
made in the meantime, it is *still* the central question:

Why can't I do what I want to do?

And the answer is, believe it or not, you *can* do whatever you
want to do. You may catch a lot of flak, but it *can* be done. And

Joyce Smith (left) and Paola Cacchi, the leaders in the 1973 International cross-country championship. (Mark Shearman photo)

it's true, if I had known what was to lie ahead, I'd probably have quit right there. Running is an amazing thing that way—the hardest part is at the beginning, and, fortunately, you never know that until you're way past the hardest point.

For all the rough times that may lie ahead, women beginning running should know that the first year is the toughest. A woman beginning as a competitor should know that she is now, to say the least, in a very competitive world, and yet competing in that world is not beyond her grasp.

Which is why I'm nearly asleep in this cab feeling this tired and thinking these thoughts. The fatigue I'm feeling now is an indicator of what is taking place in the most amazing way for women: women are getting *good*. And if they're going to compete, they're going to have to train. We're out of the jogging era. And as the idea of running (or all of women's athletics, really) emerges, what follows is a revolution in sport, because it is followed by a tidal wave of other interested people.

Women are not just becoming good because they got the idea

from someone else to do something. The boom in athletic excellence, I think, is a bit of a physical manifestation of a new psychological state which we can simply call confidence. Women's running records are being shattered, daily, with phenomenal reductions. Lyudmila Bragina ran three 1500-meter world records in
Munich. Francie Larrieu knocks 32 seconds off the old two-mile
record. Miki Gorman runs an "impossible" marathon time. I'm
sure these fantastic women know that I'm in no way negating these
marvelous feats when I say that the records are beginning to be
lowered to the point where they should be. Women haven't been
running as long as men nor in the same numbers. But as the time
and numbers increase, we will see the records tumble, then settle.

As this happens, more women will run, more women will begin to *realize* themselves, and more doors will be opened. As in
every sport, as running becomes increasingly competitive, the space
at the top becomes harder and harder to reach. This is not negative—it is wonderful. It is like the study and pursuit of an art form
—at first, a rough idea, a primitive start, and then a push for perfection.

And in this fast climb, as that spot at the top gets narrower and
narrower, the opportunities become greater and greater for others,
because the base at the bottom becomes broader and broader.
Again, it's like the ensuing diversity of the art form. Consequently, in running it allows women to run in any capacity they choose—
for fun, fitness, competition or whatever. It is their own self-ex-
pression. And, because so many others now go before them, they
are relieved of the fears of "sailing uncharted seas." They have the
capacity then to create opportunities.

Probably the most frustrating aspect of a situation like this,
though, is that opportunities come with stumbling blocks. For
example, many high schools now claim to have a women's track
team but somehow forgot to budget enough money so that they
can compete with other schools, or have uniforms, or even get to
take a shower. Another example is the woman who is encouraged
to train, pushes herself incredibly, then runs a world record marathon—only to find that that's the top. She is unable to take her effort to the Olympics because no race exists for her.

Most frustrating, of course, is when a woman does something
that to her is perfectly normal and yet someone tries to throw road-
blocks in her way rather than trying to *help* her in her effort. I'm
afraid that this is just a quirk of human nature—that people will

often expend energy being negative, when the same amount of energy being positive would soon solve the problem, and would be a helluva lot more fun besides. At any rate, this obstinance (or fear) of the new is the cornerstone to all impasses. I feel the solution is simply to press on.

Another frustrating fact is that some talented women would just like to run, but are constantly put into a position of having to fight, too. Not all persons can do both. More importantly, they shouldn't *have* to. Many women are both trying to run and be a fighter for the women's cause, and they find themselves cutting into training time and energy. My only advice is that a woman in this situation must first fulfill those needs that she personally has, hoping in so doing that she will break down a few barriers. If she cannot make changes in the system herself, she most definitely has to have the strength of character to wait it out and the conviction to know the change will come. It *will* happen. Like the proverbial snowball, once progress gets going, it grows hugely and quickly. Bear in mind, for example, that running today in any type of organized way, is infinitely easier than it was two years ago. And for the woman now who just wants to run for fun or fitness, she is limited only by her own capacity.

The opportunities for women right now are fantastic—potentially. We're only a few years away, I believe, from running scholarships for women, from equal media time, from a level of competition comparable to men's (local, national, Olympic) and for the opening of positions on the pro circuit. Additionally, more than ever before, women runners are being sought out to expand their running interests into athletic-related careers—jobs in recreational facilities, speaking, organizing, writing and reporting, coaching, sports-related business opportunites and perhaps even politics.

So, although I may sympathize with her, I believe that the woman runner who states flatly that she has absolutely no opportunity is short-sighted and/or uncreative. I grant you, running does not yet afford a wealth of opportunities—but it has a lot of future.

But the human side in all of us reveals itself from time to time. Sometimes, we wonder wearily, "Why bother, I'm too tired

"Bear in mind that running today in any type of organized way is infinitely easier than it was two years ago." (Jeff Johnson)

to fight it... I'm not going to be running long enough for it to help me, anyway"... and there are those awful, unavoidable times when opportunities come more easily to others and stab us with pangs of jealousy.

My cab jerks to a halt. I drag myself into my apartment, pour a tall glass of quinine water and flip on Wide World of Sports. Chris Evert has just beaten Virginia Wade and somebody is giving Chris a check for $10,000. That's all right, I think. It's only paper anyway. But then a man comes out and gives her the most fabulous mink coat I've ever seen. Chris looks as if she couldn't have cared less. And incredibly, stupidly, childishly, I feel a big lump forming in my throat. So I take a long hot shower, have another glass of quinine, and the lump disappears. I begin to wonder how something that petty ever bothered me.

3

PHYSIOLOGY

ATHLETES: "NEW NORMALS"

BY DR. GEORGE SHEEHAN

Dr. Sheehan is the editor of the Encyclopedia of Athletic Medicine.

Athletes have already done a thorough job of raising the consciousness of physicians interested in sports. They have, among other contributions: (a) established a new normal for man; (b) changed our concept of aging; (c) confirmed the idea of the totality of man, and (d) shifted the emphasis from disease to health.

Before we discovered that athletes were attaining maximum metabolic, muscular and cardiopulmonary steady states, we were using "average" individuals as normals. We were, in effect, using life's spectators instead of life's competitors, and were coming up with overweight, out-of-breath subjects testing well below their potential. This can clearly be shown by comparing these pseudo-normals to the athletes in their age group. Their test results are frequently as much as 50% below the athletes' performance.

One effect of this poor performance is to consider early aging as a natural process. Athletes are beginning to make physicians take a new look at this judgment. "The average man," reports Dr. John Naughton after analyzing peak oxygen intakes of 213 men from the ages of 20 to 55 years, "becomes physiologically old early in life, which may explain how many succumb to disease of chronic deterioration at an early age." What we now call aging is actually disease.

Such gloomy statistics have led Paul Dudley White to lower his estimate of the critical year at which this process begins. Previously White had set the age of 22 as the starting point. After the age of 22, he said, we must follow three rules: (1) Don't gain weight; (2) Don't smoke, and (3) Exercise regularly. Now he recommends that diet and exercise start in childhood.

The athlete has also proved that this exercise and dieting and the resultant fitness has an effect on all our processes—mental and psychological as well as physical. He is making philosophers rethink the body-mind problems which has been with us since the 17th

**Distance runners like Gary Chilton have changed the definition of
what health is and what the human body can do. (G. Beinhorn)**

century when Descartes divorced the soul from the body.

This total effect of physical fitness—the new body image, the
new self-respect, the new confidence—led Dr. Roger Bannister to
describe it as "a state of mental and physical harmony which enables someone to carry on his occupation to the best of his ability
and with great happiness."

What Bannister is describing is a state of health that can be
quantified by tests of physical fitness, by tests of muscular endurance and strength and speed and per cent body fat. But it is also
a quality, a method of living. To tell a healthy person not to abuse
his body is as unnecessary as telling a saint not to steal. Health is
really a form of behavior, a trait like honesty and a way of pursuing one's goals in life.

"Health," says Dr. Bob Hoke, a specialist in occupational medicine, "is a living response to one's total environment."

Health, then, is not merely the absence of disease just as sanctity is not merely the absence of sin. Health is man adapting, man striving, man living the present and thrusting himself into the future. Sport allows us to see purely this living to the utmost, or at least the attempt to do so.

"If there is one statement true of every living person," writes William Schultz, the author of *Joy*, " it must be this: he hasn't achieved his full potential."

The athletes whose efforts have taken him beyond our pedestrian ideas of normal and average and aging and disease sees this quite clearly. Unimpeded by the mediocrity of our vision, he moves toward a horizon where men will make the most of themselves and their world.

WHAT GOES ON INSIDE?

E. C. Frederick edits the scientifically-oriented publication Running and is the author of The Running Body. Joe Henderson is editor of Runner's World. These articles first came out in RW, February, 1973.

What Do They Test?

BY E.C. FREDERICK

This is an exciting time to be alive and running. Man's knowledge of himself is expanding at unimaginable rates. Information is perpetually accumulating, which allows us to methodically push back the limits of body and mind. Nowhere can the effects of this exponential learning be better seen than in the blossoming field of running physiology. New facts, skills, techniques and instruments are appearing daily, advancing our comprehension of what we see.

The research physiologist is unlocking the doors of our perception, allowing us to better define and understand the factors which limit running performance. As our understanding of these limits increases so do performance levels.

Modern physiological research has given us a broad picture of the limiting factors of running performance. These factors provide a framework within which to discuss methods of physiological testing and their meaning to the individual.

• **Oxygen uptake:** The maximum amount of oxygen that a runner can take in and transport to the various tissues of the body is the most basic factor limiting running performance. The measurement of this overall ability is called the *maximum oxygen consumption rate*. It is calculated by having an individual run at a given rate on a treadmill while breathing into a closed system which is designed to measure the amount of oxygen taken into the body and not returned, i.e. consumed.

These measurements are standardized in milliliters (ml.) of oxygen consumed per kilogram (kg.) of body weight per minute. This information tells the physiologist a great deal about the run-

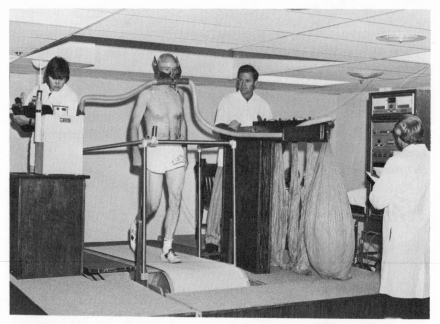

"The research physiologist allows us to better define and
understand the factors which limit running performance."

ner. It indicates the level of fitness. (Distance runners can have
twice normal levels, e.g. 80 versus 40 ml./kg./min.). It allows reasonably accurate predictions of performance. And it reflects the
relative effectiveness of various components of the oxygen transport system. These components are subject to further tests which
give us more detailed information on the oxygen transport system.

The maximum oxygen consumption rate is directly dependent
on several factors: the ventilation of the lungs, the oxygen carrying capacity of the blood, the unloading of oxygen at the tissues
and the pumping capacity of the heart. The accurate measurement
of each of these factors also is important in evaluating different
training methods and defining the capacities of the individual. Each
measurement gives us a different point of view in assessing oxygen
uptake.

● **Lungs:** Looking from the angle of lung ventilation, we can
measure the maximum amount of air which can be moved in and
out of the lungs (*vital capacity*). This is a function of the total volume of the lungs. And as you would expect, runners have much
larger vital capacities (e.g. 5.7 liters) than average untrained individuals (4.8 liters).

Besides the volume of the lungs, we are also interested in the strength and endurance of the respiratory muscles. This is assessed by measuring the maximum amount of air which can be breathed in one minute. It is referred to as the *maximum breathing capacity* and again we find runners superior in this capacity. Whereas an untrained individual may have an MBC of from 125-170 liters a minute, figures well over 200 per minute are regularly recorded for runners. Even more significant is the fact that runners can sustain a large intake (over 120 per minute for more than 20 minutes) while the untrained individual can sustain this large minute volume for only a few minutes.

● **Blood:** The lungs supply a place for the oxygen in the air to come in contact with the blood. The amount of oxygen extracted from the air is dependent on a number of things. Of major importance is the capacity of the blood to carry oxygen. This is measured by determining the hemoglobin content of the blood since the hemoglobin does the carrying. Distance training increases the hemoglobin count, so runners have a greater oxygen carrying capacity than non-runners. It is also interesting to note that altitude training can cause further increases in this capacity.

We need to know, too, how much oxygen can be unloaded at the tissue level. This can be measured by the difference in oxygen concentrations between arterial and venous blood. This function is greatly enhanced in the distance runner due to the presence of more extensive capillarization of the active muscles.

● **Heart:** Having a large vital, maximum breathing and oxygen carrying and unloading capacities is not enough if the blood is not circulated rapidly and efficiently. Therefore we need to assess the pumping ability of the heart. Two measures of this ability are the *stroke volume* (the volume of blood pumped out of the heart with each beat) and the *minute volume* (amount of blood pumped in one minute). The stroke volume of the distance runner's heart is nearly twice the normal value, and minute volumes are also correspondingly higher.

Heart rates reflect this increased capacity of the runner's heart. If your heart has a greater capacity to pump blood, it stands to reason that it will have to pump less in a normal resting state. This is true for runners who regularly record resting heart rates near 40 beats per minute.

Besides having low resting rates, the runner's heart can beat faster for longer periods of time. Say a runner has a maximum heart rate of 240 beats per minute. He can maintain 60% of that maximum (144) for a much longer time than an untrained individual. It is also significant to note that, due to increased cardio-respiratory efficiency, the trained distance runner can perform the same amount of work at a much lower heart rate than an untrained individual. This all adds up to an increased capacity to do work, which is the definition of fitness.

• **Fat:** A more indirect factor affecting oxygen uptake, and performance in general, is body composition. Researchers have shown high degrees of correlation between percent of body fat and performance.

Figures close to zero have been recorded on distance runners. And most college-class distance runners average around 8% body fat, as compared to 15% for males in the same age group.

Body fat determinations can be made in a number of ways but the most accurate and most commonly used is the "densitometric" method. An individual is weighed in air and then weighed submerged in water, and fat figures are calculated from the difference in the two weights.

Body fat calculations and other determinants of body composition emphasize the importance of diet to the runner. Not only is it helpful to maintain low body fat by eating less but also it is advantageous to control the types of food eaten.

• **Glycogen:** Using a small needle and syringe, it is possible to take a small sample of muscle tissue and analyze it for glycogen content. Glycogen is a small starch molecule which is the major energy storage unit of muscle. Many researchers feel that the depletion of energy stores is the major limitation in performance in long distance runners.

A system for increasing the pre-race glycogen content of muscle is currently in use by many runners (glycogen loading). It shows great promise in improving future performance.

• **Fluids:** Even if we can increase glycogen storage significantly, the problem of dehydration and its resulting problems (overheating, circulatory strain and electrolyte imbalance) must be overcome. By weighing an individual before and after a run, we can estimate the amount of fluid lost. And by analyzing perspiration we can predict electrolyte losses and their subsequent effect on hydration.

Besides the problems of dehydration, depletion of energy stores and electrolyte imbalance, there are the more subtle effects of depletion of vitamins and essential minerals. Analyses of blood, urine, feces and perspiration have revealed significant alterations in the amounts of various vitamins and minerals during running. We are just beginning to understand the effects of these changes.

As time and information accumulate, the research biologist, through the use of these tests and measurements, will gradually help the world class runner overcome those factors which limit performance. But, best of all, this new information will allow runners on all levels to make the most of running.

How Do They Test?

BY JOE HENDERSON

In October 1972, an experienced distance man named Larry Vollmer collapsed after a half-marathon race in Eugene, Ore., and died before reaching the hospital. He had a heart ailment that was symptom-free until the fatal day. Vollmer was 31.

In November, police found a body in a park near my home where where I often run. They learned that the man was a regular jogger with no previous history of heart disease. He was 29.

Physiologists have devised tests to spot these latent problems in a large percentage of cases. They call it "silent heart disease." The preventive is the "stress test." Kenneth Cooper writes of it in *New Aerobics*, and uses it in his aerobic testing facilities in Dallas, Texas. It involves taking electrocardiogram (EKG) readings while exercising—generally either walking-running on a treadmill or pedaling a stationary bicycle. This method is far superior to a resting EKG as a gauge of heart capacity. Dr. Cooper estimates it is 85% effective in detecting silent heart disease.

Stress testing facilities are mushrooming. The National Jogging Association's newsletter recently published names and addresses of nearly 100 offices equipped for such testing. Medical doctors or exercise physiologists are in charge. These laboratories, it turns out, do more than look for dangerous lines on the EKG graph. They are pioneers in preventive medicine—the basis of health and fitness.

Jack Wilmore is a slim, intense exercise physiologist-in-residence at the University of California's Davis branch. Wilmore is a marathoner ("I've run two of them") whose main exercise interest is running. He has tested top international runners and has taken measurements on most of the country's best over-40 athletes. But Dr. Wilmore's big push is in the area of adult fitness. In the last year alone, he has run some 500 beginning exercisers through his "Human Performance Laboratory." Based on the test data, he prescribes individual programs.

Wilmore is in the treadmill room. Surrounding him are a cardiologist (who monitors every second of every treadmill run), a graduate school assistant, and about a million dollars worth of gadgetry ("most of it is on loan," the assistant says). A computer gushes out great typed bursts of information on heart rate, respiration and the like. An EKG keeps a constant tracing of heart activity.

A 61-year-old is on the treadmill. He has a half-dozen leads attached to his shaven, shirtless chest. An air collection mask is on his face, and he's beginning to labor.

The gradulate assistant, steeplechaser Ed Haver (one-time NCAA college division champion), watches the computer print-out with one eye and the 61-year-old with the other. Ed shouts encouragement like a cheerleader. Dr. Wilmore is more subdued, but he urges the man on, too.

"Okay, that's good," Wilmore says as he shuts down the machine that was traveling uphill at brisk walking pace. The subject slumps to a stool to recover.

"Very good," Wilmore says as he holds the corner of the printout. "You're in great shape. Either you're doing more than you think you are, or you chose your parents wisely when you were born." The old man beams, as if it were the first time in years that anyone had praised his physical capacity. Wilmore sends him off to be tailored for an exercise program.

The next subject has just come from the water. There's an oversized wine vat at the other end of the room. Wilmore's helpers weigh people there by dunking them in the warm water. That tells them how much of their weight is expendable fat.

"This man had a heart attack several years ago," the cardiologist says. "He has been on a closely supervised exercise program since last year." The 50-year-old goes through the treadmill routine. "He has no symptoms now that would prevent him from exercising," the heart doctor says as he watches the green line on his EKG.

Weight itself is a myth. Alone, it doesn't say much about the person carrying it. Fat percentage gives a better picture.

Dr. Wilmore says, "Such an assessment allows an accurate estimate to be made of what an individual's ideal weight should be. This is important since the traditional approach of using standardized weight tables adjusted for sex, height and frame size has been shown to be grossly inaccurate for a rather large percentage of the population. The 'ideal' weight within any one category of these tables can vary up to 22 pounds... It is not unusual for an individual to fall within the normal range for his or her category but actually to have 10-30 pounds of excess body fat."

Ed Haver adds that while testing the San Francisco Forty-Niners football team, the "gargantuan linemen weighing 250, 300 pounds" had almost no body fat. If anything, they were over-muscled, but they were solid.

The first phase of the testing is a submerged weighing in the vat. This simply gives absolute lean body weight. This is compared with normal weight to find the fat percentage. For instance, a wet weight of 100 pounds and an actual weight of 120 equals 20% fat.

"Standards will vary from one clinic or laboratory to another," Wilmore says, "but it is generally accepted that men and women should not exceed 15-20% and 25-30% respectively." He says most trained runners go under 10% fat, and some—because of heavy bone structure—actually register "negative" fat. Their submerged weights are higher than their actual ones.

Wilmore remembers testing women runners Doris Brown, Francie Larrieu and Cheryl Bridges. Since women tend to test considerably higher than men, he was impressed by the fact that they all had about the same fat content as male runners.

"Cheryl Bridges," he says, "had only 7% fat. She had lost something like 30 pounds when she became a runner. Now she's a very well put together girl."

I always thought I was skinny. The weight charts say so, and so does the mirror. But apparently they lie. I came out of the tank to the news that I'm carrying about 14% fat—average for an average healthy person, yes, but twice normal for runners.

Ed Haver types at the top of the computer sheet: "FAT MAN TEST."

"Relax," Dr. Wilmore says as he switches on the treadmill to gentle walking pace. "You have your fists clenched, and it makes General (the cardiologist) nervous. He thinks you're going to hit him."

The EKG silently traces its heartbeat line. The computer clatters out heart and respiration readings every 15 seconds. Wilmore gradually boosts the "hill" on the treadmill, then kicks me into running pace, gradually taking the breathing and pulse up to their maximum while the machines record them. After 10 minutes, as I'm about to gag on the air tube, he shuts down the moving belt.

He explains that maximal oxygen uptake is the most important thing he's measuring on me. This tells the body's ability to take in and use oxygen. Normal for runners is in the range of 56-81 millilters per kilogram of body weight per minute. Jim Ryun and Kip Keino have registered about 85. Mine is in the mid-60s.

Oxygen uptake relates directly to weight. I ask Ed Haver what a 5% loss in body fat would mean.

"About a 5% rise in oxygen uptake," he says. "Just flip-flop them." Since weight is part of the oxygen uptake formula, fat loss means one can run easier at a higher level of efficiency.

"Weight really has a big effect," Ed explains. "We had one runner here—I won't mention his name because he'd hang me—who was an All-American cross-country runner as a freshman. He had a maximal oxygen uptake of about 80, and only 6-7% fat. He laid off of running for one semester and his fat percentage doubled. He hasn't run well since."

Haver tells of a current runner at UC Davis whose oxygen uptake measures 81. "It is almost as high as Ryun and Keino. But others who test lower run faster. He doesn't have it up here (pointing to head)."

There's a "basic speed" factor involved, too. But Haver says that in five-mile cross-country races at Davis, the runners place according to their maximal oxygen uptake capacities almost right down the line.

How much can it be improved? Dr. Wilmore says, "We're still trying to resolve that. We know you can't take everyone and make him a runner. Heredity has a lot to say about it."

Running performance capacity is predictable. Body fat and oxygen uptake capacity have a lot to do with it. But Wilmore isn't primarily concerned with people who have half the normal quota of fat and twice normal uptake volumes. He mainly operates down around the minimum standards, with people who need his advice most. These are the beginners. They get the real value of his testing.

"About 10-15% of the population has abnormalities of one sort or another in the heart," Wilmore says. "This doesn't mean they can't exercise. But the exercise has to be well within their capabilities."

His main job is spotting the abnormalities and handing out

customized programs based on measured work capacity. His main tool is the stress test on the treadmill.

"In the adult fitness program (at Davis)," Wilmore advises beginners, "we use the level of 75% of your capacity at the intensity level. If you have a maximal oxygen uptake of 40, you exercise at 30. But since you can't easily monitor oxygen consumption during routine exercise,the same concept has been applied to a related physiological variable—your heart rate. You can easily monitor your heart rate by taking your pulse periodically during the exercise session and then adjusting your intensity to bring your heart rate either up or down to the 75% level. This is referred to as the "training heart rate."

Wilmore says 500 people have gone through his stress testing in the last year—including heart patients and "silent" heart disease sufferers. There have been no coronary accidents.

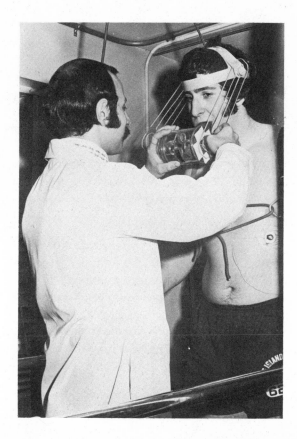

Testing oxygen uptake at the Human Performance Laboratory, Long Island University. (Steve Sutton photo)

Simplified Self-Testing

Physiologists are precise scientists, and as such are skeptical of self-testing methods outside the laboratory.

"Most self-type tests," writes one of the country's leading running researchers, David Costill, " are inaccurate and often misleading."

Of course nothing can replace the controlled conditions and apparatus of the lab, and the trained judgment of the physiologist. Exact measurements of physical capacity can only be made under those conditions.

But physical feedback is too important a body of information to stay in isolated testing centers. So certain field tests have been devised to give approximate data. A runner can do these himself, with little or no equipment or special technical know-how.

Actually runners are self-testing every time they run. It's them against time. The most obvious and reliable test is how well you, the runner, run at the distance you choose. Timed distances put the whole system on trial.

We have isolated two factors which contribute to running performance or block it. These can be self-tested fairly objectively and with a reasonable degree of accuracy.

The two—oxygen intake, body fat percentage— measure running capacity.

Remember that no testing program, in the laboratory or on your own, can precisely predict running ability. There are too many intangibles involved on the emotional side acting as modifiers.

OXYGEN INTAKE

Maximum oxygen intake rate (often called "maximal uptake") is one of the key tests of endurance fitness. Readings are taken in the laboratory from controlled treadmill runs.

Champion distance runner have readings of 70-80 (milliliters per kilogram of body weight per minute) or sometimes higher. It does not necessarily follow that the people with the highest oxygen intake levels make the best runners, but this is still a reliable indicator of personal fitness. The higher *one's own* reading, the faster he should be able to run.

Exercise physiologist Jack Daniels supplies the following self-test devised by Bruno Balke.

1. Run as far as possible in 15 minutes.

2. Record the distance run in meters (one mile=1609.334 meters).

3. Divide total metric distance by 15 to find speed in meters per minute.

4. Compute maximum oxygen intake using this formula: (speed minus 133) x 0.1.72 +33.3.

(For example, a runner does 5000 meters in 15 minutes. This is 333 meters per minute. Subtracting 133 from that gives 200. Multiply by 0.172 gives 34.4, plus 33.3 is a final estimated oxygen intake of 67.7 milliliters per kilogram per minute.)

A level of about 40 (depending on age) is considered a minimum standard of everyday fitness, but even casual joggers tend to score much higher than that. Increased aerobic training adds to this capacity, as does lowered body fat.

Jack Daniels warns, however, that "this formula underestimates oxygen intake for some people and overestimates it for others. This is particularly true for growing youngsters, since it will probably underestimate his aerobic capacity—which could be discouraging."

BODY FAT LEVEL

Body fat, translated into extra weight, has a limiting effect on running. Since weight is part of the oxygen intake formula, it stands to reason that a 5% increase in body bulk shows up negatively in the oxygen system's efficiency, and vice versa.

Average mature men have 15-20% fat. For women, the figures are 25-30%. Runners of both sexes, however, tend to be below 10% fat. This is tested in the laboratory by weighing people underwater.

E.C. Frederick, who wrote the introduction to this feature, has come up with a mathematical method of measuring a runner's fat content. He says it appears at best to vary about 2% either side of actual figures, but that it gives a ballpark estimate of body composition. It comes closest with individuals of average bone structure and proportions and is least accurate for extremely lanky or portly persons.

It is based on the "ponderal index," which is a ratio of height to weight. This is calculated by dividing the height (in inches) by the cube root of the weight (in pounds). Here is a chart of cube roots for various weights.

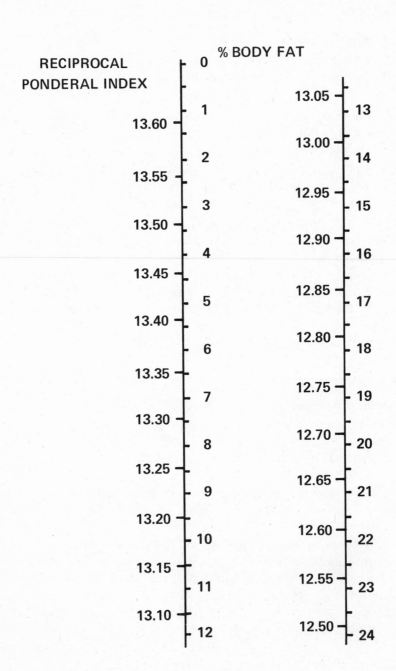

% BODY FAT

RECIPROCAL
PONDERAL INDEX

91 lbs. = 4.5	133 lbs. = 5.1	175 lbs. = 5.6
97 lbs. = 4.6	141 lbs. = 5.7	185 lbs. = 5.7
104 lbs. = 4.7	149 lbs. = 5.3	195 lbs. = 5.8
111 lbs. = 4.8	157 lbs. = 5.4	205 lbs. = 5.9
118 lbs. = 4.9	166 lbs. = 5.5	216 lbs. = 6.0
125 lbs. = 5.0		

Once the ponderal index is calculated, find it on the left side of the scale on page 76. The approximate corresponding body fat percentage is on the right side of the scale.

Runners showing fat percentages over 15% (and particularly if they have thick waistline skin folds to match) could profit by reducing their weight. Most runners, regardless of body build, do better when they cut down their fat levels.

THE YOUNG RUNNER

This article was first published in The Young Runner, June 1973.

Arthur Lydiard and Ernst van Aaken maintain that moderate endurance running is the true activity of children. They're made for it, the two coaches say, and as long as they don't go too hard they can go all day.

On the other hand, long sprint and middle-distance racing are somewhat foreign to pre-teenagers, and they should only work into them gradually as they mature.

These contentions raise questions:

● What is the scientific basis of their claims, if any?

● Is the child different, physiologically speaking, from the grown-up runner?

● Is there any more reason to worry about the effects of running on a growing child than on any other runner?

● What types of races, if any, best match a young runner's physical capabilities?

Taking the last question first, evidence increasingly points to the conclusion that youth programs start children from the wrong end. The general—and apparently erroneous—feeling is that youngsters, particularly before puberty, aren't able to run long distances. So they're limited to short ones and to jumping and throwing, which are "easier."

"What children do badly," says Dr. van Aaken, are "such exertions as sprinting, particularly in excess of 100 meters. On the other hand, any healthy boy or girl is able to run as much as three miles at moderate pace. The play of children is nothing more than a long distance run because in a couple of hours they cover many kilometers with several pauses."

At this age, the German says, general endurance is high but strength and skill have barely begun to develop. This development can't be rushed, as it comes only through growth. No matter how hard they try, children can't overcome their nature. It's in the trying that they get hurt.

Independent research in a number of countries supports van Aaken's claim. Perhaps the most convincing arguments that young runners are indeed different than mature ones in their abilities and limits come from Soviet studies. Dr. A. Viru, an exercise physiologist, conducted extensive testing on young athletes of all ages and compared them with adults.

"Any healthy boy or girl is able to run as much as three miles at a moderate pace." (Horst Muller photo)

Viru writes that runners in all events reach their maximum racing potential "in the third decade," or between the ages of 20 and 30. That's the time when youthful vigor and mature speed-strength-stamina should combine best, if training is adequate.

There are several physical reasons for this:

1. **Heart and Circulatory System**—Viru says although there is no great difference in heart volume relative to body weight when comparing adults and children, "the pulse rate at rest is higher in younger athletes and the minute volume (pumping capacity) for each kilogram of body weight is inversely proportional to the age. This indicates that the child's circulatory system is required to work

Mary Etta Boitano started setting age-group marathon records when she was six years old. She ran 3:01 at age 10. (George Beinhorn)

harder at rest than the adult's, making up for the smaller minute volume and lower contraction capacity by a higher working rate."

In other words, the heart grows stronger (therefore slower and more efficient) with age. Athletes in the 9-13 age group get only one-third to one-half the oxygen supply of adults from each heart beat, according to Viru. "The differences decrease with age," he says, "but even the 16-18 age group reacts to the same work load with a higher pulse rate."

Not only does the young runner's heart have to work harder for comparable results; the blood being pumped also is lower in oxygen-carrying hemoglobin until about age 14 or 15. This gives young runners lower oxygen reserves.

Additionally, there is less blood sugar available for quick conversion to energy under conditions of high stress.

This adds up to the fact that young runners can't possibly do as well as adults in efforts that rely on maximum oxygen and carbohydrate burning.

2. **Respiration**—Even "untrained" children have high rates of oxygen intake, which is considered a good measurement of endur-

ance fitness.

Jack Wilmore, a physiologist at the University of California in Davis, tested 100 children ages 8-12. Many of them had oxygen intake readings in the neighborhood of 60 milligrams per kilogram per minute. Only well-trained mature distance runners routinely score higher.

But these results are somewhat deceiving. High oxygen intake doesn't mean youngsters can use this oxygen efficiently. They can't. As Viru said earlier, red blood cell counts are still rather low, so the oxygen doesn't have good transport through the system.

And, he says, young runners have less of a tolerance to oxygen debt. "While untrained adults are capable of (tolerating) an oxygen debt to 80-85%, the percentage for youngsters is only 90-92%."

Viru's test showed that oxygen consumption in younger runners at rest and at set work loads is higher than adults'. They needed more oxygen just to keep going, and they drop into oxygen debt at lower levels. Young runners also have a smaller capacity to deal with the fatigue product lactic acid that collects in the system during anaerobic work. They tire quicker than mature runners when breathing is strained.

3. **Muscle Strength**—The changes with age in this trait are dramatic, with a spectacular spurt coming at puberty.

"From the age of about five until the third decade," Viru says, "the muscle mass grows 7.7 to 8.5 times and muscle strength nine to 14 times.

"At the age of eight, the muscles form about 27% of the body weight and are still low in contraction capacity. The main development begins at the age of 12, and at 15 the muscles make up about 32% of the body weight. While for the first 15 years the muscle mass, relative to body weight, increases 9%, in the next two or three years the growth is 11%."

Viru measured the amount of weight the young athletes could lift with one hand and carry a few steps. For the eight- and nine-year-olds, it averaged only about a third of body weight. By age 12-13, the relative weight lifted had doubled. At 16, his subjects could lift and carry their own weight.

The sprints and middle distances are "muscle" events, relying heavily on strength and power which are slow in developing.

4. **Speed**—This relates to anaerobic capacity and muscle strength as well as to reaction time and coordination. Since these factors are

related to maturity, too, speed also comes along slowly. It doesn't reach its highest level, Viru says, until between age 20 and 30.

5. Endurance—Here is the one area in which children excel from the earliest years.

While watching children play at a "steady-state work load where no oxygen debt occurs and the nervous system is not under stress," Viru found that they have "excellent endurance for extended workloads, especially where there is sufficient variation in the intensity of the load and they are truly motivated. In these cases, they are virtually capable of non-stop activities—running, jumping, and climbing—for hours."

Any adult who has tried to keep pace with a playing child knows this without an exercise physiologist having to verify it.

Dr. Viru is reluctant to draw any conclusion himself on how this tests translate into practical running experience. The apparent message, though, is to give young runners the type of exercise they're capable of handling, when they're capable of handling it: relaxed, endurance running first, to take advantage of their inherent stamina, adding hard speed and strength work later.

According to Dr. Wildor Hollman, one of Europe's leading sports doctors, "tempo runs"—better known as intensive interval training—should be used only very moderately before the age of 17. Weight training, he says, should be avoided completely because the muscles, bones and joints still aren't sufficiently mature to take it until after high school.

This advice leads to the great unanswered question. What is the effect of early sport on the growing body? We don't have *the* answer yet, but young runners may be susceptible to structural problems from abnormal stress.

A *Medical World News* article on high-stress training in young athletes reports that rats forced to swim strenuously suffered retardation of growth and various deformities. Young runners aren't rats, but as the magazine says, "Recent animal experiments suggest that the effect of early sports training on children's structural development should be studied in detail."

THE OLDER RUNNER

BY DRS. MICHAEL POLLOCK & HENRY MILLER

Drs. Michael Pollock and Henry Miller did their research at the exercise lab, Wake Forest University. Their article appeared originally in Runner's World, February 1973.

There is much research information available concerning the effects of various exercise regimens on young, middle-aged and older men and women. Most of this information deals with either the effects of short-term training investigations conducted over a period of four weeks to six months or with special groups or persons, such as highly trained Olympic athletes.

The recent boom in masters (over age 40) track and field competition has raised many questions concerning training and competition in middle age. Are there harmful effects related to training for competition after 40? Are there certain precautions one should take prior to joining an endurance training program? What kind of physiological changes can be expected? What are some of the differences between trained and untrained young and master athletes? We have tried to answer these questions in several research investigations conducted at the Wake Forest University physical fitness reserach laboratory.

● **What preliminary precautions are needed for a middle-aged or older runner just beginning an endurance training program?**

In order to properly prescribe a training regimen, a thorough physical examination and physical fitness appraisal are important. The fitness appraisal should include a variety of tests evaluating the areas of cardiopulmonary function, body composition (bone-muscle-fat relationships), and certain aspects of motor fitness, such as strength, muscular endurance and flexibility. (Many of these are described in other parts of this series.)

To support the fact that masters competition participants should all be evaluated, the following study is presented. Five years ago, in our initial evaluation of approximately 40 masters runners ages (38-65) from the track club at North Carolina State University, we found 25% to have abnormal EKGs at maximal stress. Most of

these abnormalities were associated with a flattened ST segment
depression which became normal again after 1-2 minutes of rest.
ST segment depression is primarily associated with a relative lack
of circulation to the heart muscle (ischemia). The exact significance
of ST segment depression with maximal exercise and its potential
danger to trained competitive runners is questionable.

Our recommendation is if one encounters more than 1.5 mm.
flattened ST depression at maximal stress then competition should
be avoided. It is safer to train at a heart rate level at which one
knows his heart and its circulation is functioning properly.

Within this group, one runner had aortic valve disease with an
enlarged heart. When asked about medical supervision (physical examination, etc.), it was found that he had had none. His performance on the treadmill elicited multifocal premature venticular beats
as well as 3-4 mm. ST segment depression. Multifocal premature
ventricular beats are beats which originate from different areas of
the heart muscle, and occur before and replace the normal beat.
This phenomenon is potentially dangerous during exercise and can
trigger the heart into fibrillation (uncontrolled beating). Unless
remedied quickly, this results in sudden death.

Heart valvular problems are also potentially dangerous and
can result in sudden death under stress. In this condition, the
amount of blood leaving the heart may be greatly reduced, thus
reducing the blood supply to the heart muscle and the body. This
will cause the heart to be constantly overworked and result in an
enlarged heart. Under exercise conditions, the work of this type
of heart frequently exceeds its blood supply, at times causing ischemia, premature beats and possible sudden death. The man with
this problem was referred to his local physician. It was recommended that he avoid competition and moderately stressful activities.

● **What are some of the physiological characteristics of champion masters runners?**

The table below illustrates data collected on 26 champion
American runners from 40-75 years of age. All subjects had recently placed in a regional or national meet.

All groups have excellent cardiopulmonary function and body
composition characteristics. It is particularly interesting to note
the high maximum oxygen intake results of the men over 60 years
of age. One of these men, Dr. William Andberg (age 61) had the
highest on record for his age group—61 milliliters per kilogram per
minute. Young champion distance runners generally go over 70,

Physiological characteristics of champion Masters track athletes.

Age (Years)	Number of Athletes	Height (inches)	Weight (pounds)	Percent Fat	Skinfold Fat (millimeters)	Max. Ox. Intake (ml./kg.)	Max. Heart Rate	Resting Heart Rate	Blood Pressure	Miles per Week
40-49	11	72.3	158	11	59	57.5	178	49	117/76	40
50-59	6	68.1	150	12	51	54.4	178	42	129/81	40
60-69	6	69.3	147	11	53	51.4	163	46	122/78	30
70-79	3	69.3	147	14	70	40.0	166	60	141/83	20

while young, middle-aged and older sedentary men have values averaging 45, 37, and 30 respectively. Moderately trained middle-aged joggers average about 40-50.

Resting heart rate, body fat and serum triglycerides (fats in the body fluids) were much lower in the tested runners than in the sedentary population, while blood pressure and serum cholesterol were approximately the same. The latter agrees with other research findings in that serum cholesterol appears to be affected more by diet than exercise per se, and normal resting blood pressure values are not usually affected by exercise.

The masters champions' per cent fat was comparable to that of college age men, while sedentary middle-aged men average 22%. Total skinfold fat was determined by measuring skinfold fat at six sites (chest, side of chest, back of arm, abdomen, above hip and thigh) with a skinfold fat caliper. Young college men at Wake Forest University averaged 105 mm. while sedentary middle-aged men averaged 145 mm.

It is evident that the masters athletes possess extraordinary physiological capabilities for their age. The question arises as to whether these characteristics are a result of heredity or from years of continued physical activity, or both. In looking over the questionnaires filled out by these men concerning their past training experiences, most of them had some previous experience in competitive track. Most of the men had not continued their training after college age but resumed running again only after many years of sedentary living.

The runners described in the table were mostly distance runners, with a few walkers and sprinters included. In further analy-

sis of the data, the walkers and sprinters were shown to be lower in cardiovascular function and higher in fat. This was not surprising since their training routines were less demanding. They trained-few miles per week and, in the case of the walkers, at a lesser intensity. The sprinters trained approximately 8-10 miles per week compared to 60-80 miles per week for many of the distance runners.

● **What effect does the aging process have on training and performance?**

Many physiological functions have been shown to be affected by the aging process. As mentioned earlier, working capacity and cardiopulmonary function show marked reductions and fatness increases to alarming proportions. Many studies have shown that these deteriorating effects of sedentary living can be reversed with endurance training.

But the question as to what extent training can slow down the deterioration processes of aging has not yet been quantified. Until data can be obtained from large groups of people over a period of many years, this question cannot be answered.

As shown earlier in the table, although masters champions possess extremely good physical fitness characteristics, they are significantly lower than younger champions. Other factors are involved, but the differences in training regimens associated with age would account for some of this. The fact that the 70-year-old group shows much lower fitness status than the other groups could be partially a result of their training characteristics.

In analyzing the many questionnaires we have received concerning training characteristics of masters athletes and in discussions we have had with many of them, it appears that the aging process eventually limits the amount and type of training one can adjust to. Athletes of all ages have to design their training regimen in accordance with how their body can adapt to the training stimulus. We all have a point in which training becomes straining. When the straining stage is reached, athletes often experience a regression in performance and/or become candidates for an orthopedic disorder.

In our experience with masters runners, intensity (speed) and duration (mileage) of training are the two big problem areas. As one gets older, and in the case of most of the masters runners who have had many years of sedentary living prior to resumption of

"The aging process eventually limits the amount and type of training one can adjust to." (Steve Sutton photo)

training, the joints do not adapt as well to speed work or marathon training. Variability as to what type and how much training one can adapt to is quite wide. Thus training regimens should be adopted on an individual basis. The notion that a runner must train 100 miles a week to be a winner may be true for some individuals but may not be a realistic goal for many masters runners.

● **Should sprinting events be eliminated from masters track competition?**

We have heard many comments concerning the possible safety of older runners competing in sprint type events. Sprinting requires a tremendous amount of energy over a short period of time. Most of this energy is derived anaerobically (without oxygen) and thus places the heart and circulation in great demand. The question arises as to whether or not the heart can cope with this stressful exercise as one gets older. The data at hand cannot answer this question completely. The questionnaires on training characteristics which we received from sprinters revealed the lack of year-round endurance training regimens. In fact, some of the sprinters had no regular training program but just ran occasional sprints to get ready for a particular race. It would appear that sprinters should maintain a year-round program for improvement and maintainence of good cardiopulmonary efficiency. Keeping the heart and circulation in good condition may help to improve the safety of sprint events. Certainly, adults should be discouraged from entering sprint events without previous conditioning. Another important point would be to be sure and have a stress test. This, of course, is the main prerequisite for all older persons entering running.

THE WOMAN RUNNER

BY JANET HEINONEN

Janet Newman Heinonen, runner and frequent contributor to Runner's World, wrote this article for the July '72 magazine.

The so-called lonely world of the distance runner had belonged almost exclusively to the male. But the beauty and the joy, as well as the solitude, of long distances have been experienced by increasing numbers of women over the last decade.

Such organizations as the Amateur Athletic Union have proceeded at a cautious rate in sanctioning long distance events for women. But even without sanctioning, well over 100 women ran marathons in 1971, and countless others competed in road runs all at distances. None dropped dead.

1972 was the first year for the 1500 meters in the Olympics. The women's cross-country distance is 5000 meters or less. The woman who wants to run longer distances must usually compete in men's races (which she can do, says the AAU, only if she is scored separately).

Physiological evidence is accumulating to confirm the experience of women runners: that running feels good. (The first national women's AAU marathon took place Feb. 10, 1974, in San Mateo, Calif. More than 60 women ran the distance.)

The range of distance is increasing as many top female runners now log 70-100 miles a week. The pace is increasing, too, with women running under 2:50 in the marathon (less than 6:30 per mile), and correspondingly fast at other distances. In other words, they're running as fast as or faster than many adequately trained males.

As more women participate in longer distances, both range of distance and pace will increase. Clearly, women's physiological makeup has not kept them from doing as well in the distance events as they have in the shorter ones. Yet questions remain about male/ female differences are related to *how* they run, not to *whether* they should.

Data on female distance runners is scanty and we must rely, for now, on studies of women in athletics generally, not just running.

Fears, prejudices and misinformation exist concerning women in sports. Yet, says women's coach Dr. Harmon Brown, "From a physiological point of view, females can participate in the same sports as males." However, it is important for the athlete, coach and official to be aware of the physiological differences which indicate that men and women cannot compete together *on an equal basis.*

H. A. de Vries, in *Physiolgy of Exercise for Physical Education and Athletics,* sums up existing information:

● The differences in sports performances can be attributed partially to the ratio of strength to weight—which (after puberty) is normally greater in the male. Women have a smaller proportion of muscles in relation to a considerably larger amount of adipose (fatty) tissue.

● The ratio of heart weight to body weight in women ages 10-60 is also a factor limiting sports performance. Women have only 85-90% of the heart size of men.

● Males have a higher basal metabolic rate. But when evaluated in relationship to muscle mass instead of surface area sex differences disappear. Thus the difference would have significance only in respect to resting heat dissipation, not for the efficiency of muscle capacity.

● Men have an advantage in blood content. Many women are chronically anemic, due to iron deficiency. Men, in the age group 20-30, have, on the average, 15% more hemoglobin per 100 milliliters of blood and about 60% more erythocytes per cubic millimeter. This combination of factors gives men a greater capacity to carry oxygen.

● DeVries points out that women have a lower Erbolungs Quotient, which indicates the degree an individual must encroach upon her anaerobic reserves to perform at a given level.

● Cardiac cost, the measure of stress on the heart for a given workload, shows that girls 12-13 work most efficiently. There is no further improvement with increasing age. The male, on the other hand, at age 12-13 has only one-third the cardiac capacity of males in the 31-36 age group.

● Maximum oxygen consumption peaks at an early age for women, too. Eight- and nine-year-old girls have the highest oxygen consumption, then they decline to age 15; after that, it remains constant. Boys peak at 15-16 and maintain that level through young adulthood.

• There seems to be disagreement about the trainability of women. De Vries reports that the female adjusts to heavy training in
much the same fashion as males. Yet researchers Klaus and Noach
say that at the age of greatest trainability (20-30) women respond
to training with only 50% improvement of men. They feel that women shouldn't compete in events longer than 1000 meters.

By contrast, though, de Vries states that by far the greatest
percentage of injuries is found in sports that require explosive efforts: short runs (53%) and the long jump (31%). It is difficult to
avoid the conclusion, says de Vries, that such activities are not suited to the female's musculoskeletal system.

Women in general have bones, muscles, tendons and ligaments
that are more delicately constructed than those of men. And the
overall incidence of athletic injuries to women is double that of
men. The incidence of injuries involving overstrain—such as con-
tractures, inflammations of tendons and tendon sheaths, periosteal
injuries—is four times as great as for men.

As far as gynecological problems are concerned, no distur-
bances of the onset of menarche have been found, nor is there evidence of dysmenorrhea as a consequence of athletic participation.
Athletic women generally have quick and easy deliveries. Women
shouldn't train during pregnancy, says de Vries, because of hazards
to respiration and circulation. Unfortunately, he didn't specify at
what point in pregnancy one should terminate training. Several
women have won Olympic medals while pregnant, and one prominent distance runner whom I know nearly delivered her healthy
son at the track.

The effect of the menstrual cycle on athletic performance has
long been a subject of debate. Different conclusions have been
drawn from different studies. In one study of 70-80 female athletes
at the Tokyo Olympics, gold medals were won by ladies during all
phases of the menstrual cycle.

In a study that tested training response in a female long distance runner, Ona Dobratz was the subject. While the conclusions
are limited because only one runner was tested, they still give some interesting facts about Ona, who later ran a marathon under three
hours.

Ona's oxygen transport capacity increased with training, as
well as her contractile heart force. Performances on maximal exertion tests improved dramatically as her training progressed. Her
hemoglobin level increased during periods of exertion, although

Nina Kuscsik (left) and Beth Bonner were the first women to go below three hours in the marathon. (Walt Westerholm photo)

there were no differences in resting state hemoglobin as training progressed.

The most significant conclusion of the study by R. G. Knowlton at Southern Illinois University was that "many of the results of this experiment parallel anticipated findings based on results from trained males. The training program was considered to be extremely severe (compared with) convention for female runners. Although there were periods of detraining due to physical injury, training was graded and progressive, and there were no signs or indications that the physical stress was inappropriate for the subject."

In future studies of female long distance runners, serious questions must be posed to determine the difference between biological constraints and societal/environmental constraints. Do females have more fatty tissue because of the role they play in society—that of the "weaker" sex? Are females as slow by nature as world track records indicate, or is it due to the fact that proportionately fewer women compete in athletics? Questions along this line could make for hours of lively debate among AAU officials, physiologists, athletes and coaches.

But, as indicated by the findings here, available evidence is lining up on the side of the women who run. The more that's learned, the more credibility is given to the observation by famed New Zealand coach Arthur Lydiard. He wrote in the early 1960s in *Run to the Top:*

"Females have a lighter and weaker build and an inferior capacity for physical performance than males. Their bones are lighter and smaller, their muscles are smaller in proportion to their total body weight, and they have less muscle bulk. Usually, the female is one-third less strong than the male in either individual muscle or total strength capacity.

"The cardio-pulmonary reserve capacity of the female is about two-thirds that of the male, and she is therefore unable to obtain the same maximal oxygen intake, ventilation volume and cardiac output that the male can achieve during physical performance.

"The female's loosely-constructed abdominal organs—the inclined pelvis, producing a greater abdominal area, and the pelvic floor—constitute weaknesses in her physique. But in spite of that, she has the qualities to perform the same types of movement and engage in the same physical activities as the male, limited only by intensity and duration. At her own level, she can match the male in engaging in activities requiring speed, strength, endurance and skill.

"...They (women) can train as long as men can train, can run as far as men can run, like men can do it seven days a week all year through. A few years ago, most people would have considered this either impossible or unwise."

RUNNING FASTER, LONGER

BY J.L. MAYHEW

Jerry Mayhew is with the physical education department at the University of Illinois.

Two recent studies by C. G. Williams and his South African colleagues have revealed some facts which could be vital to runners.

The 1967 study (3) trained men for as much as four hours daily at aerobic levels. Each day's work was followed by "exhaustive" bouts at maximal effort. While maximal oxygen intake increased an average of only 7% (range = 0 to 20%), the percent of maximal oxygen uptake at which excess lactate appeared in the blood rose 16% (range = 5 to 33%).

The change in the two factors did not appear to be related. Before training, excess lactate appeared in the blood at an exercise level requiring approximately 46% of maximum aerobic power. After training, this level had risen to 62%. Therefore, after a period of training (4-16 weeks), the maximal oxygen intake—felt by many to be the prime criterion for endurance performance—may not change greatly, while the ability to work at a greater percentage of that intake without lactic acid buildup shows a relatively larger increase.

In light of recent findings (1, 2, 5) that show relatively little change in maximal oxygen intake over a season of training, an increase in the level of exercise at which anaerobic metabolism begins can be vitally important. It means the runner is able to carry a faster pace for a longer period with less fear of fatigue from lactic acid buildup. If a cross-country runner performs a five-mile race at approximately 80% of his maximal oxygen uptake capacity, fatigue would set in at a later stage of the race and he would have a greater capacity for a sustained drive at the end.

A 1968 study (4) further confirmed that trained men could work nearer their maximum without increases in blood lactate. Furthermore, the researchers found that lactate levels had decreased after one hour of ergometer exercise from the level observed at six minutes into the work. That is, blood lactate reaches a peak early in the transition from rest to work and then decreases even with a constant work rate.

   This finding has several implications. The initial stress of the race will be slightly relieved as the lactate produced is removed. The lag in the oxygen transport mechanism makes it somewhat improbable that the transition from rest to exercise can be met by aerobic means. The initial anaerobic process that allows the body to get into race pace produces some lactic acid. However, as the constant pace is held over an hour period, much of this lactate is removed. Runners would do well to exhibit some caution in choosing the initial pace in that too great a lactate buildup early might not be removed as quickly to allow a continued fast pace.

   Jim McDonagh broke 2:30 in the marathon and made the US Pan-American Games team when he was well into his 40s. (Walt Westerholm photo)

Additional implications related by the physiologists were that at higher air temperatures, the level of oxygen consumption at which lactate increased in the blood was lowered. When the environmental temperature is low relative to the "comfortable" temperature, the percent of maximal oxygen uptake at which lactate accumulates is raised. In hot environments, the runner's endurance capacity is lowered while in cold environments it is raised.

CONCLUSIONS

1. Once oxygen intake capacity has reached its maximum for the individual, further training will increase the level of performance at which lactic acid accumulates in the blood.

2. The initial rise in lactate during the first few minutes of exercise is lowered as the run continues.

3. Hot weather reduces the level at which lactate accumulates in the blood, although this may not be related to the reduced maximal oxygen intake in hot climates (6).

REFERENCES

1. Dainty, D.A., J. Kollias, R.C. Nelson. "A Longitudinal Investigation of the Physiological and Biomechanical Characteristics of Experienced Runners." Paper presented at American college of Sports Medicine Conference. Philadelphia, Pa. 1972.

2. Mayhew, J.L., P.M. Gross. "Functional Variation of Highly Trained Athletes during a Season of Competition." In preparation.

3. Williams, C.G., *et al.* "Effect of Training on Maximum Oxygen Intake and on Anaerobic Metabolism in Man." *Int. Z. angew Physiol.*, 24:18-23, 1967.

4. Williams, C.G., *et al.* The Capacity for Endurance Work in Highly Trained Men." *Int. Z. angew Physiol.*, 26:141-149, 1968.

5. Wyndham, C.H., *et al.* "Physiological Requirements for World–Class Performance in Endurance Running." *S. African Med. J.*, 43:996-1002, 1969.

6. Wyndham, C.H., *et al.* "Relation betweem maximal oxygen uptake and Body Temperature in Hot Humid Air Conditions." *J. App. Physiol.*, 29:45-50, 1970.

CHAMPIONSHIP FIBER

BY DR. GEORGE SHEEHAN

George Sheehan, a cardiologist from New Jersey, is medical editor of Runner's World.

While Dr. David Costill was reporting his findings on muscle biopsies of distance runners at the American College of Sports Medicine, I sat thinking of a long past Boston marathon. That Patriot's Day I had hit the 20-mile barrier and had come apart. From Boston College on, I was reduced to nine- and 10-minute-mile pace, finally finishing in a state just short of collapse some hour and a quarter behind the winner. As I lay splayed out on the terrazzo floor of ground level minus one at Pru Center, a track buff leaned over me hoping to hear the wisdom and eloquence that sometimes fills the common man after surviving such agony. "Those guys up front," I told him, "they must have some alternate metabolic pathway."

Not eloquent perhaps, but certainly wise. I had finally learned that those guys up front were different—different enough that no scientific training schedule, no newly discovered diet, no amount of vitamins would never make me like them. And in realizing this, I finally accepted my place in the middle of the Gaussian bell curve that nature uses so often. I gave up the fantasy of superior performance.

Now, almost a decade since that day, Costill was telling his audience what it was those guys up front really had, what went into a champion, what made men excel, or at least what made distance runners excel. What Costill did was simple. He assembled 16 distance runners ranging in ability from excellent to poor, from champions to also-rans. He then had them compete in a 10-mile race and thus established their performance capabilities. He then inserted a needle in each runner's leg muscle and obtained a specimen for staining and examination.

Leg muscles are composed of two types of muscle fibers: (1) fast-twitch related to speed and power; (2) slow-twitch related to endurance. All runners, good or bad, have these fibers. The way runners differ, Costill discovered, was in the ratio of the two types. As the percentage of slow-twitch fibers increased, so did the runner's speed and performance. In fact, plotting percent slow-twitch fibers against improving time for the 10-mile (and previous personal best time) showed an almost exact correlation. The runner with the highest percent of slow-twitch was the fastest 10-miler. Further, it has already been established that our slow-twitch fast-twitch ratio is built in and is not altered by training, diet, or any known physiological sleight-of-hand.

So there you are. You are either born with it or you're not. The slow-twitch fibers carry the glycogen or sugar source, and when this is used up it cannot be replaced in any reasonable time. Hence, the more slow-twitch cells, the more sugar available for the long distance run. The calculation is simple. If the runner has 90% slow-twitch fibers, he is carrying almost twice as much sugar-fuel as the poor slob who only has the 45%. He has, therefore, an endurance only those similarly endowed can match. Training allows you to reach your maximum potential, but unfortunately that maximum has already been determined from birth by the composition of your muscles.

"I am convinced," said Per-Olof Astrand, the Swedish exercise physiologist, some years back, "that anyone interested in winning Olympic gold medals must select his or her parents carefully." Costill has given a physiolgical basis for Astrand's intuitive statement.

It will only be a matter of time until these studies are expanded to solve other mysteries. How does a marathoner like Frank Shorter differ from a miler like Jim Ryun, for instance? Can we arrive at a muscle profile for each event? Can we pick out the champion sprinters as readily as the distance runners? Is the time coming when the first day of track practice will see the coach line up the candidates for their muscle biopsies and pick his team right there?

MEDICINE

AVOIDING ALL INJURIES

BY TOM OSLER

Tom Osler, a college mathematics professor, is author of the booklet Conditioning of Distance Runners. The following article originally appeared in the Encyclopedia of Athletic Medicine, June 1972.

The purpose of this article is to discuss, in practical terms, the nature, detection and prevention of overstress from distance running. I confess a certain missionary zeal in preparing these words, for after 18 years of running I feel that most runners I have met would do well to contemplate this most important subject.

The material which follows was learned through trial and error. The first 10 years of my running (ages 14-24) left me with injuries of the achilles tendons, arches and knees. Also, my racing performances were very unpredictable. Repetition of a particular training method could not guarantee repetition of racing times. Ten years of running had taught me nothing.

Finally, a severe injury of the hip left me feeling that I might never recover, and in this atmosphere of frustration I decided to "run for fun" and forget serious racing. Away went words like "strain against pain," and "the harder you work, the better you get," which I had trusted so long. In place of the previous hard discipline, I substituted slow, painless running.

Naturally, I expected my performances would gradually decline, but to my surprise I slowly began to improve. In a few years, I won National AAU titles at 25 and 30 kilometers and the RRC 50-miler. More important, I have enjoyed robust health and have been injury free for the eight years following my "enlightenment."

And what is this revelation I claim? Is it some startling fact never previously observed? No indeed! How magnificent is nature in her understatement! I suffered for 10 years with injuries and erratic racing performance, only to find that nature herself has provided us with a simple common sense guide to determining when we are performing healthy work in contrast to self-abuse. It is simply this:

When we feel good, look good, and are alert and productive, our bodies will be adapting effectively to stresses (like running) which we place upon them. If we feel tired, pain and are washed out, we need rest, not stress.

Simple common sense? Yes! But how many times have I heard runners and coaches say, "I felt tired in that race; I must need more work," or "A workout's no good unless it hurts," or "I did not try hard enough," etc.

If we train too little, we do not improve. If we overtrain, our bodies not only fail to improve, but injury and/or illness are likely induced. How can the runner decide upon the quantity of training which produces improvement?

I believe that a practical determination of this optimum quantity can be arrived at by first learning the symptoms of initial overstress. The optimum quantity of running is, then, the largest amount which *fails* to produce these symptoms. In practice, the amount varies from day to day, and the experienced runner learns to "feel in his bones" the appropriate training for that moment.

Here is a list of key symptoms:

1. Mild leg soreness.

2. Lowered general resistance (evidenced by sniffles, headache, fever blisters, etc.).

3. Washed-out feeling and I-don't-care attitude.

4. Poor coordination (evidenced by general clumsiness, tripping, stubbing one's feet, poor auto driving, etc.).

5. Hangover from previous run.

I cannot overemphasize the importance of this list. If any of these symptoms is observed today, it is likely that yesterday's run was too hard to allow the body to adapt effectively to its stress and to improve. Instead of getting a little better, you've gotten a little worse. Easy running should now commence, and harder running be resumed *only* after all these symptoms disappear.

One should also note that all these symptoms are quite mild. They are not dramatic and are, unfortunately, all too often ignored because they seem trivial. But remember that when training effectively you should feel good.

The first symtom, mild leg soreness, is perhaps the most important. It means that the legs are too tired for any real work. It is in this fatigued state that the opportunity of injury becomes fertile. We might say that the legs are pregnant with injury. If the runner continues training hard for several days, so that this leg soreness remains, an injury will likely be born. If he rests or runs easily until the soreness disappears injury will likely be aborted.

I believe that my discovery of this simple principle has largely been responsible for the fact that I have had only one injury since 1964, in spite of the considerable quantity of long racing my legs have endured.

Thus we see that the runner can best decide if workouts are too hard by observing their effects over the following 24 hours. Runners must avoid following a predetermined training schedule with ascetic zeal. A flexible mental attitude is required so that necessary corrections can be made. There is no surer way for a runner to drive himself into injury, illness and poor performance than to religiously follow a training schedule which is more than his body can effectively handle.

Athletes should also consider that continual overstress can produce problems from which they might never fully recover. Buddy Edelen's sciatic problems, Jim Peters' collapse in the 1954 Empire Games marathon, as well as problems endured by several lesser known runners I have observed, all marked the end of promising running careers. Symptoms of overstress must not be taken lightly.

Besides recognizing the symptoms of overwork and stress, it is well to incorporate the following habits into the athlete's training program. These reduce the likelihood of overstress.

1. **Frequent easy days**—Some athletes train hard every other day, running easily on the remaining days. This makes good sense, as it tends to insure recovery.

2. **Flexible mental attitude**—There is no surer path to injury, poor health and bad racing than a stubborn dedication to a strict training schedule. No one can design in advance a training schedule which can anticipate the many variables the runner will encounter. Thus, "common sense" must always prevail, and a schedule must be abandoned or altered as the need arises.

3. **Good diet**—The runner's needs are not much different than those of the general public, except for perhaps increased fluid and caloric input. The runner should attempt to get his nourishment from *fresh natural* sources. Artificial food supplements, such as manufactured vitamins, are of dubious value.

4. **Wear good shoes**—A poor shoe is a sure source of injury. The shoe should have a *soft flexible* bottom to absorb road shock. The elevation of the heel is critical. This elevation should be iden-

tical on the runner's training and racing shoes, and at least as high as his dress shoes. If not, he will likely injure the tendons near his heel. The shoe must fit well, and must be kept in good repair. A great number of injuries are caused by worn shoes. In particular, the heel must be kept square at all times. As you train, the heels tend to wear on the outside. The runner must continually glue rubber to the worn area, or replace the heels. I replace the heels on my shoes about every 200 to 250 miles.

   5. Quit races when exhausted—Long distance races can be brutal on the runner's health. If the athlete runs too fast in the first few miles of a race, he should elect to retire rather than flog his body on while his nerves cry out for relief. Every marathon race features a number of runners who make a point of seeing how much they can suffer. To be sure, they pay a high price in resultant injury and illness for disregarding nature's warnings.

   6. Watch body weight—A gain in weight of even a few pounds places a heavy additional strain on the runner. He should compensate by running slower, and adjusting his caloric input so as to return to his desired form.

   While sprinting and running long distances at an easy speed are natural activities for man, racing long distances are not. One could appropriately describe participation in long distance racing as an act of *self-abuse*. Thus, the runner must consider carefully the frequency he will engage in this unnatural activity. He must also take special precautions to see that his body recovers from racing as quickly as possible.

   Generally speaking, the longer the race, the longer will be the recovery period. The better the runner is conditioned, the sooner he will recover from a race of a given distance.

   How often should one race? This is a complex question, which I try to answer in the following table. I assume that the runner is mature and is training about 65 miles per week.

   This table is only a general guide. Some athletes are naturally heartier than others and can take more stress. Still others, better conditioned, will recover sooner. Nevertheless, I believe it realistically reflects the increase in stress caused by increasing racing distance, and the recovery periods required.

   Meaning of the table:

   Column 1: I assume that the runner goes "all-out" in this race.

   Column 2: This minimum recovery period is the least time

1. Distance of Race	2. Minimum Recovery Period	3. Minimum Time Recommended Until Next Race	4. Special Notes
2 miles	24 hours	3 days	
5 miles	3 days	7 days	
10 miles	7 days	2 weeks	
15 miles	2 weeks	1 month	Not more than 5 15-milers recommended in a given year.
Marathon	1 month	3 months	Not more than two all-out marathons per year.
50 miles	3 months	1 year	Not more than one 50-miler every two years.

interval before the runner can repeat his performance. For example, if a runner clocks 54 minutes for 10 miles today, he can expect to repeat this performance in about one week. However, he could not continually race 10 miles each week without seriously risking damage to his health.

Column 3: While Column 2 gave the minimum recovery period, this column gives a realistic time interval after which the next race should take place. Thus, our 54-minute 10-miler, mentioned above, could expect to race 10 miles all-out every other week without risking eventual health damage.

Column 4: Races of 15 miles and more are sufficiently difficult that special precautions are necessary. These precautions are described.

My friends are likely to accuse me of hypocrisy, for I do race more often than I recommend in this table. *However, I do not race all-out.* For example, while I often race the marathon distance three, four or five times a year, only once, or perhaps twice, will I try to run as fast as I can. At other times, I run considerably slower than I can on that day, so as to avoid abusing my health.

As this article closes, it is well to repeat the "Common Sense Principle" stated in the first section. *You should look and feel good—be alert and productive when training effectively.* While many specific points were touched on such as shoe repair, racing frequency, etc., there is no substitute for your own analysis of your particular situation. Reflection on your own experience, in the light of this basic principle, should lead to a running career which not only provides satisfying racing performances, but robust health as well.

STRUCTURAL TROUBLES

BY DR. GEORGE SHEEHAN

Dr. Sheehan's feeling is that most injuries originate in the feet. He develops that theme here.

The human body is a marvelous instrument. When in perfect alignment and balance, there is almost no feat of endurance the body cannot handle even on a regular basis. However, structural imbalance of even minor degrees can result in incapacitating injuries and persistent disability. Prevention and treatment of muscoskeletal problems in the athlete, therefore, rests on the establishment of the structural balance and architectural integrity of the body—and its re-establishment should injury occur.

There is very little place in the treatment of these diseases for injections, medications and manipulations. Treatment rests almost completely on the following:

● **Biomechanical treatment of the foot.** This means providing a foot support or orthotic which keeps the foot in proper balance. Ordinarily, this entails the preservation of the neutral position of the foot. What we do is bring the ground up to meet the foot, thus preventing it from flattening or coming over on the inside (pronating).

● **Flexibility and strengthening of the muscles.** Ordinary training involves the continual repetition of one motion and the use of one main axis of muscles. This results in two unwanted effects: (a) shortening and loss of flexibility in the exercised muscle, the prime mover, and (b) weakness in the antagonist which opposes it. Additional exercises are needed to prevent this.

It would be wrong to consider these measures as "either/or". Both are necessary. Biomechanical problems in the foot are accentuated as the muscles tighten and their opposing muscles weaken. Treatment to the muscles, therefore, lessens the required corrections of the feet. Conversely, using orthotics for the shoes can lessen the symptoms due to muscle imbalance in the leg, thigh and back. This is particularly true in instances of the " short-leg syndrome," now thought to be due to muscle spasm and to be helped by both heel lifts and muscle re-education.

Using these general principles, one can move on to a general preventive program. First, the runner must review his feet with three major abnormalities in mind:

● **Morton's Foot:** This is a short first toe with a long second toe. The short first metatarsal tends to pronate the foot and cause failure of the long arch as well. This (and other pronatory influences) can cause such problems as:

1. *Heel spur syndrome.* This is improperly called a heel spur. Actually, it is a fasciitis, an inflammation of the plantar fascia which attaches to the heel spur and spreads across the foot like a fan reaching to the toes.

2. *Posterior tibial tendinitis.* This causes pain on the inside of the leg along the shin bone. Sometimes it is mistakenly called shin splints, a term reserved for pain along the front of the leg between the two shin bones.

3. *Chondromalacia or "Runner's Knee."* This causes the pain and occasionally tenderness under the kneecap and sometimes to either side. It results from the foot flattening out and transmitting a torque to the knee, causing the kneecap to ride over on the knob of the thigh bone.

● **Loss of the long arch.** This can cause all of the above.

● **Unstable heel.** This movement can result in achilles tendinitis and "runner's knee."

Prevention for these conditions would include a heel cup, minimal heel lift, a longitudinal arch and a Morton's extension. Judicious use of arch "cookies," heel cups and felt for heel lifters, arch supports and Morton's extensions can be done on a do-it-yourself basis.

Next, the runner should review his muscular status. The distance runner will shortly find that he has established tightness of the muscles running from his foot to his low back. The achilles will tighten, as will his gastrocnemius, hamstrings and iliopsoas. Meanwhile, his front muscles, the anti-gravity muscles, will become weaker. When this happens, he is in trouble. The difficulties to look for are as follows:

● **Inflexibility of the achilles.** This leads to achilles tendinitis and worsens any biomechanical problem in the foot. It also overbalances the shin muscles and makes them unable to handle stress.

● **Tightening of the hamstrings.** This contributes to low back and sciatic problems. It also sets the runner up for a quadriceps pull through relative weakness of that group. It contributes to the short leg syndrome.

● **Shortening of the iliopsoas.** This is almost always present in sciatic and low back pain. It also may contribute to the short leg syndrome.

● **Weakness of any of the opposing muscles,** including the anteroir chamber muscles (shin splints) quadriceps (quadriceps pull) and stomach muscles (rectus pull), sciatica and low back problems.

Preventive maintenance therefore involves the following: (1) foot care, (2) flexibility exercises, (3) strengthening exercises.

When faced with an injury not due to a collision or a fall, the runner must assume that he is out of structural balance. No medication is going to restore that balance. He must get down to basics, diagnose where he is out of line and correct it. He will get temporary relief with whatever the doctor recommends, i.e., rest, butazo-

Highly competitive runners are prone to injury because of the effort and the specialized nature of their activity. (Mark Shearman)

lidine, cortisone shots or whatever. But as soon as he resumes running, he will quickly get into trouble again.

With this in mind and remembering what we have said about structural balance let us consider some of the most frequent running ailments and proposed treatment:

- **Achilles tendinitis**: Cause—short achilles, gastroc, hamstring axis; unstable heel; inverted heel; weak arch; excessive use of toe flexors. Treatment—stretching of achilles; heel lifts; arch supports; anterior crests.

- **Heel spur syndrome**: Cause—no shank in shoes; Morton's foot; weak foot; forefoot varus. Treatment—"doughnut" for heel; full foot orthotic for forefoot problems as well as arch; shoe with good shank (Tiger or Nike Cortez, Puma 9190, Adidas Country or SL-72).

- **Stress fracture, metatarsal**: Cause—weak forefoot; Morton's foot. Treatment—full orthotic with metatarsal help; Morton's extension.

- **Stress fracture fibula**: Cause—unstable heel; weak arch; other pronatory abnormalities and forefoot problems. Treatment—full foot orthotic with attention to Morton's foot; forefoot varus and unstable heel.

- **Runner's Knee**: Cause—pronatory foot influences including the unstable heel, weak foot; forefoot varus and Morton's foot. Treatment—heel stabilizer; arch; possible full foot orthotic.

- **Numbness of the feet** (distance runner's neuropathy): Cause—sciatic nerve pressure. Treatment—stretching of hamstrings and iliopsoas along with abdominal situp (bent leg) and isometric tummy tucking.

- **Other sciatic syndromes**, pain in the thigh and buttock: Cause—tight hamstrings, iliopsoas, weak abdominals. Treatment—use same flexibility and strengthening exercise; use of a Sacrogard belt (usually $6-$8 at drugstore).

- **Shin splints**: Cause—weakness of the anterior chamber muscles. Treatment—strengthen muscles by flexing foot with weight over toes; anterior crest to lessen use of flexors; stretching for the opposing muscles, the achilles and gastroc and hamstrings.

- **Groin pain**: Cause—unknown but probably a mixture of weakness of the adductor muscles, the short leg syndrome and biomechanical difficulties in the foot. Treatment—advise flexibility exercises along with exercises drawing leg toward the mid-line; attention to any biomechanic problem of the foot, however mild.

We are dealing in problems measured in millimeters. Often the injury is precipitated by wear of the regular training shoe down to a critical point—the heel, for instance, where an eighth of an inch makes the difference. Use of a totally new type of shoe for a major effort will also bring on difficulties, as will change of surfaces and even change of direction when there is a slant in the road.

I cannot emphasize too strongly that this is a structual, almost architectural problem, not a medical one. You would almost be better off in the hands of an engineer than a doctor when these illnesses strike. At least you would not have your problem complicated by medication which in the long run will do no good. What the runner needs is to be restored to structural balance. Acupuncture, surgery or wonder drug will not do that.

ABDOMINAL PAINS

BY DR. GABE MIRKIN

Dr. Mirkin is an allergist practicing in the Washington, D.C., area. He is heavily involved in promoting age-group running and is a regular columnist for Starting Line magazine.

Abdominal pains recurring with hard exercise has perplexed many a competitive athlete. The pain, usually in the upper right quadrant, can occur anywhere in the abdomen or back. It usually comes with hard and fast running requiring deep and rapid breathing. Several different mechanisms responsible for the pain have been reported.

Hepatic flexure distention: Most exercise-induced right upper quadrant pain probably is due to swelling of the last part of the intestinal tract, called the transverse colon. Gas is formed throughout the entire intestinal tract and is pushed by muscular contraction, which is markedly increased by hard exercise, towards the colon. As gas rises, it gathers in the right upper part of the transverse colon, called the hepatic flexure. As the gas is prohibited from passing further by stool in the colon, it causes pain by distending the walls of the colon.

Therapy should be aimed at softening the stool so that the gas will be able to pass along the colon. A diet rich in starch yields hard stool, while a diet rich in fruit and vegetables yields the opposite. A runner who gets frequent right-sided pain should eat more fruits and vegetables and limit his intake of bread, potatoes, spaghetti, etc.

If the pain occurs in a race, bend forward as far as you can while still running and squeeze the site of the pain with your hands. This will push the gas along and ease the pain.

Distended liver capsule: When the heart beats rapidly, excess blood is stored in the liver and distends it. This, in turn, stretches the capsule surrounding the liver. As the liver can stretch and the capsule cannot, the runner feels pain. Treatment during the race is the same as with pain caused by a distended colon.

Weak diaphragmatic muscles: Diaphragmatic pain can come from the accumulation of breakdown products from muscular exercise. The diaphragm, like any other muscle, must be trained to get rid of these breakdown products. Accordingly, racing hard and fast should be done at least once every two weeks.

One can also take some of the work off the diaphragm by increasing the intra-abdominal pressure through better abdominal muscle control. Sit-ups done with the knees bent are strongly recommended. The knees are bent in order to put more of the workload on the upper abdominal muscles.

Pre-race meal: The breakdown products of ingested protein metabolism called organic acids, can only be eliminated by the kidneys. Large amounts of organic acids, from exercise in addition to ingested protein, can cause abdominal pain. Accordingly, one should never eat significant amounts of protein for 24 hours before a race. Steak and hamburgers are very poor pre-race meals.

The night before a race a competitor should eat a diet rich in carbohydrate (spaghetti, marcaroni, bread, potatoes). The day of the race, very little should be eaten and it should certainly not be protein.

Milk or wheat intolerance: A significant number of people get abdominal cramping with either milk or wheat. This is due to the absence of an enzyme in their intestinal tract to break down these foods. A person given to abdominal pain should experiment first by not taking milk for 48 hours before a race and then by omitting all wheat products.

Summary of Recommendations: (1) Do sit-ups with your knees bent. Work up to at least 150 per day every second night. (2) Run hard and fast at least every two weeks. (3) Diet: Switch to a diet primarily of fruit and vegetables and limiting carbohydrates. Three days before an important race, switch back to a diet rich in carbohydrates and cut back on the protein. The day of the race, eat nothing or a small amount of dry cereal. Do not eat wheat or milk. (4) If the above fails, see your physician for blood tests, x-rays or other tests.

EXERCISE AND THE HEART

BY DR. GABE MIRKIN

Dr. Mirkin's article appears for the first time in this book.

America has a heart-attack-prone society due, in part, to over-eating. A middle-aged man who has overeaten all his life may be asking for trouble by plunging into an exercise program without proper preparation. Prevention of heart attacks should include both exercise and food restruction.

"A close look at all of the coronary risk factors reveals that what is good for the heart is good for the distance runner." (George Beinhorn photo)

What is a heart attack? Heart attacks are the leading cause of death among middle-aged Americans. The heart is a large muscle which pumps blood to the body. All muscles require a constant source of oxygen and nutrition through their blood supply. If for any reason the blood supply is blocked, the muscle, unable to be maintained without oxygen and nutrition, dies.

Although the heart pumps blood inside its chambers, it receives almost no nourishment from this blood. The heart depends on blood vessels (coronary arteries) on its outside surface for survival. Evidently, as people get older, deposits of fat are laid down on these blood vessels. When enough fat exists to block the blood flow, a heart attack occurs.

Who gets a heart attack? How one chooses one's parents is extremely important. Heart attacks, strokes, high blood pressure, diabetes and generalized hardening of the arteries (arteriosclerosis) run in families. All of these diseases are associated with each other. If either parent had a heart attack before they were 60, one is a likely candidate for a heart attack.

Presumably because of their female hormones, women have an extra 20 years protection against heart attacks. For example, brothers get heart attacks 10-20 years before their sisters.

Laboratory data: There are several tests that a person can get to help determine the statistical probability for getting a heart attack.

● *Electrocardiogram*—Resting EKGs (heart tracing) are not worth much, as many people with severe heart disease still have normal resting EKGs. To be of real value, an EKG must be done during exertion. A "stress" cardiogram may pick up left ventricle strain or a poor blood supply to the heart.

● *Blood pressure*—An elevated blood pressure markedly increases one's chance for a heart attack.

● *Blood tests*—Elevated fat (cholesterol, triglycerides, fat fractions) and uric acid are associated with an increased risk for a heart attack.

Food: For years, medical scientists have argued about what type of food causes fat build-up in the arteries. Ancel Keys, through epidemiologic studies, has blamed saturated fats. However, Eskimos and Samurai warriors eat most of their calories as saturated fats, and have a low amount of fat in their blood and a low incidence of heart attacks. Almost all the fat in the body is manufactured by the body from any foods presented to it. Ingested fat is a miniscule portion of the fat in the blood vessels.

Overeating is probably the single most important environmental susceptibility factor. With the refrigerator and pre-packaged foods, one has a constant source of palatable food available.

Actuarial tables tell us that one has to be almost 50% over-

weight to increase one's chacnce for a heart attack. It takes massive
overeating to become 50% overweight. However, skinny people can
be taking in too many calories. There are many people who can
eat massive amounts of food and still not get fat. Yet, these people store their extra calories in fat plaques in their blood vessels
and markedly increase their chance for a heart attack.

Lack of exercise: Many studies show a higher incidence of
heart attacks in sedentary than in physically active populations.
Accordingly, there are many jogging programs for middle-aged
men. These are not completely safe. A middle-aged man with a
poor blood supply to his heart makes his heart require more oxygen during exercise. The oxygen cannot get through the blocked
pipes and an irregular heart beat may develop. This could be fatal.

For this reason, everyone who has exercised should continue
to do so. Before starting an exercise program, a middle-aged man
should get a stress cardiogram to detect whether his arteries are partially blocked.

Smoking: Smoking markedly increases one's chance for a
heart attack, and the incidence of heart attacks is proportional to
the amount of cigarettes smoked.

Eating salt: In susceptible people, a heavy salt intake will ele-
vate the blood pressure and increase one's chance for a heart attack.

Conclusion: A close look at all of the coronary risk factors
reveals that what is good for the heart is good for the distance runner. Overeating, smoking, lack of exercise and a heavy salt intake
predisposes one to heart attacks. Food restriction, being away from
pollution, vigorous training and restricted salt intake enhances performances.

THE RUNNER'S HEART

BY DR. GUNNAR SEVELIUS WITH JAMES WOODRUFF

Woodruff and Dr. Sevelius are employed by the National Aeronautics and Space Administration.

Sedentary living increases the risk of heart attack. Exercise is prescribed by many physicians as a means of preventing heart disease. But exercise must be approached with caution and a full understanding of its effect on the heart. A number of guidelines must be observed if an exercise program is to improve resistance to fatigue and decrease the risk of a heart attack.

First, a few anatomical and physiological facts. The volume of blood the heart pumps each minute is called "cardiac output." The volume the heart pumps with each contraction is called "stroke volume." Stroke volume can be increased by training the heart muscle. Cardiac output varies with the oxygen demands of the body. A person who has a strong heart will have a large stroke volume and a low pulse rate (less than the normal 72 beats per minute) while resting. A person in good physical condition can do more work at a given pulse rate than an untrained person because of his larger stroke volume.

The blood leaves the left side of the heart through a large artery, the aorta. The blood then flows through other arteries, through the capillaries, and returns through the veins to the right side of the heart. Venous flow, back to the heart, is pumped mainly by contracting muscles in the arms and legs, and by low pressure in the chest each time air is inhaled.

The heart is supplied with blood from the aorta by a pair of vessels called the coronary arteries. If a coronary artery is blocked by a blood clot, a portion of the heart is deprived of blood and dies. This is called a heart attack, or myocardial infarction. Blood clots are more likely to form when the blood stream is slow because of low cardiac output.

The heart muscle, unlike the skeletal muscles, works all the time. The heart works more when we do physical work and when we are upright, and less when we lie down—especially when we sleep. Since the heart works all the time, it gets the rest it needs only when it works less. Some time is required each day for the heart to rest. For most people, about one-third of the 24-hour day is sufficient time for this.

Cardiac output during rest decreases 1% during each year of adult life (past 21 years of age). For this reason, a young adult usually needs less than an eight-hour recovery period and an older person more. Also for this reason, we should eat fewer calories each year past the age of 20.

The work load of the heart is greater for a person who is overweight or has high blood pressure, emphysema or an abnormally large blood volume. Any of these conditions increases the time required for rest and diminishes fatigue resistance.

To help a fatigued heart meet the oxygen demands of the body, blood flow through the kidneys is decreased. Waste products which the kidneys normally remove from the blood, particularly sodium and water, are retained. The fluid retention results in increased blood volume, possible elevated blood pressure and edema, which is manifested by a slight swelling of the ankles. This swelling can be checked by pressing with the thumb over the lower third of the shin bone for five seconds. A thumb mark with a depth of more than one millimeter indicates an accumulation of fluid and a need for more rest.

A fatigued heart has a small stroke volume and pumps blood more slowly than usual. This, combined with a large blood volume, causes a slow blood stream. A slow stream tends to precipitate clots where an artery is narrowed by arteriosclerosis. The reason for arteriosclerosis is not fully understood, but high levels of serum cholesterol tend to predispose to this premature hardening of the arteries. A heart attack results if the clot precipitates in a coronary artery; a stroke if it precipitates in the brain.

The heart meets the demands made on it during exercise by increasing the pulse rate. Two critical pulse rates are of interest. A pulse rate of about 140 is the lowest at which the oxygen demand of the heart muscle is sufficient to stimulate strengthening of the heart. At pulse rates above 160, the venous return is not sufficient to fill the heart, and the heart is inefficient. At either of these heart rates, a strong heart with a large stroke volume can pump more blood than a weak heart, permitting the body to do more work. A strong heart also recovers faster after work.

The purpose of exercise is to improve fatigue resistance by developing a strong heart with a large stroke volume. The same exercise also enlarges the arteries, thus decreasing the resistance against which the heart must pump. An artery with a larger diameter is also less likely to be blocked by a blood clot.

The heart, like any muscle, strengthens if it is made to work under a high oxygen demand. This demand can be sustained for the longest time with a pulse rate of about 140. Running and many other forms of exercise will bring the pulse rate to this level. Exercises which do not bring the pulse rate to 140 beats per minute are generally of less value.

The beginner wishing to improve his condition should start his training by bringing his pulse rate to 140 beats per minute three times in the same session, letting it drop back to 100 in between. As his heart grows stronger, he will have to work harder to bring his pulse to 140. Various exercises may be used. Running is one of the better exercises because the repetitive contractions of the leg muscles and the accompanying deep breathing assure a good venous return. Daily training will usually enable a beginner to run a mile in a few weeks. A person with a known heart disease should check with his doctor, but this program is safe for most people. Any exercise program based on a present work load, disregarding the pulse rate, is unsafe.

The person who wishes to enter into competitive running for a given distance should divide the distance into three or more sections. He can start by running 80% of each section with a pulse rate of 140 and the final 20% of each section with a pulse rate between 160 and 180, with recovery periods between sections. The added oxygen demand at these pulse rates will stimulate his heart to rapidly grow stronger. As his speed comes closer to his set goal, he should add the sections together so that he finally runs the total distance without any rest periods.

Young people may train everyday. People past 40 years of age, and those with a condition that places an extra load on the heart, should allow themselves one day each week for complete rest. Lack of sleep should sometimes be taken into account in the following day's training. Swelling of the ankles and any sudden increase in weight should be checked for daily. Both are an indication of fluid retention and a need for rest. Training should never extend into the third of the day which the heart needs for rest and for supplying blood for the visceral functions.

Exercise should start with a short warmup period. During

Heart rates go quickly to near-peak and stay there for the duration of races like the International cross-country. (Mark Shearman)

this period, the blood circulation shifts from the viscera to the muscles that will do the heavy work. It is important to jog immediately after a race to assure good venous return. Jog until the pulse rate returns to about 120 beats per minute. Failure to do this can result in fainting.

Prolonged exercise causes heavy perspiration which may lead to to a small blood volume and poor venous return. The fluid can be replaced with water and salt tablets (0.5 grams of salt for each pound of fluid lost).

Keeping fit for a normal work day requires only enough exercise to keep the pulse rate at 140 for 15-20 minutes every other day. To become a good athlete, it may be necessary to exercise for hours with a pulse rate of 140 and several periods of peak pulse rate. The oxygen deficit which develops during peak pulse rates causes severe pain in all muscles. The degree of pain a person can stand in training determines, in part, how good an athlete he will be. There will be no fame without pain.

Page 120: Jacki Hansen, winner of the women's division at the 1973 Boston marathon. (John Marconi photo)

5

NUTRITION

WHAT DIET CAN DO

These articles on diet first came out in the July 1973 Runner's
World.

Once it would have been unthinkable to do what Park Barner
did in the fall of 1972 before two ultra-marathons. One of these
races was a double marathon—the 52½-mile London to Brighton
race in England. The other was a 36-miler just two weeks later.

It would once have been unthinkable to run two races so long
so close together, but that's another story. The subject here is running nutrition. Long runs such as these gobble up calories at the rate
of perhaps 100 per mile. Ultra-marathons like Park was running require 3000-6000 calories, at least.

So the logical thing for the 28-year-old Pennsylvanian to do
would be to eat heartily the last hours before racing, stuffing himself with as much energy as he could store.

But instead of fueling up, Barner fasted. "A week before the
London-Brighton," he says, "I tried juice fasting. I also ate my
last meal 24 hours prior to the race instead of the usual 3-6 hours."

Not only did he finish without having his energy run dry, he
ran almost a half-hour faster than his previous best for 50 miles.
Two weeks later, in the 36-miler, he used the same fasting technique.
He passed the marathon within minutes of his best time at that distance, and went on another 10 miles at the same pace.

Park had picked up the fasting notion while reading *The Runner's Diet*, a booklet that is full of radical approaches to the feeding
and watering of runners. It points out a number of so-called "myths"
in established nutritional theory and proposes alternatives.

It has been assumed, for instance, that runners need more food
than most people because they exercise more. The booklet flatly
states, though, that even runners usually are overfed and therefore
overweight.

A leading nutritional expert has said, "The ideal diet only provides a neutral atmosphere." In other words, it can only hurt performance if it is inadequate, not measurably improve it by being
adequate or super-adequate.

Perhaps runners are simply coming up with a new definition of "adequate," but in case after case they've shown that diet juggling gives immediate and positive results. This is true of reducing weight to well below established norms, loading with carbohydrates and/or fasting before races, and with taking special drinks on the run. Some support is also offered for the beneficial effects of vitamins and minerals in heavy doses.

Admittedly, many of these techniques are controversial. Now that the booklet has been out for years, there has been plenty of time to argue over the practices, to practice them, and in some cases to add to them.

This series of articles isn't duplicating *The Runner's Diet* but summarizing what has happened in this area since the booklet was published in August of '72. The articles include some of the arguing, some of the practice and some of the additions.

We're concentrating on the positive benefits of diet-watching, the effects that can be seen in terms of faster times and longer distances, instead of the practices that merely prevent or correct dietary inadequacies. Those are problems for a doctor. We're interested in what already healthy runners can do to help themselves run better.

The emphasis is on long distance racers who go continuously for more than 30 minutes. This isn't meant to exclude non-racers, sprinters and middle-distance people because they are runners at their maximum. They're pushing to the limits of their resources, and diet often can extend those limits—sometimes dramatically—by increasing available fuel supplies and simultaneously reducing the load that has to be carried.

If these dietary practices help runners at the extreme end of the effort scale, they should have application to all other runners who sometimes get tired, hot or thirsty.

Dietary Habits of Runners

The athletic image is closely linked with dietary faddism. Athletes are thought of as pill-poppers who are easy prey to advertising claims. They think of themselves, it's said, as needing special menus which translate into improved performance. Smoking and drinking? Never. Drugs? Maybe, if the rewards are high enough.

RW recently polled its readers to see how realistic this image is. Questions involved weight gain or loss through running special dietary practices, and smoking-drinking habits. (We didn't want to touch the drug matter.)

The survey measured only prevalence, not effectiveness, of these diet-related factors. But runners tend to do what they think is good for them, and to avoid what appears to be harmful. So effectiveness can be inferred from these figures.

Weight: How effective is running as a weight reducer? Amazing claims have been made for it, but what are the experiences of long-term runners?

We looked at runners who'd started as adults, since obviously most of those beginning as children show weight gains unrelated to running.

Of the sample, two in every three runners lost weight, while the other one usually eight showed only slight gain or no change.

Losers typically dropped between 10 and 20 pounds. One-fourth of those surveyed did this, while 11% shed less than 10 pounds, 14% between 20 and 30, and 15% over 30 pounds. One runner claimed to have lost 100 pounds.

Of all the diet-related factors, reduced body weight seems to have the most dramatic effect on running performance. Fat is the enemy. And as was pointed out in Chapter three in the series on physical testing, weight charts alone can't measure fat. The charts are deceptive because they don't take variations of body build into account. The only sure way to find one's own best weight is to have body composition studies taken. Regardless of structure, 10% or less fat is said to be ideal for runners.

Fat beyond 10% is the weight that slows them. "If you don't believe the difference five pounds can make," Hal Higdon has written, "then consider how fast you could run tomorrow if you had to carry a five-pound weight on your back."

Higdon said the best way to get rid of excess weight is to combine distance and dieting: "One of the important benefits of hitting high mileage is that you burn off calories. However, there is an easier method—dieting. To control your weight, limit your intake of calories."

Fewer calories means fewer miles are needed to burn them off, several writers say in *The Runner's Diet*.

● **Fasting:** One way to reduce weight is to take periodic fasts.

When water isn't enough, distance runners head for the ERG container. The drink was devised specifically for runners. (Beinhorn)

Weight-reduction, however, is only one of the benefits claimed. Another is giving the digestive system a rest, and a chance to clean itself out.

Only a small percentage of our readers do any serious fasting. Some 13% reported regular fasts of at least 24 hours. Typical runners' fasts were 1-3 days, taken several times a month with water and juices being the only nourishment.

Park Barner's case is covered in the previous article. He fasts for a full day before races, on the theory that his body already will have enough to do without having to digest food.

● **Vegetarian diets:** Non-meat eaters number only 6% of our sample. Though true vegetarians are rare, however, new evidence suggests that runners have no unusual need for protein. Even people who normally eat meat are now replacing it with starches on pre-race menus.

● **Carbohydrate loading:** This is a technique designed to super-charge energy reserves in the form of glycogen (which carbohydrates produce). In simplest terms, it involves three days of high-protein eating followed by three days of high-carbohydrates. It first drains fuel supplies, then packs them back in just before the race. Carbohydrate loading is said to be increasingly effective in races lasting a half-hour or more.

It has growing popularity among racers. Though the technique has only been widely known the last couple of years, about one in three (32%) of the racers we surveyed now use it. Users claim it lets them run longer while feeling stronger. But at least one doctor, Gabe Mirkin, has doubts about its safety for some individuals. More on this controversy later in this chapter.

● **Vitamin-mineral loading:** This subject is even more controversial. Widespread medical opinion is that overdoses of vitamins and minerals, beyond recommended daily allowances, is somewhere between useless and dangerous.

But one of the world's leading figures in sports medicine. Dr. Ludvig Prokop of Austria, says in *The Runner's Diet* that runners' needs are greater than non-athletes'. Runners, he says, need 2-4 times the intake of certain vitamins.

In our survey, 46% of the runners said they take vitamin-mineral supplements. The most popular are vitamins E and C. Twenty-six percent take E, 23% take C, and 16% use a combination of the two.

Magnesium and potassium reportedly are key minerals for athletes, but almost no one in this group supplements his diet with either of them.

● **Special "athletic drinks":** An immediate need in long races, anything much beyond a half-hour in length and particularly on hot days, is liquid. Tom Fleming, second-placer at Boston this year, said afterwards, "There were thousands of people lining the way and each of them gave me a tremendous round of applause when what I really wanted from them was something wet to swallow. I felt like I had cotton inside my chest."

Water is good, but other substances are better because sweat contains more than water and more has to be put back in. Water + sweetener + electrolyte drinks are available commercially, in an assortment of mixture and flavors.

About 28% of our runners use such drinks before, during or after running. Most of them drink Gatorade, the most heavily advertised product. Gatorade drinkers account for 22%, with most of the others favoring ERG ("Gookinaid"), a drink specially formulated for distance runners.

• **Smoking and alcohol:** Few, if any, runners smoke (tobacco cigarettes, anyway). But one in five of those questioned had smoked regularly before starting to run. Running apparently has some effect in motivating a runner to stop and in keeping him off the weed.

But while runners abstain from smoking, a large majority sees little harm in a friendly drink now and then. One in three allows himself this pleasure.

A Case for Undereating

Even the scientific community isn't quite sure how the Tarahumaras do it. The Indians of the high mountains in northern Mexico subsist on what by American standards is a near-starvation diet. Yet they are the greatest endurance runners in the world. (See "The Super Runners," May 72 *RW*.)

The Tarahumaras race among themselves, in kick-ball relays, for 100 and 200 miles at a time. The runs go continuously for up to two days. American physiologists who have studied these Indians estimate that they burn up more than 10,000 calories during the runs.

Ten thousand calories, to a Tarahumara, is at least a week's worth of eating. They eat barely half as much as nutritionists recommend for athletes. Yet they can run for hours without tiring.

Where do they get their energy? Part of it, of couse, comes from the highly adapted systems they have developed by running every day of their lives in the thin air of the mountains. They eat what is available, which isn't much. There are no fat Tarahumaras.

Drs. Richard Casdorph of California and William Conner of Iowa studied the primitive tribe in 1972. They said the Tarahumaras "are essentially vegetarians deriving most of their calories from corn and beans. Additional nutrition is derived from a variety of vegetables and fruits, including potatoes, squash, pumpkin, chili peppers and citrus fruits. Occasionally, an egg will be eaten, and about once or twice a year as part of their festivals, goat meat will be ingested. But this is a rarity."

The Tarahumara diet, the doctors said, is quite high in carbohydrates and extremely low in protein. They naturally follow the "carbohydrate-loading" practice that modern runners only recently adopted. They are forced by environment, not fad, to be vegetarians. And they practice a form of fasting before their big races.

Michael Jenkinson wrote in *Natural History Magazine* that the Indians eat no fat, eggs, potatoes or sweets for 2-5 days before their day-long kickball matches.

You might ask, "But what would happen if these Indians were put on an 'adequate' diet? Would they run better?"

The Mexicans have tried that, with dismal results. They tried to recruit Tarahumaras for Olympic training. Jenkinson reported, "The Tarahumara lives mostly on corn gruel in the mountains. When he comes to an Olympic training camp, he is given beefsteak to eat, and his gaunt gut is filled with eggs and milk and other strange foods. His metabolism begins to run crazy. He doesn't sleep much, and when he does he has weird dreams."

These Indians aren't quirks of nature. In other areas scientists are finding, often to their surprise, that light eating and endurance are complementary. Other studies have centered on another kind of endurance besides the ability to run long. These have involved long, healthy, vigorous lifespans.

The World Health Organization recently reported on tests by Dr. Joshua Cohen of Switzerland. Cohen measured the longevity of rats, comparing those on "normal" diets with those who were "underfed." The light-eating rats lived twice as long as their heavier brothers and sisters.

Dr. Cohen is now planning the same kind of testing with human volunteers, to see if light eating slows physical deterioration. He feels that by restricting calories, an individual can add decades to his life while giving him the strength and vitality to enjoy the extra years.

Dr. Alexander Leaf, professor at the Harvard Medical School, agrees. He has visited three isolated areas of the world—Hunza in Pakistan, Vilcabamba in Ecuador and Abkhazia in the USSR—where men and women routinely live beyond 100. He wrote of these centers of longevity for *National Geographic.*

Dr. Leaf said these three groups shared several traits: (1) they live in mountains; (2) they are somewhat cut off from the mainstream of modern life; (3) they give high status to the aged and let them participate fully in the community; (4) their everyday lifestyle demands constant endurance activity; (5) they eat lightly, with the diets including little or no meat.

These features are least true of the Soviet Abkhazians, who live in lower mountains than the other two groups and are now beginning to enjoy "the good life." They now eat heartily and consume a normal amount of meat. But the old folks remember leaner days when they were young.

The diets of the Hunzans and Vilcabambans, however, are still sparse. Dr. Leaf wrote, "A US Department of Agriculture study lists average daily intake for Americans of all ages at 3300 calories, with 100 grams of protein, 157 grams of fat and 380 grams of carbohydrates.   By contrast, I found the diets of Vilcambaba and Hunza strikingly similar to each other and substantially lower than the US recommendations."

The averages among adults in Hunza were about 1900 calories, 50 grams of protein, 36 grams of fat and 354 grams of carbohydrates. Meat and dairy products made up only 1½% of the protein intake.

A study of the elderly of Vilcabamba showed that they ate only 1200 calories daily, 35-38 grams of protein, 11-19 fat, 200-260 carbohydrate. Protein and fat again were mainly from vegetable sources.

"The old people of all three cultures," according to Leaf, "share a great deal of physical activity. The traditional farming and household practices demand heavy work, and male and female are involved from early childhood to terminal days. Superimposed on the usual labor involved in farming is the mountainous terrain. Simply traversing the hills on foot during the day's activities sustains a high degree of cardiovascular fitness as well as general muscular tone."

The doctor tells of struggling to keep up with a 106-year-old on a six-hour mountain hike. When Dr. Leaf, then 52, returned to Massachusetts, he immediately cut his caloric, fat and protein intakes and started a running program.

Do We Need Extra Pills?

Ludvig Prokop is not a food faddist. The Austrian is one of the world's most respected sports physicians. His stand in the great supplements-for-athletes debate is that they are needed and can improve performance. But he's careful to qualify his statements.

Dr. Prokop wrote about vitamins in *The Runner's Diet*. He cautioned that vitamins only produce "a demonstrable and subjectively noticeable influence on performance when errors are made in composition and amounts in the diet. With full-valued diet, if one adds even high amounts of additional vitamins, he can expect little positive effect."

His position is one generally held among doctors and dieticians: Added amounts of vitamins and minerals, beyond supplies in the normal diet, only improve running results by correcting deficiencies. If no deficits exist, nothing good happens. Money spent on supplements is wasted.

The debate centers on deficiencies. How common are they? And are they likely to occur in athletes more than in non-athletes? The lines on these questions are clearly drawn.

Some experts feel that the Recommended Daily Allowances (RDA) drawn up by the Nutritional Board of the National Academy of Sciences are more than satisfactory, and that the typical American diet provides all the nutrients required to stay healthy.

However, the US Department of Agriculture found in 1965 that two-thirds of the American population was below the recommended level in at least one nutrient. Another study showed that one in 10 school-age boys and more than half of the girls had deficiencies in vitamin C.

A conservative diet expert's answer to this would be that the RDAs have built-in safety margins, and that most people can get by quite well on less than those figures.

Ludvig Prokop says a non-athlete may be able to do this, but not an active individual. He says, "In hard work, the need for various vitamins increases markedly, so that even with so-called 'normal' doses a deficiency can result."

Take vitamins C and E, for instance. They're the most common ones that athletes take in large doses. The American recommendations are 60 milligrams of C and 30 international units of E daily for grown men. Prokop, a European, quotes a slightly higher

The race will go on around
the clock. It's a 24-hour
relay, and the runner
hopes he has packed
enough nutrition in
his case to keep him go-
ing all day and all night.
(Stan Pantovic photo)

figure for C (70 mg.) and slightly lower for E (7-10 i.u.)—these for
non-athletes.

But for speed/strength athletes, he has found the daily needs
to be twice to three times as high. And for competing distance runners, he recommends 200-240 mg. of vitamin C and 30-50 i.u. of
E. Both vitamins are said to be related to endurance and recovery
powers.

Prokop warns, though, that these increased doses are only
used to make up for deficiencies. Overdoses "can easily disturb
the balance and thereby *decrease* performance capacity."

But another part of the argument over supplements is what
constitutes an overdose? Dr. Gabe Mirkin tells of an experience he
had several years ago.

"I would take 500 mg. of vitamin C twice a day. I noted that
whenever I stopped taking it, my recovery period from long runs
was prolonged and my mileage would go down. I even wrote a newspaper article stating that vitamin C appeared to improve my endurance."

Then Gabe was injured. He quit taking his C. When he recovered, he found he didn't need the vitamin. His workouts were as good as ever and his races better than before.

"I attributed my earlier dependence to the fact that when I took large doses of vitamin C, my body required large doses," he says. "I didn't think much more about it until I read in a medical journal that mothers who took large doses of it during pregnancy have infants that developed scurvy (C deficiency) symptoms early in life."

Perhaps of more immediate concern to endurance runners is any deficit in minerals—particularly magnesium and potassium. Dr. Kenneth Cooper reported in *The Runner's Diet* that the most significant loss in distance running is magnesium. Drains in this mineral result in extreme muscle fatigue and cramping.

Now Cooper has backing from a team of French scientists working with another kind of athlete. Drs. B. Boursier and A. F. Creff tested soccer players. While normal blood maganesium levels are 50-62 milligrams per liter, the doctors found that only five players on a 14-member team fell in this range. The others were all below. Boursier and Creff said both endurance and recovery times were impeded in these players, and that the team had been doing poorly in recent games.

They gave the players supplemental magnesium, combined with potassium, salt and vitamin C. Magnesium doses were 8-10 mg. per kilogram of body weight. On game days, extra amounts of C (2 grams) and potassium were supplied.

Blood magnesium levels climbed back to normal, even above-normal levels, after this treatment, indicating the athletes would be able to work harder and bounce back quicker than before.

Ultra-marathoner Ken Young experimented with magnesium supplementation last year during a 100-mile run. He took Dolomite—a magnesium-calcium blend—to prevent cramping in the last half of the race.

"I found that two Dolomite tablets washed down with 3-4 ounces of Gatorade every three miles from 50 on worked quite well for me," he says. "In fact, I did not suffer muscular cramps during or after my 100-mile ordeal, although I was rather stiff for a few days."

Special diets: Are they a "total waste of money," as some nutritionists have suggested? Distance man Tom Hovey has one answer:

"A society that annually spends $4 billion on candy, $3 bil-

lion of soft drinks and $11.5 billion on alcohol should think twice
before criticizing those who spend a little money on stone ground
flours, whole grain breads and cereals, pressed oils, or fresh fruits
and vegetables grown without chemical fertilizers and insecticides."

He concedes, "There is no magic food or food supplement
that is going to turn the athlete into a super performer. I am 43
years old and hope to break three hours in the marathon. I wish
it only took a vitamin pill."

It obviously takes more than that. But when diet is inadequate,
runners may need to spend some money on supplements to keep
themselves from going deeper into nutritional debt.

CARBOHYDRATE-PACKING

BY PETER VAN HANDEL

Peter Van Handel works in the Human Performance Laboratory at Ball State University, Muncie, Ind., site of a great deal of ground-breaking research involving running physiology.

Much has been written concerning the relationship of carbohydrate stores (glycogen) to endurance performance. However, many of the comments on the matter of "carbohydrate-packing" to improve running time seem to be based on misinformation and/or prejudice. Many of the critical statements come from athletes who have tried "packing" but for one reason or another failed to achieve the desired results. However noble their intentions in passing this information on, the result is often the spread of more misinformation. I am attempting here to clear up some of these misconceptions and to present a workable protocol for those who may wish to "pack."

The energy used during distance running is obtained from the breakdown of foods both with and without oxygen. The relative contributions of these aerobic (with oxygen) and anaerobic (without oxygen) processes change with the intensity and duration of activity.

In endurance events, both the ability to take in large amounts of oxygen and the ability to utilize a high percentage of this oxygen seem to be requirements for success. Thus, it has been shown that top-flight endurance runners are able to function above 80% of their maximal oxygen capacity for an entire marathon.

In work of this duration, fats are the major source of energy. However, numerous investigations have indicated that at the same time the carbohydrate (glycogen) stores of the working muscles are rapidly consumed and at fatigue they are nearly depleted. Based on these data, researchers have suggested that (1) the available stores of carbohydrates may be the limiting factor in endurance work, and (2) there is a positive relationship between muscle glycogen concentration and exercise tolerance in man. The evidence also indicates that there is an enhanced capacity for prolonged work after a carbohydrate-enriched diet, and this is due to an increase in the muscle glycogen stores.

For example, in one study subjects on a normal diet had depleted glycogen stores after a cross-country run of 30-kilometers and had showed a marked reduction in running speed as the glycogen levels approached low values. The same subjects on a carbohydrate-enriched diet completed the run in a shorter time and could hold the pace for a longer time. The authors point out that the greater carbohydrate stores do not have a direct effect on the speed the runner can maintain. Rather, this is primarily determined by the individual's ability to take in and use oxygen.

Along this same line, Dr. David Costill has shown that the rate of glycogen utilization is greatest during the early stages of a race. The runner who selects too fast a pace early in the run may prematurely reduce the glycogen stores and severely limit his performance. This in effect means that if you have "packed" you are *not* going to be able to go out faster. You should, however, be able to hold your best pace longer, which then results in a faster running time.

The value of carbohydrate-packing or enriching diets seems to lie with athletes participating in events relying on the aerobic processes. Most research studies have concentrated on exercise tasks of 30 minutes to several hours in duration, so that the benefits of increased carbohydrate stores on performance in events of 10-30 minutes duration or in events requiring repeated performance in a short time period are unclear.

Included in this group would be high school and collegiate two-, three- and six-milers, cross-country runners and any runner competing in more than one event as occurs in conference, national and international championships. For example, Costill examined the effects of three successive days of running (10 miles each day) on the carbohydrate stores. He found a marked reduction of muscle glycogen from day to day, and also showed that a normal diet between runs was not able to restore the glycogen to pre-exercise levels. In effect, the runner was starting each run at a progressively lower level. This would seem to have important implications for those athletes using solely long-hard runs for training. Numerous other investigations have shown that the glycogen stores have no real effect on short, high intensity tasks (sprints, etc.).

There seems to be no doubt, however, that increasing the body's carbohydrate stores will enhance endurance performance.

The question is, how does one go about carbohydrate packing?

Swedish researchers summarize the experimental work done by stating that the initial glycogen stores can be lowered by a high-fat/protein diet and/or exercise, and can be increased by a high carbohydrate diet. The athlete is then ready for the race.

Carbohydrate stores can be increased by (1) eating a carbo-hydrate-rich diet, (2) exercise depletion followed by packing, and (3) exercise and diet depletion followed by packing. All three methods will increase the glycogen stores by significant amounts, though the third method seems to achieve the highest levels. This indicates that it is not necessary to suffer through extreme dietary changes in order to produce some results.

Here is a suggested protocol for carbohydrate-packing. On day one, a long run is followed by a fat-protein diet until after the workout on day three. From day three to competition, he packs. The workout on day five should be very light or not taken at all. (Note: research has shown that the chemical processes responsible for glycogen restorage are most active 5-10 hours after depletion, so that the first packing meal may be the most important one. The meal the night before the race is probably the least important. Note also that gorging yourself is not necessary and in fact may be a cause of angina-like pains.)

Several important points need to be mentioned here. First, it has been our experience that runners using this protocol experience symptoms similar to those found in hypoglycemia (low blood sugar) on days two and three. Since the brain can only use blood sugar, one may expect some disorientation, inability to concentrate and irritability on these days. We are assuming that all runners have had a thorough physical exam which includes a "stress test" electrocardiogram, glucose tolerance test, and measurement of various blood and urine factors. This type of information identifies the person with tendencies towards diabetes or other disorders which would presumably preclude carbohydrate-packing and possibly even distance running itself.

Secondly, it is important to maintain caloric intake during the depletion period, i.e., don't starve yourself. I have seen runners lose 5-10 pounds over 1-3 days by not maintaining adequate intake. Such weight losses may negate the packing effects by causing reductions in strength. Concerning weight changes with "packing," there seems to be no cause for worry by adding weight by storing water with the glycogen. Since there is a maximum amount of glycogen that can be stored in the body, and we know how much water is stored with glycogen, the amount of possible weight gain can be calculated.

Assuming maximal glycogen storage, the water weight gain would be at most 3% of the individual's normal weight—a rather insignificant amount. Indeed, this excess water may be of benefit if the run is in the heat where large sweat losses can occur. The possibility of the extra glycogen "sucking up" the water of the cell and blood causing dehydration is highly unlikely if the runner is sat-

Pax Beale (left) and Ken Crutchlow take a drink break on their 1973 Death Valley-Mt. Whitney trek. (Joan Ullyot photo)

isfying his thirst to any degree. If any dehydration does occur, it is most likely due to the failure of the runner to replace the fluids lost via sweating during the training runs.

Third, though it is theoretically possible to deplete and pack once every 6-7 days, it is recommended that this technique be used to peak for some important race. It probably shouldn't be used more than once or twice a season, as our experience indicates that the process is rather unpleasant and seems to place severe stresses on the individual. It should by all means be tried for some unimportant race before one makes the commitment to "pack" for the big one.

Fourth, any concern over the effects of repeated carbohydrate depletion on cholesterol and triglyceride levels when packing seems to be unfounded. True, one form of hyperlipidemia results from excess dietary carbohydrates being converted to fats. However, this is a disease state that is not compatible with the requirements of distance running. If anything, the high blood fat levels found in athletes are due to the repeated days of distance training causing increased reliance on the fat stores for energy. It is also known that following endurance exercise, the fat levels of the blood show an increase.

Fifth, disorders of metabolism or other disease states may cause cellular destruction. There are diseases where abnormal amounts of glycogen are stored and/or the glycogen cannot be broken down once it is stored. However, these diseases are rare and incompatible with life so that death usually occurs before the age of five, or are such that the individual cannot exercise beyond a limited amount without extreme fatigue and muscle cramps occuring. Indeed, if glycogen was to cause cellular destruction, we would all be in sad shape since there are always carbohydrate stores present in muscle and liver tissue.

This leads me to the sixth and last point. It is important to realize that this technique may have different effects on the same individual if repeated during a season. In addition, "packing" does not seem to help some runners. Indeed, it may not be advisable for some athletes even to attempt packing. Whether this variability in effects is due to weight losses, inability to recover from the fatigue during depletion, "slow" restorage processes or some other factor isn't quite clear. We suspect that the individual's age, state of training and the environmental conditions may also affect the results.

In summary, carbohydrate-packing seems to be an effective tool for improving performance in events longer than six miles. However, some individuals do not respond as expected. It is important that the stresses of training, depletion and packing don't overload the individual so that excess fatigue and weight loss result.

REFERENCES

1. Christensen, E. H. and Hansen, O. "Arbeitsfahigkeit und Ehrnabrung. *Skand. Arch. Physiol.* 81: 160-171, 1939.

2. Costill, D., Sparks, K., Gregor, R., and Turner, C. "Muscle Glycogen Utilization during Exhaustive Running. *J. Appl. Physiol.* 31: 353-356, 1971.

3. Costill, D. "Muscle Glycogen Utilization during Prolonged Exercise on Successive Days." *J. Appl. Physiol.* 31: 834-838, 1971.

4. Saltin, B., and Hermansen, L. "Glycogen Stores and Prolonged Severe Exercise," in G. Blix (ed.), *Nutrition and Physical Activity,* p. 32, Almqvistand Wiksell, Uppsala, 1967.

Additional information on this topic can be found in the following:

Astrand, P. O. and Rodahl, K. *Textbook of Work Physiology*, McGraw-Hill Book Company, New York, 1970.

Bergstrom, J. and Hultman, E. "Nutrition for Maximal Sports Performance." *JAMA.* 221: 999-1006, 1972.

Costill, D. L. "Health Hazards During Distance Running." *Amer. College Sports Med. News.* 8(3): 6, 1973.

Hoffman, W. S. *The Biochemistry of Clinical Medicine.* (4th Ed.), Year Book Medical Publishers, Inc. Chicago, 1970.

Karlsson, J. and Saltin, B. "Diet, Muscle Glycogen and Endurance Performance." *J. Appl. Physiol.* 31: 203-206, 1971.

DRINKING ON THE RUN

by J.L. MAYHEW

This article by University of Illinois physical educator Jerry Mayhew deals with drinking during long runs.

The questions of fluid loss and hypoglycemia (low blood.sugar) are not new in distance running. However, recent research has produced interesting prospectives along two distinct lines, one dealing with the immediate amelioration of the problem and the other with a relatively long term cycle for forestalling fatigue.

The immediate solution to the problem is just that—a glucose solution which can be consumed both before and during the event. In short duration runs (under 10,000 meters), lowered blood glucose is not a major problem. Besides, no one can afford to interrupt his running rhythm to take a drink. However, in longer races the reduction in blood sugar (glucose) is a major problem and may be credited with the fatigue felt in the latter stages of a marathon.

The drink (e.g., Gatorade, Quick-Kick, ERG) is a glucose solution with electrolytes (inorganic chemicals for cellular reactions) added. It is often present among runners before the race and is usually provided at each aid station, along with plain water. But what does research say about the two liquids?

First, heavy exercise (above 70% of maximal oxygen uptake) causes inhibition of the emptying process of the stomach. Over years of experimentation, J. N. Hunt has shown glucose, even in small amounts, to further retard the emptying rate of the stomach. In addition, plain water has been shown to leave the stomach as much as 50% faster than a glucose solution.

Therefore, which is better: get in water fast or absorb glucose at a slower rate? No one has a certain answer. If 5-6% of the body weight is lost by dehydration, serious symptoms may result: high pulse rate, high body core temperature, dizziness, nausea, etc. As is well known among distance runners, if these symptoms are not reversed, serious consequences can result. Thus, the immediate problem becomes to prevent as much dehydration as possible

The art of taking a drink without missing a stride. (G. Beinhorn)

but also to forestall the drop in blood glucose.

Sufficient studies now show that a glucose solution taken during prolonged exercise can improve performance. The reason given is that it offsets the fall in blood sugar in the latter stages of the race. Since intestinal absorption of glucose is not markedly affected by exercise, and because ingested glucose is taken up and used by active muscles, it seems quite appropriate that runners should take in small amounts of a glucose solution during long runs.

In addition, the recovery from extreme effort is markedly enhanced by taking a glucose solution during the run. Costill, Kammer and Fischer report that after treadmill runs of approximately 18 miles, trained marathoners were able to perform an additional 5-10 miles in a second workout only on the day in which they consumed glucose solutions during the treadmill run. On days when no fluid or only water was taken during the treadmill run, the runners were too tired to perform a subsequent training session.

However, it should be noted that for those who find these solutions distasteful or nausea-producing, plain water can successfully hold down the rising body temperature during the race, no less an important factor in long runs. This fact may prevent the dangerous heat syndrome: high pulse rate, reduced blood volume, syncope and cessation of sweat production. Additionally, it has been observed that drinking rather large quantities of water (about two liters) prior to exercise may reduce exercise heart rate and increase sweat production.

CONCLUSIONS

1. Blood glucose levels may be maintained during exercise by periodic ingestion of a glucose solution.

2. Water is removed from the stomach 50% faster than a glucose solution.

3. Overhydration prior to the race may aid physiological responses to severe exercise.

4. All fluids taken during exercise should be cool (about 41 degrees F) when ingested to enhance gastric emptying.

5. Sponging the body offers little heat dissipating advantage.

REFERENCES

1. Cade, R., et al. "Effect of Fluid, Electrolyte and Glucose Replacement during Exercise on Performance, Body Temperature, Rate of Sweat Loss, and Compositional Changes of Extracellular Fluid." J. Sports Med. Phys. Fitness, 12:150-156, 1972.

2. Costill, D. L., W. F. Kammer, A. Fisher. "Fluid Ingestion During Distance Running." *Arch. Environ. Hlth.*, 21:520-525, 1970.

3. Costill, D. L., Sparks, K. E. "Rapid Fluid Replacement Follow Thermal Dehydration." *J. App. Physiol.*, 34:299-303, 1970.

4. Costill, D. L., *et al.* "Glucose Ingestion at Rest and During Prolonged Exercise." *J. App. Physiol.*, 34:764-769, 1973.

5. Costill, D. L., *et al.* "Factors Limiting the Ability to Replace Fluids During Prolonged Exercise." *Med. Sci. Sports*, 5:57, 1973.

6. Fordtran, J. S., B. Saltin. "Gastric Emptying and Intestinal Absorption during Prolonged Severe Exercise." *J. App. Physiol.*, 23:331-335, 1967.

7. Gisolfi, C. V. "Evaluation of Hyperthermic Preventive Techniques during Endurance Running." *Med. Sci. Sports*, 4:vi, 1972.

8. Gordon, B., *et al.* "Sugar Content of the Blood in Runners Following a Marathon Race." *J. Am. Med. Assoc.*, 85:508-509, 1925.

9. Green, L. F., Bagley, R. "Ingestion of a Glucose Drink during Long Distance Canoeing." *Brit. J. Sports Med.*, 6:125-128, 1972.

10. Hunt, J. M. "The Site of Receptors Slowing Gastric Emptying in Response to Starch in Test Meals." *J. Physiol. (London)*, 154:270-276, 1960.

11. Hunt, J. N. "The Osmotic Control of Gastric Emptying." *Gastroentro.*, 41:49-51, 1961.

12. Levine, S. A., B. Gordon, C. L. Derick. "Some Changes in the Chemical Constituents of the Blood Following a Marathon Race." *J. Am. Med. Assoc.*, 82:1778-1779, 1924.

13. Mayhew, J. L. "Causal Analysis of Distance Running Performance." *Brits. J. Sports Med.*, 6:129-137, 1972.

14. Moroff, S. V., D. E. Bass. "Effects of Overhydration on Man's Physiological Responses to Work in the Heat." *J. App. Physiol.*, 20:267-270, 1965.

15. Thomas, V. "Some Effects of Glucose Syrup Ingestion Upon Extended Sub-Maximal Sports Performance." *Brit. J. Sports Med.*, 5:212-227, 197.

16. Whichelow, M. J., *et al.* "The Effect of Mild Exercise on Glucose Uptake in Human Forearm Tissue in the Fasting State and After Oral Glucose Administration." *Metabol.*, 17:84-96, 1968.

Page 144: Wisconsin's Paavo Nurmi marathon, largest between the two coasts. (Jay McNally photo)

6

LIFE-STYLE

RUNS THAT NEVER END

This feature series originally appeared in Runner's World, August 1973.

Exact figures are impossible to come by, but a safe guess is that of every 10 runners who were active last New Year's Day, nine of them won't be running by this Christmas.

The overall trend in running is to growth. But the dropout rates are still astonishingly high. If you were on a high school or college track team as recently as a year ago, count the number of your teammates who are still running. If you have a figure higher than 10%, your school is most unusual. Your coach planted a wonderful seed of interest in his athletes.

This doesn't happen in most schools, which account for all but a small percentage of US runners and therefore most of the dropouts each graduation day.

Hal Higdon is 42. He has been running most of those years, and probably will keep running the rest of his life. Hal recently went to his college class' 20-year reunion in Minnesota.

"Three or four classmates came up to announce that they were now doing some running themselves," Hal says. "But the thing that really struck me was that the current runners from the class of 1953 were not the athletes. They were the non-athletes who seemed to have discovered this thing later in life. None of them had been on the track team. The one former track man I saw there does no running at all. Maybe this says something about our sport."

It says several things. For one, Hal Higdon is the exception and his former teammate the rule. Few runners continue, and the reasons for quitting are many—and often quite legitimate. Some are discouraged by unfulfilled goals, some are satisfied by fulfilled ones, some are disabled by chronic injuries, and some are unable or unwilling to make room among their responsibilities for this type of activity.

Curiously, it is often the "athletes" who quit early and the "non-athletes" who pick up the sport later to stick with it. (Higdon, again, is an exception. He was a capable runner in college who later bloomed into an American record holder and later still set world marks as a veteran.)

The pursuit of excellence is so fast and hard that runners who choose this road don't often stay on it for long—"long" in this case meaning 10, 20 or more years, with no desire to stop. Pursuing excellence means suffering, sacrificing and gambling. It isn't easy to keep doing any of these unless a person keeps meeting his high standards, and it is all but impossible to meet these standards year after year.

One long-term runner was quoted in the *Racing Techniques* booklet as saying, "You have to look at your career as if it's a race, then pace yourself accordingly. If you're planning to run indefinitely, you don't blow everything by sprinting the first mile. You find a pace you can comfortably carry all the way. One year to me is like the first mile of a marathon, and I have to be careful not to go out too fast."

This isn't to suggest, though, that a runner can't be fast some of the time, have high-level success for awhile and still enjoy dec-

Hal Higdon is an exceptional runner, if only because he kept running after college—and on into his 30s and 40s. (Jay McNally)

ades of running. It's just a warning against suffering, sacrificing and gambling *all* the time. The odds are against you.

Running without end is first a matter of pacing. Also of (2) maintaining an appetite for running; (3) fitting it into one's everyday lifestyle as comfortably as possible; (4) adapting gracefully to inevitable changes in age and living-family-work situations; (5) avoiding injuries and illnesses.

Is it important to run endlessly, or is it a wise man who knows when his prime has passed? This is a question of values, to which there is no single answer. The answer is in each runner's view of the sport, and what he wants from it. The individual who runs a mile a day for 50 years looks at it differently than one who runs one mile on one day in 3:50.

One says, "If it's worth doing, it's worth doing as fast as possible." The other says, "If it's worth doing, it's worth doing forever—no matter how slow it might get."

Those Who Keep Going

Running, of course, is the oldest of sports, and most other sports trace their ancestry back to it. But in two important ways, running is still quite young—young because the bulk of the runners are under 20 years old and because runners hadn't participated in bulk until the last five or 10 years. Until recently, it was rare to see a runner still active after leaving school. It is still rare to see one who has stayed active for more than a decade.

No one knows this better than Mike Kish. Kish ran his first race when he was seven years old. That was in 1913. Mike has run steadily since then, and has watched the sport go through waxing and waning cycles, the latest being the present unprecedented boom phase.

Kish is the leader of a very select group of enduring runners. He has been running and racing for 61 years now. We surveyed these readers last March, and nearly 1700 of them responded. Of that number, only Kish and two others had run for more than a half-century straight. We found 62 runners—about 4% of the sample—who had lasted as long as 20 continuous years, a commendable accomplishment in itself.

Think of it. They started in 1953 or earlier. If you're 30 years or so, remember what 1953 was like and how long ago it was. The

Mike Kish (left)—a runner since 1913. (Jeff Johnson photo)

Korean War had just ended, and Eisenhower was in the White House. Running outside of school was all but non-existent.

Mike Kish recalls, "I came to California in 1948, and they were just starting races. I started most of them myself, in fact, or got others interested in running." Los Angeles, now one of the three or four leading running centers in the country, was unusual. Most areas had nothing then, had no Mike Kish to spur them, and wouldn't start any open races for another 10 or 15 years.

Think what these 62 runners had to go through in years when running wasn't so easily accessible or acceptable as now. It's surprising this many survived.

If you're too young to remember 1953, or you're just now

beginning running, think ahead 20 years. That's 1994. Will you
still be running then? And if so, can you imagine the changes the
world and the running environment will have gone through by then?

Those of you who want to last that long might be able to learn
from those who already have—the 62 runners who have been at it
for 20 years or more and don't intend to stop now.

Several features link them.

• They're all at least 30 years old. Most are over 40, which
they almost have to be to have logged this many running years.
This usually means they are men with careers and growing families,
and in some cases retired men with families that are grown and gone.
These runners apparently have successfully adapted running to other
responsibilities.

• All but a few of them raced from the beginning, and most
of them still do it. (About 87% began as racers, and 72% race now.)
Then, as now, racing can serve as a valuable central focus, a goal
or motivator, to one's running. Those who have this focus seem to
stay with the sport longer than those who don't race. But remember, too, that almost no one ran in 1953 unless he was a racer.

• Early success at racing has something to do with establishing
a lasting interest. Four out of five of these runners have run the
equivalent of a five-minute mile or a three-hour marathon in years
past. However, few if any any of them were among the very top
runners at their prime and few are the leading veterans now. (Peter
Mundle and Hal Higdon, both present or former over-40 record
holders who have run for almost 30 years, go against the general
trend.) Reasonable success appeared to spur these runners, but it
left them hungry for more. Milers in the 4:30 range and marathoners around 2:40 seem the hungriest, according to this survey.

Remember again, though, that few runners had a chance to
keep going in 1953 if they didn't race well from the start. That has
changed.

• While most of these people still race, the races are fairly infrequent. Sixty-two percent of the racers compete fewer than 20
times a year, and 42% of them fewer than 10 times. This indicates
that races are well enough spaced—typically about once a month—
so there is adequate recovery in between.

• The majority of these racers, present and past, consider themselves middle distance runners. Exactly 50% run or have run races
mainly in the 880 to six-mile range. Most of the rest are long distance men; very few of them are sprinters.

• These runners are thoroughly hooked on day-to-day running. Seventy percent of them run at least five days a week, most do seven, and many go out both morning and evening. Running is an essential part of the daily lifestyle, a habit.

• Though running is an everyday affair, it isn't too strenuous or time-consuming in most cases. Only one runner in five trains more than an hour a day. Typically they average 3-6 miles per session, which is quite low by current standards but more than adequate for purposes of maintaining condition and interest.

• A surprisingly large portion of this sample does strength and flexibility exercises in addition to running. Sixty-one percent do one or the other, or both. These exercises are said to "balance" and stretch muscles in ways that prevent injury or speed recovery.

• These runners, however, are injured only slightly less often than the general running population. The overall survey shows that about 76% of runners had been hurt seriously enough to require a layoff. The figure for the enduring group is 61%, but keep in mind that these men have had many more opportunities to be injured through the years. They've run through, recovered, adapted to prevent recurrence.

There are no special secrets or surprises in these results. The runners who have lasted have established a hunger for running early, and have maintained it through changing times. They saw running as something more than a youthful game to be tossed aside at the precise moment it becomes more important—the time when they leave school and settle into a sedentary routine which isn't as comfortable as it appears.

RUNNING IN THE FAMILY

This group of articles came out first in **Runner's World**, May 1973.

"If you want to be successful as a runner, really successful," a man we'll call Harvey Davis said, "you have to be one of two things—unemployed or unmarried. Preferably both."

Harvey was serious. The runner, who is in his mid-30s and is quite successful as a marathoner considering he's only been running a few years, was recently divorced. He has a job allowing him more than enough training and travel time.

"You can't take running seriously if you're too tied down with other responsibilities," Harvey said.

Running is a self-centered sport with high demands on time, energy and attention. When it gets to be like a second job or a mistress, family stresses often show up. There undoubtedly is truth in what Harvey says about marriage and mileage not mixing well.

With every one of her husband's evenings taken up by training, and every weekend taken up by racing, a wife gets annoyed. If she doesn't run, she can't understand this strange preoccupation of his. If he started running after they were together, she may be justified in saying, "He's no longer the man I married." The changes in his personality, appearance and interests may have been dramatic.

One runner's wife wrote to *RW* pleading that we do an article on him. "It seems to me," she said, "that since I have to put up with his daily training schedule, his picture-taking instructions at races, his careful diet and his running magazines scattered hither and thither, I should get to read about the bastard in one of those magazines. How about it?"

She was semi-joking. But what has happened to a number of former Olympians isn't so funny. Three women runners from the '72 team—all middle-distance runners who had been married—were separated from their husbands. Two Olympic distance men from 1968 have seen their marriages flounder.

Of course we're not saying that running alone caused the breakups. At best, marriage in the 1970s is a risky proposition for anyone. But it is safe to assume that the stresses of high-level competition contributed to these divorces.

If running can pull families apart, though, it can also bring them together. It can relieve some of the pressures that send marriages to the rocks.

The Cunneens on the cover of the May '73 issue belong to a unique club in the San Francisco area: the "Pamakids." Pa, ma and the kids all run and race together. The club has dozens of family members.

One woman in the club said, "I got tired of going to those races all the time and standing around bored. I didn't see much point in running then, but I was curious why my husband was so addicted. So I decided to try it myself. Now I'm as involved as he is."

Increasing numbers of family men have started running for fitness and then graduated to the harder stuff. As barriers against women and children runners have come down, they've joined papa. When they're equally committed, the running-related conflicts subside. The family that runs together doesn't necessarily stay together, but it has a much-needed common tie.

Whether running fits comfortably into any family's routine depends on which comes first—the family or the running.

The Price of Being Alone

Runners are "self-battling, inward-looking loners," says Dr. Bruce Ogilvie, who should know. The Institute for the Study of Athletic Motivation, which he operates along with Dr. Thomas Tutko, has probed the personalities of thousands of athletes.

Three traits show up strongest in runners—particularly distance runners—Ogilvie says: aggression, autonomy and introversion. Runners like to be alone, and they prefer turning their aggressive feelings on themselves instead of others. This happens, Dr. Ogilvie says, not only to men but often women runners too.

"Outstanding women competitors," the San Jose State University psychologist noted in the booklet *Practical Running Psychology*, "show a greater tendency toward introversion, greater autonomy needs and a combination of qualities suggesting that they are more creative than their male counterparts. They show less need for sensitive and understanding involvement with others. Women competitors are more reserved and cool, more experimental, more independent than males..."

Ogilvie attributes this in part to "cultural repression of women. To succeed in *any* field, a woman has to be able to stand up and spit in the eye of those in charge."

Women, and men to a smaller degree, seem to be more interested in their running than in how outsiders view it. It is a self-imposed loneliness, and they glory in it. They are saying, "This is mine. I'm doing it on my own, my way. I don't care what you think of it. Just don't interfere."

British Olympian Dave Holt greets his wife Laraine at the end of a road race in New York's Central Park. (Steve Sutton photo)

In general, runners want to be apart, not together; to escape, not join; to feel unique, not alike; to find self, not company.

All this is honorable and innocent enough as long as everyone involved accepts these premises. If both partners in the marriage are runners, chances are they'll understand each other. But what happens when a wife, for instance, has little use for her husband's obsession?

"There's a camaraderie and general acceptance among the competitors themselves," Bruce Ogilvie says, "because they are identifying with the same things. But it's the girl friend or the wife in the life of the (runner) who often has to suffer. A man who loves to run has to have a very special wife or girl friend to understand and accept his running, which may be a competitor to her."

No woman can love her man's running if it shuts her out, if the sport is his mistress and more attention goes to the mistress than to the Mrs. A non-running wife can't share in it because it's too personal to be shared. If she hasn't accepted running as one of her mate's "vices," and the man isn't willing to tone down his running passion for her sake, a serious conflict is set up.

Running can be beautiful for him but a bore and an irritant to her. She can think of far better ways to spend her Sunday mornings than standing with other running widows on strange street corners watching runners disappear and waiting for them to drag their exhausted bodies back.

It's no better when they finish. Runners stand and jabber about each bump in the road, talking to themselves if no one else will listen. Meanwhile, the widows hang unnoticed in the background. One of the ladies could strip and dash through the crowd of runners, and they'd go right on talking.

Most wives eventually shake their heads and give up. "You can tell how long a guy has been married," one runner says, "by whether or not his wife goes to races. All the girl friends and fiances go. Some of the newlyweds are there. But you know the honeymoon is over when runners are alone again."

We're All in This Together

Running had already made vast changes in the lives of the Epsteins of Brooklyn. Irving and his wife, Marion, and their children, Ed and Laraine, had been running for several years.

"To us," Irving said, "running has ceased to be a sport. It is a way of life." The family raced on the roads in and around New York because, the father explained, "the fun is mostly in seeing and running with people who enjoy life as we do."

Then Laraine, who was 24 and had marathon ambitions, traveled to England last summer for hard training. She didn't realize then that family running was going to take another nice turn for her.

Two days after she arrived, Laraine met David Holt. Dave was getting ready to run the British Olympic marathon trials. (He missed in that event, but made the team later in the 10,000.)

"David and I started running together," Laraine said, "and we decided if we could live through that experience together, we could live through anything."

They announced their engagement at Munich. In December they were married. They planned to come to the US in April '73 for a big family reunion at the Boston marathon. They all would run it.

"Perhaps it's selfish or sentimental," Irving Epstein said before the race. "Mama and I want to run with our children." Run with them in the spiritual sense, not side by side.

"It would be nice to run together," said Dave, whose twin brother Bob also is one of Britain's leading distance men, but a bit of a wasted trip for me I'm afraid. I know I'm capable of a 2:12 marathon, and I'd like to think I could do it at Boston."

That's the healthy paradox in family running. The group shares the experience while running as individuals. They're in it together, yet they're on their own. Regardless of ages or abilities, the family members are equal when it comes to running. Each one has to do his own work. He can't shove it onto daddy or brother. But each one gets to collect his own prize too.

Running this way lets children act a little more grown up than they normally can and it lets parents act a little more like kids. Traditional parent-child, husband-wife roles temporarily break down, perhaps letting each one understand the other somewhat better. Even if it doesn't go that deep, they at least get to do together something they all enjoy.

"I could go on and on about running and the joy it has brought us individually and collectively," John Butterfield wrote in the booklet *Beginning Running*. His wife and three children all run with him. "As a family, we have something we can share, and that we enjoy sharing."

Laraine Epstein Holt and her husband Dave (left) with her parents, Marion and Irving Epstein. (Steve Sutton photo)

The Myths about Sex

As if Dave Wottle didn't have enough problems already with an Olympic race to run on gimpy legs, he had to watch his honeymoon be made a matter of public record back home.

Dave got married shortly before leaving for Europe in the summer of '72. His bride went with him, but once in Munich, he was cloistered in the Olympic Village and she had to sleep outside.

"I can't concentrate on track very well," Dave told the press, "when I know my wife is almost an hour away from the Village, must eat all of her meals alone, and can't speak a word of German."

Dave, along with other athletes, began sneaking his wife into the compound. Many of them set up housekeeping there during the games. And Bill Bowerman, the US men's coach, wasn't at all happy with this arrangement.

"Dave Wottle is having a nice honeymoon," Bowerman told Blaine Newnham of the *Eugene Register-Guard* before the Games, "but he'll be lucky to get past the first round in the 800 meters."

Wottle of course did advance past the first round. But the coach remained set against the rooming-in situation that existed.

"I don't want anybody to get the idea that I'm a prude," Bowerman said, "I'm as interested in sex as anybody. But the most important thing we're doing here is competing in the Olympic Games. We should remember that."

He used the Bible and horse-sense to bolster his arguments. "There is evidence to support my contention in the Old Testament," Bowerman noted. "It tells us that a warrior should not go to battle shortly after he is married, and that his neighbors should help him with his farm work so he can adjust to matrimony."

The Olympic coach added that "until after Man O'War ran his last race, he didn't know there were two sexes of horses."

In saying all this to Wottle and his teammates, Bowerman was echoing the prevailing athletic attitude that running and sex don't mix, and that if you're serious about your race you must abstain from pre-meet sex.

This comes partly from confusing moral with purely physical considerations, and justifying the moral question on physical grounds. Yet in the "strength sapping" sense, there's little solid evidence on the side of the abstainers.

Dr. George Sheehan, father of 12, writes, "Statistics on sexual activity suggest that actual energy expenditure is in the order of a 50-yard sprint. I cannot see how this would affect anyone's competitive efforts. Any problem then would by psychological. Perhaps the lowering of tension and loss of competitive drive would be a problem. However, there are some coaches and psychologists who think that such relaxation can be beneficial.

"My personal experience has convinced me that peak performances in middle and long distance races are possible within hours of sexual activity."

Dr. Craig Sharp, Britain's chief medical advisor at the 1972 Olympics, goes along with Sheehan. He has been researching this question for some time, "mainly because of the bad advice that people have been getting." Dr. Sharp said some athletes "upset their personal lives on non-physiological advice given either for puritanical reasons or through old wives' tales."

The doctor has written: "I can find no factual evidence either in scientific literature or in discussion with many athletes and sportsmen of world class that sexual activity in moderation up to and including the night before a match has any detrimental effect on the sport in question."

Without mentioning names, Sharp cited the cases of an Olympic middle distance runner who set a world record an hour after making love, and of a British miler who broke four minutes shortly after sex.

Sharp said married runners do face problems when they've competing, but only because they need to be with their wives rather than separated from them.

"It would be a good idea," he advised, "for wives to have accompanied their husbands to the Olympic Games. The sex would only have been about 10%; 90% would be sheer morale."

Perhaps Casey Stengel's earthy observation is most pertinent here:

"It isn't sex that wrecks these guys, it's staying up all night looking for it."

Running and Motherhood

Paola Cacchi's and Joyce Smith's one-two finish in the 1973 International cross-country championships was a victory for motherhood.

Cacchi, of Italy, won the race. Defending champion Smith, of England, finished second this time. They are 28 and 35 years old respectively and both have had their running careers interrupted by childbearing. Both came out of the experience faster than ever. (And both, incidentally, are coached by their husbands.)

Paola Cacchi missed two crucial years during and after her pregnancy. She ran little and raced less during 1970 and 1971. Yet with only a year's intensive work she finished third in the Olympics 1500 breaking the old world record.

These cases emphasize the fact that pregnancy, a complication male runners don't have to deal with, doesn't have to be any more disruptive to a running career than any other kind of long layoff.

Madeline Manning, the 1968 Olympic 800 champion, retired to marriage and eventually motherhood after those Games. She returned to running in 1972 and tied the world half-mile record.

Judy Ikenberry was one of the early women marathoners in the US. She quit running seven years ago, and since then has given birth to two children. Judy is back in long distance running now, and won the first national AAU women's marathon championship by running 2:55.

Nina Kuscsik, the first women's winner in the Boston marathon, was a mother of three before she took up racing.

It's obvious that women can come back from childbirth and run as well as before, if not better. With their doctor's okay, they may even continue running during early pregnancy—thereby reducing the total time away from training.

"According to Dr. Evelyn Gendel, director of the Kansas Division of Maternal and Child Health," George Sheehan wrote in "Medical Advice," "there is no reason for women not to continue in athletics during pregnancy, if they are continuing what is customary for them. Assuming a normally implanted pregnancy, physical activity is not only permissible, but desirable. It not only increases the joy of living; it also maintains cardio-pulmonary efficiency and muscle tone and prevents back problems."

Difficult deliveries of course are harder to overcome. Israeli writer Abraham Green tells of the case of Hanna Chezifi, who won the 800 meters at two Asian Games—before and after having a child.

"Hanna's achievements in reaching top form again were by no means easy," Green says. "This small woman, slim and narrow-hipped, had a very difficult and painful delivery. Her child was too big, relatively, at eight pounds. It was pressing on her heart. The delivery of the child had to be made through Caesarean operation.

"All her troubles prior to delivery and afterwards left Hanna weak and exhausted. Notwithstanding her physical condition, the moment the stitches were removed, she began to exercise very lightly. Against doctors' warnings, she began a month after the delivery by jogging 300 yards. Normally her heart beat would be around 42. Now it was 80-90. She was almost 20 pounds overweight, and even the 300-yard jog exhausted her.

"Less than a year later, however, 27-year-old Hanna set Asian Games and Israeli records in the 800 with 2:06.5 and the 1500 with 4:25.1."

Judy Pollock set the world half-mile record several years ago. She was a favorite for the gold medal at 800 meters in Mexico City. Then she learned she was pregnant. She decided to retire.

"I was sure that was the end of my running career," the Australian said later. "I had no thoughts of ever coming back. I settled down to being an ordinary housewife."

Hanna Chezifi of Israel, winner of the Asian Games before and after having a child. She won the 800 and 1500 less than a year after a difficult delivery.

In the space of three years, Judy had three children. None of the deliveries was easy. The first child was the easiest. The next one died at birth. The third, born in 1971, was delivered by Caesarian.

Three months after having the last child, Pollock began thinking of re-entering running—and possibly competing at Munich a little over a year from then.

"Most of all," she said, "I had to build up my confidence after what I had been through. It took a while."

Once she had that, 31-year-old Judy came back quickly. Before Munich, she ran 800 meters in 2:01.5—about equal to her best of five years earlier. However, a leg injury knocked her out of the running before the Games.

Pollock finds the logistical problem of combining running and motherhood to be tougher than the physical ones. She once marked out a 400-meter strip of road in front of her house and practiced there, popping in every few minutes to make sure the dinner was not burning or to see that the children were asleep.

She says, though, that "having a family isn't a handicap; it's a help. Everybody rallies around to help, and I enjoy having plenty to do. You have to be well-organized to live the crowded life I do, and I am a fairly well-organized person."

During peak training, Pollock organizes herself this way: "My husband comes home from work with the car at about four o'clock, and I leave to drive up to one of the tracks in Melbourne. On the way, I leave the baby with Mum, who gives her an evening meal. I usually take my son with me to the track and he has a picnic tea while he watches us train. He thinks it's great fun. Then we drive home, picking up the baby on the way, and I put them to bed before we have dinner."

I'm lucky to have an understanding husband. I couldn't do it unless he approved. He isn't the kind who stands around grumbling when I come home at eight o'clock from training to get dinner ready. He is used to the demands running makes. But it is difficult for the children—and their needs always come first."

GUIDING YOUNG ATHLETES

BY E.R. SANDSTROM

The Australian technical journal "Modern Athlete and Coach" published Sandstrom's article in 1973.

There is a fairly widespread belief that track and field athletics is a sport which is essentially the preserve of an elite. This belief is, no doubt, strengthened by both the relative ease of measuring and comparing performances and by the adulation accorded to the champions who emerge at the different levels of competition. The tragedy has been that a selection process has evolved which is primarily on a success-failure basis, with the decision frequently being made very early in the period of exposure to athletics. In the past, the decision has been taken in the secondary school where attitudes towards athletics have tended to crystallize by the age of 15 years, after only two or three years of very limited experience. Possibly one of the major contributing factors is that the child has become disillusioned by his initial lack of success.

The whole approach to the teaching and coaching of beginning athletes of any age should be to arrange for the attainment of some measure of success. The younger the child is when introduced to athletics, the more important this aspect becomes. It would be an even greater tragedy if adverse attitudes towards athletics were formed at earlier and earlier ages. Everything must be done to guard against emphasis upon the development of champions at different age levels and the earlier disillusionment of young athletes. The primary aim of all organizations concerned with track and field athletics must be upon participation so that the thrill and joy of competition can be experienced by as many as possible for as long as possible.

Greater involvement in physical activity is discernible at both ends of the age range, yet there is little evidence concerning the influence of physical activity upon growth and development. There no doubt is need for considerable research into the effects of physical activity, particularly of extensive training programs which involve high levels of energy expenditure, upon young children.

Per-Olof Astrand and associates have reported the results of a longitudinal study of 31 girls swimmers from 7-15 years of age. Some of the girls had started intensive training as early as 10 years of age, yet their growth had in no way been impaired. This study supported earlier studies on both animals and humans which showed that regular physical activity favorably affects animal studies which indicate that the time in the life cycle at which an exercise program is introduced is less critical than its duration and intensity.

However, it could be suggested that greater gains, if desirable, could be made if an exercise program were emphsized at the time when the growth impulse is dominant. M. Ikai has shown, in his studies of training for muscular endurance in relation to age, that

"Ideally, a form of indirect competition would predominate, in which the aim is not always to produce one winner per age group, leaving the remaining participants almost inevitably viewing themselves as losers. . ." (Doug Schwab photo)

the greatest improvement with training took place between the ages of 12-15 years. He concluded that the possible cause of this beneficial training effect could be easier capillarization in the muscles of boys aged 12-15.

Astrand and Rodahl point out that the factors of importance for maximal aerobic power can be "influenced by training early in life, between 10 and 20 years of age, during the period of growth and development." While natural endowment may be the most important factor in determining the oxygen uptake of an individual, it is stressed that regular training can increase the maximal oxygen uptake by up to 20% and maintain it at the elevated level.

Assessment of maximal oxygen uptake and of strength in relation to age shows that before puberty there are no significant differences between boys and girls, and consequently it would be feasible for them to undertake similar training programs and participate in the same track and field events. After this, women on the average achieve 70% of the oxygen uptake and strength of men and hence performances differ markedly.

The place and type of competition need to be carefully considered in the context of declining numbers of competitors with increasing age. It has to be recognized that competition is the very essence of athletics. Without a doubt, the thrill of competition and desire to prove themselves motivate the majority of athletes to train hard in order to participate. In considering competition for the young athlete, it should be borne in mind that it is not obligatory to emphasize the formal, adult-type of competition of a direct nature.

In fact, it may well be that this is the least desirable form of competition in that it stresses winning above all else, focussing attention on a single individual. It would be preferable to place the emphasis upon personal performance so that the individual can compete against himself, against his own previous performance. Ideally, a form of indirect competition would predominate, in which the aim is not always to produce one winner per age group, leaving the remaining participants almost inevitably viewing themselves as losers and, hence, possible failures. It is possible to modify the customary form of competition in different ways to reduce the emphasis upon a single winner for each event.

One possibility would be to dispense with chronological age as the basis for organizing different levels of competition. For any given chronological age of children there are marked differences in those measures which reflect skeletal and physiological maturity. Clarke and Wickens have reported that when boys of the same chronological age were assessed within two months of their birthdays, skeletal age ranges of 32-62 months were found. For example, boys assessed at the age of 13 years could show a physical maturity level typical of boys from 10 up to 15 years. Marked differences in height and weight occur among children of the same chronological age.

It is obvious that the performance levels in a wide variety of physical activities will be affected by such differences in maturity, height and weight. There would seem to be a place for competitions based on a classification index in which age, height and weight are taken into account.

It would appear that there will be a minority of performers of high ability who will emerge and attain a considerable measure of success in a number of activities, whatever the competitive system. It is questionable whether highly individualized and direct competition is a desirable objective for all. The majority of performers tend to be discouraged by such a system.

An English study of attitudes towards athletics showed that there was a significant difference in atitudes between those who were good at athletics and those who were not. Attitude deteriorated from the age of 11-15 years, with the most marked deterioration occurring in the low performance group. J.E. Keogh has pointed out that participation in sport is directly related to the degree of skill (level of performance) developed in the activity. It would seem that the success of an organized program of track and field athletics could be better judged in terms of its retention of participants rather than the level of performance achieved by a few participants.

It is felt that the number of participants continuing in athletics to a large extent is related to the way in which competition is organized. The customary orientation towards the production of "champions" at an early age could have a deleterious effect on the continued participation of the majority of performers as well as the few young champions.

If children were exposed to regular individual competition from the age of 7-12 years, it is likely that the crystallization of attidues towards track and field athletics will take place for many during these years. It would be preferable for children to experience a broad program of physical activity in which there is an opportunity to develop the ability to run, hurdle, high jump, throw and pole vault. In such a program, the major emphasis would be upon the development of skill and not upon the demonstration of a high level of skill by a few in a selective series of competitions. The objective would be to maintain the interest of a large number of participants and extend the length of time for which they participate, recognizing that athletic training and competition can provide enjoyment and pleasure—particularly if divorced from a need to provide a champion.

Competition, per se, does not bring benefits in terms of increased growth and development. One ought to be conscious of the risks associated with highly individualized competition by parents, coaches and club officials, some of whom put their own ambitions and fulfillment before the interests and welfare of the children.

REFERENCES

1. Astrand, P. O., *et al.* (1963). "Girl Swimmers," *Acta Paediat* (Suppl. 147).

2. Astrand, P. O. and K. Rodahl (1970). *Textbook of Work Physiol.* McGraw-Hill, NY.

3. Clarke, H. Harrison and J. S. Wickens (1962). "Maturity, Structural Strength and Motor Curves of Boys 9-15 Years of Age," *Res. Quart.*, 33:26-39.

4. Ikai, M. (1069). "Training of Muscular Endurance Related to Age," *F.I.E.P. Bulletin*, 3-4:19-27.

5. Keogh, J.F. (1963). "Extreme Attitudes towards Physical Education," *Res. Quart.*, 34:27-33.

6. White, G.B., *et al.* (1965). "Attitudes to Athletics in Second and Fourth Year Boys in Secondary Schools," Reserach Paper in P.E. (C.C.P.E.) No. 1, June, 51-54.

EXERCISE AND LONGEVITY

BY DR. HAROLD ELRICK

Dr. Elrick, a San Diego medical researcher, has a special interest in the relationship between endurance activity and long life.

For several years, I have been carrying out studies comparing unconditioned and highly conditioned (distance runners of the San Diego Track Club) individuals: physical, biochemical and psychological aspects. At the same time, I have been gathering similar data on certain long-lived population groups. The findings to date indicate that the distance runners have much in common with long-lived individuals. Both groups do much daily strenuous physical activity. They have similar body composition and build. They have similar cardiovascular and biochemical findings.

It is intriguing to speculate that distance running as an integral part of daily life (along with an optimal diet) may be one practical way for the individual living in the highly developed society to achieve the physical and biochemical characteristics of longevity. In any case, this is my present working hypothesis.

I am interested in knowing why some people live a long time and remain vigorous—like Michelangelo and Picasso, who were active and productive in their 90s. I decided years ago that it might be fruitful to study population groups which are supposed to be exceptionally long-lived and vigorous. The prospect of finding a real-life Shangri-la excited me very much.

In the summer of 1970, I first learned of a long-lived population in Ecuador. Because this area is easily reached, I felt it would be a good place to start. Shortly before setting out, I learned that a group of Ecuadorian physicians headed by Dr. Miguel Salvador had already carried out studies of these people. The information to be presented here includes that gathered by Dr. Salvador's team in 1969 and 1970, as well as Dr. Alexander Leaf and I in September 1970.

Our attention was focused on the tiny village of Vilcabamba in the Andes Mountains. The name Vilcabamba means Sacred Valley in the langauge of the Inca Indians. The Vilcabamba area had

been cited as being free of heart disease. In addition, outsiders
with heart disease reportedly had been much improved by living in
the area. The inhabitants of the area were rumored to show remarkable longevity.

In 1969, the Ecuadorian government requested Dr. Salvador
to investigate the rumors about Vilcabamba. He organized a team
of physicians and technicians who worked for three days to complete carefully planned studies of the villages. Before undertaking
our own studies in 1970, we spent several days in Quito analyzing
the findings of Dr. Salvador. Then we spent three days in Vilcabamba examining the village and its inhabitants.

The village covers an area of about 250 acres and looks like
anything but a Shangri-la. Its appearance and style of life is very
primitive. It is at an altitude of 4500 feet, 100 miles from the Pa-
cific Ocean and 600 miles south of the equator. The average temperature is 68 degrees, with very little variation throughout the year.
The average humidity is 67%. The community is an agricultural one,
whose products are corn, yucca, coffee, tobacco, bananas, potatoes,
oats, wheat, sugar cane, grapes, barley and peanuts.

Although it is only 25 miles from the capital of the province,
Vilcabamba remains isolated because of poor roads and lack of motor vehicles. The homes are made of adobe and wood. All buildings
appear very old and in bad condition. The hygenic conditions of
the inhabitants and their homes are poor. But the scenery of the
countryside is beautiful, with lush green vegetation, crops, trees, all
surrounded by high mountains and traversed by streams.

Dr. Salvador's team tested 340 natives of the village. The ex-
aminations were done in the village school or private homes with the
help of the local school teachers and priest. The ages of those examined were between 7 and 120 years. Thirty-one individuals over
the age of 80 were found. The ages were proven by baptismal records. Seventy-five percent of those examined were judged to be of
European origin, and 25% of mixed Indian and European stock. Ecuador as a whole has a distribution of 40% Indians, 40% mixed, 10%
Europeans and 10% black.

A detailed dietary history was obtained from 25 adults by Dr.
Guillermo Vela of Quito. The daily food intake was chiefly cereals,
fruits, and occasionally meat (lamb, jerky, chicken and hog). Eggs
and dairy products were rarely used. The average diet contained
1200 calories with 35-38 grams of protein, 200-260 grams of carbohydrates and 12-19 grams of fat. Everything in the diet is local-

ly grown. Compared to the average diet in the United States, the Vilcabamba diet is extremely low in calories, protein and fat.

All of the natives examined are active physically, irrespective of age. The chief occupation is farming, and the work day is 10 hours long. The women are also very active both at home and in the field.

Many of the men smoke the locally grown tobacco. However, this is done in small amounts only. Cigarettes are handmade by the individual, with a few flakes of tobacco and a piece of wrapping paper. These cigarettes last only a few puffs.

Small amounts of alcoholic beverages made locally from sugar cane are commonly imbibed daily by adults. However, only a very small percent use alcohol excessively.

Blood pressures were measured in 340 villagers. Less than 2% had high blood pressure. Of the 134 adults over the age of 40, only 4.5% had high blood pressure. These findings are much different from the US, where many studies show that more than 20% of adults have high blood pressure.

Blood cholesterol was measured in all individuals over the age of 30. Eighty-two percent of them showed a level less than 250 mg%. This is considerably lower than statistics in the US. The amount of heart disease found was very low, and tended to be mild. No evidence of old or recent heart attacks was found. There also saw no evidence of strokes. Everyone, including the few that had heart disease, was without symptoms and in good general condition.

Our objectives were to check the ages and numbers of the old people in Vilcabamba, to observe the living habits of the people, and to collect information as to body build, mental and physical vigor. By examination of the baptismal records, we were able to verify the ages of 45 (total population: 900) individuals ranging from 75-121 years.

The village contains no restaurants, hotels, movies, clubs, recreation areas or motor vehicles. The atmosphere is tranquil and quiet. One hears no machine noises, only human and animal ones.

We examined 110 inhabitants of the village. They were from 15-121 years of age (about two-thirds of them men). All seemed friendly, relaxed, cooperative, alert and healthy. The people were not shy or retiring. No idlers were seen on the street. Everyone seemed busy. The appearance, features, eyes, etc., were European in type. Some may have had some Indian mixture, but this was not prominent. In general, the villagers appeared taller than the Indians seen in other parts of the country and their names were of Spanish origin rather than Indian.

As a group, they were slender and well muscled with good posture. They appeared vigorous and younger than their age. Only nine of the 110 examined were not working regularly, but none was confined to bed. It is noteworthy that 43% were at perfect weight in contrast to only 3% of a large sample from San Diego. Most of the inhabitants were born and had always lived in Vilcabamba. Nearly all of the remainder were born in nearby villages but had lived in Vilcabamba many years.

An unusually high percentage of elderly people live in Vilcabamba, Ecuador. More than five percent are over the age of 75. This is remarkable in a country which is not noted for its longevity. It is noteworthy that the elderly individuals were examined and were mentally and physically vigorous. Their life-style in general conforms to our ideas of the type that prevents heart disease and hardening of the arteries—i.e., the simplicity; the abundance of exercise; the simple low-calorie, low-fat diet; minimal cigarette smoking, and the freedom from the stress of competitive society.

The Vilcabamba diet is thought-provoking. Do we have to revise our ideas on nutritional requirements? It is clear that one can live a long time and work hard on what would be considered a near starvation diet in the US. The high frequency of optimal weight is of interest and is undobutedly a manifestation of a healthy life-style. The level of blood cholesterol found in these villagers is in the range generally associated with a low risk for heart disease and hardening of the arteries. Heart disease is very infrequent.

The situation in Vilcabamba seems to be a happy combination of good genetic endowment and a healthy life-style. It would appear to fit our preconceived notions regarding longevity.

Page 172: Alain Mimoun (center) won the Olympic marathon in 1956 and is active nearly 20 years later. (Jerome McFadden)

7

ENVIRONMENT

WHEN IT'S COLD OUTSIDE

BY JIM SEXTON

Jim Sexton is a Canadian runner well acquainted with the cold. Ernst van Aaken is a West German physician and running coach. Their articles are reprinted from the January 1974 Runner's World. (Van Aaken's article appeared first in Condition magazine and was translated by George Beinhorn.)

"The current temperature is..." How many times last winter did you listen to your friendly local TV or radio announcer tack a number on the end of this sentence so low that you decided to call off your run until tomorrow? If you live in any of the northern states or Canada, this thought probably crossed your mind quite often. If you were inclined to give in to temptation then I have advice you might use, since I live and run in Canada where temperatures can go far below zero.

The most important factor to remember when running in subzero weather is that nothing, short of a blizzard, should stop your running—*if you are prepared!* "Prepared" is the key word. Running in cold weather can be as harmful as running in hot weather if you are not adequately prepared. The problem then is how to get prepared. Here are a few guidelines I follow:

• Probably the most important "rule" to remember when running is to avoid heavy, bulky garments. Use several layers of light-weight clothing. Running in severe winter conditions often dictates the use of up to four layers.

The first layer should be absorbent and non-irritating. Fishnet underwear made of wool is excellent.

The second layer should be a good insulator. For this layer, I often use a turtleneck shirt as this allows me to retain important warmth in my arms and neck without adding the extra weight of a sweater and scarf.

The third layer, if chosen carefully, can allow you to run at all but the coldest temperatures. This layer is, of course, the age-old sweatshirt. But a sweatshirt made of the wrong materials, or with the wrong "features" is of no use to anyone. A good sweatshirt should have: a hood, preferably with a tie around the neck, long arms (especially welcome when running into a wind without mittens), a pocket to keep mittens, kleenex or a stop watch handy, and proper materials. Proper materials? Wool, fleece-lined cotton, anything that is not made of nylon and keeps you warm.

The fourth layer is the most important when it comes to running in extremely cold or windy weather. It is the wind-breaker. Although it is possible to use any type of material in a windbreaker, it is better to use cotton poplin. Cotton poplin allows sweat to evaporate without condensing on the inside of the jacket. At the same time, it will not allow wind to penetrate. A jacket of this type is available at any cross-country ski store.

● Guidelines for leg care: *no more than two layers of clothing for the legs!* I don't care how warm and cuddly you feel wearing two pairs of underwear and three pairs of sweatpants. What good are all those clothes going to do if you can barely walk? A pair of wool or nylon warmup pants and long underwear are more than adequate for all types of weather. I do not wear more than one pair of pants unless the weather gets below minus-100 with the wind-chill factor.

I have found that it is more comfortable to wear shorts instead of a jock strap. If you don't believe me, just try and adjust a jock when it is 50-below and you are wearing mittens!

A word of caution: be sure that you wear a good pair of cotton twill shorts beneath your sweat pants. This is vital (particularly for male runners) and, unless you're willing to undergo considerable agony, take this bit of advice to heart.

● Footwear is, thank goodness, the simplest part of all as far as dressing is concerned. The cardinal rule is always wear socks. One pair will suffice for nearly all conditions (as long as you keep moving).

If you are planning on doing a lot of running in deep snow, a rather interesting gadget to keep the snow out of your shoes is a gaiter. Gaiters are tube-shaped pieces of nylon or poplin which are pulled over your pants legs then fastened at the bottom of your shoes with an elastic strap. One warning: the elastic piece used to keep the gaiter on is not very strong, so it is a good idea to limit your gaiter-wearing to snow.

As far as shoes are concerned, leather and nylon work equally well, with leather being preferred for running through puddles.

It is a good idea to protect leather shoes with a silicone agent available at any shoe repair shop.

● If you have run cross-country during the fall and early winter, you will have noticed that the first parts of your body to get cold are your hands and arms. This is equally true in winter and spring training, and it is of prime importance to keep your hands well protected. Mittens are very good for this purpose and are far superior to gloves. Probably the best mittens are those made of leather with a high cuff. Although it is not vital, a liner made of wool or silk can be added.

A trick which mountain climbers often use to increase their resistance to cold while working at high altitudes is to avoid wearing gloves while skiing and doing lower-altitude climbing. Because of the constant exposure to cold atmosphere their spleen enlarges, which enables them to carry more blood to the surface of the skin. Those of you who ski and have the internal fortitude to do this, go ahead. People who suffer frostbite while getting a dish of ice milk out of the freezer are better off sticking to mittens.

A rather interesting variation among people regards the circulation in the hands. If you're right-handed, you'll find that your left hand gets cold first and tends to stay colder, and vice versa if you're left-handed. The degree to which this affects people varies immensely. After only a short run, some are so cold that it takes a full day to defrost. Others can run for miles at sub-zero temperatures with no noticeable effects.

● Head gear is probably the most important piece of equipment that you can have if doing a lot of training in extremely cold and windy conditions. Insufficient protection against cold and wind in this area is asking for a whopping case of pneumonia or a bronchial infection. Just ask me. During the fall, I picked up a slight cold, nothing serious. Or at least it wouldn't have been serious if I had stopped racing. I continued—with disastrous results. I might add that most of my competing was done in very windy conditions. I think that this is a very important factor as it is not so much the cold which caused damage, but the cold and wind combined (more on this later).

The most important function of a head covering is to keep your face warm. The best material for keeping your face (and breath) warm is wool. Wool, because of its ability to absorb great amounts of moisture without losing its insulating properties, should be used in as many places as possible when collecting a winter uniform. The cost is well worth it. A ski mask made of either wool or orlon is far superior to anything else I have tried. (Don't take my word for it, though. Experiment!)

At this point, I should comment about the safeness of the cold and the meanness of the wind. In Saskatchewan, we have very severe weather conditions, both in winter and summer. It is not unusual for temperatures to go to 40-50 degrees below zero for weeks on end during the winter. Nor is it unusual for the temperature to go to 100 above for weeks during the summer. Add a 40 m.p.h. wind to either of these conditions and it can become pretty uncomfortable. I have learned to respect that wind.

Winter is hard in Finland, but runners don't stop racing. Seppo Nikkari leads a February race. (Markku Pekola)

A person can run for up to two hours a day in 50-below weather without any fear of "freezing lungs" or, if properly protected, frostbite. Add a 10 m.p.h. wind to this, though, and everybody goes scurrying for ski masks. This is why it is so important to take the direction of the wind into consideration when planning a workout. This is crucial.

Always go into the wind at the start of a run and with it on the way back. Running with the wind causes the body heat to build. Having to run back into the wind with your outer garments sweaty can be disastrous. It is a very good idea to tell your next of kin where you are running and the expected time of return, in case you are overdue on your schedule.

While most articles on cold weather running include a chart on the wind-chill factor, I'm skipping that detail. (Okay, if you're really interested, there's one in the Feb. 73 *RW*.) The reason I don't have it is because by the time you're finished figuring out the wind-chill factor, you will already have decided to take up a sensible indoor activity, like ping pong.

But if you're well prepared, you'll be warm at any temperature. True, a person from California who has just moved to Saskatchewan would not be able to run at 50-below immediately, but adaptation comes fairly quickly. When it does, there is little further trouble.

To give you an idea of how much a runner's body can take, I relate an experience I went through in January 1972. Sometime around noon, disregarding the pleas of my parents and assorted other kin, I went out and ran 7½ miles when the wind chill reading was 125 below zero. That's right, one hundred and twenty-five below. I really did not feel cold—just slow. Of course I was wearing all five layers and then some, but I had absolutely no trouble with frostbite. Although this has not been verified by the Guinness people, I think this must be a world record for cold running. It had better be, because I'm never going to attempt a stunt like that again.

Winterized Running Training

BY DR. ERNST VAN AAKEN

In earlier years, athletes used to take a break in winter in order, they thought, to regenerate their strength. However, this we found to be valid only on a psychic level nowadays. If you're sick of running month after month on the road or the track, you should change athletic gears for a while, but by no means rest or get rusty. Getting rusty happens fast.

During California winters, the only problem is rain. (G. Beinhorn)

Emil Zatopek once said, "If I miss one day, I can tell them I'm several seconds slower." Famous pianist Arthur Rubenstein said of pauses in practice, "When I take a day off, I notice it. When I miss two days, the audience notices it." And so it is with running training.

There should be no such thing as sitting out cold, wet weather. You just have to protect yourself accordingly. Obviously, you don't have to work for maximal hardness and natureboy exhibitionism. Just dress warmly and conserve energy. In very cold weather, hands and face must always be protected. Running shoes should be waterproof or coated with water repellent.

Even in great cold, distance runs in winter have to lead to perspiration—not because of running speed but because of the length of the runs. This slow heating of one's own inner oven strengthens the runner's resistance. If you change clothes immediately after running, there's no danger of catching cold. Even when you don't feel quite right or have a mild fever, distance running in winter can accelerate a cure.

A mistake often made—especially among marathoners—is to believe that the most miles ought to be run during the rawest part of the year, in January. There are no great losses of heat, even freezings. Runners doing this kind of training don't build their reserves but squander their capital to the point of depletion. Naturally, they catch cold easily.

During very cold weather, then, only run as many miles as you can while staying comfortably warm and reasonably dry. There should be no more effort to force more miles out of yourself in winter than in summer. You can always make it up in March and April during the early good weather.

Though winter training consists of slow runs and perhaps less miles than in fall or spring, it is done daily, regardless of the weather.

Winter training should strengthen the heart, increasing oxygen uptake capacity and keeping the circulation tuned. This is true for sprinters as well as distance runners. It's best to do long runs all winter long, finishing the season with gradually increased tempo runs (maximum length of 700-1000 meters at 70% of top speed).

Every long run can be followed by just one tempo run a day, or a few sub-maximal accelerations of 60 meters or so. This way, you will be sure to have practiced all the possible variations of tempo from warmup to sprint, and you won't have to go through a radical change at the end of winter.

The runner should be ready to race at any time on this base of training, but actually he should only race playfully and without any great attachment to results—just to test his form or learn tactics. The most important thing is for the runner to very seldom give his all during winter.

Muscles are best irrigated by slow running and a heart rate of 130-150, and they are strengthened only by tension. The running muscles require formation during the winter of a great number of fine, hair-like blood vessels to insure a better blood supply. The runner has to make his body an oxygen supermarket in winter, and avoid as much as possible all consumption of energy in oxygenless (anaerobic) reactions.

In winter, it comes right down to the vital stuff of life, oxygen. In summer competition, you can occasionally overdraw your account and incur an oxygen debt. You survive these overdrafts better when you have a nice, fat oxygen account.

HAZARDS OF THE HEAT

BY DR. DAVID COSTILL

Dr. Costill, pioneering researcher in distance running physiology, wrote this originally for the "American College of Sports Medicine Newsletter."

The requirements of distance running place great demands on both circulation and body temperature regulation. Numerous studies have reported rectal temperatures in excess of 105 degrees after races of six miles and more. Attempting to counter-balance such overheating, runners incur large sweat losses that may total 6-10% of the body weight. Dehydration of these proportions severely limits subsequent sweating, places severe demands on circulation, reduces exercise capacity and exposes the runner to the health hazards associated with hyperthemia (heat stroke, heat exhaustion and muscle cramps).

Bob Scharf—a heat-collapse victim at the 1968 Holyoke (Mass.) marathon. (Jeff Johnson photo)

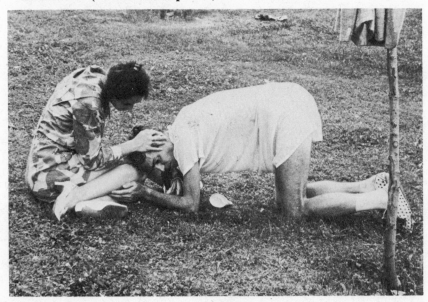

Even under moderate thermal conditions (e.g., no cloud cover, relative humidity 49-55%), the risk of overheating is a serious threat to the highly motivated distance runners. Nevertheless, distance races are frequently conducted under more severe conditions. For example, the air temperature at the 1967 U.S. Pan-American Marathon trial was 95 degrees. Many of the pre-race favorites failed to finish the race, and several of the men demonstated overt symptoms of heat stroke (no sweating, shivering, lack of orientation).

In recent years, races of six miles and more have attracted several thousand entries. While distance runners recognize the hazards of competing on a hot, sunny day, most cannot resist the challenge of responding to the starter's gun. Since it is likely that distance running enthusiasts will continue to sponsor races under adverse heat conditions, specific steps should be taken to minimize the health hazards which accompany such endurance events.

Fluid ingestion during prolonged running (two hours) has been shown to effectively reduce rectal temperature and minimize dehydration. Although most competitors consume fluids during races that exceed one hour, current international distance running rules prohibit the administration of fluids until the runner has completed 11,000 meters (about seven miles). Under such limitations, the competitor is certain to accumulate a large body water deficit (-3%) before any fluids can be ingested.

Measurements made at the 1968 Olympic marathon trial demonstrate that most runners are unable to judge the volume of fluids they consumed during competition. We observed body weight losses of 6.1 kilograms (13-14 pounds), with an average total fluid ingestion of only 0.14 to 0.35 liters. It seems obvious that the rules and habits which govern fluid administration during distance running preclude any benefits which might be gained from this practice.

Runners who attempt to consume large volumes of a sugar solution during competition complain of gastric discomfort (fullness) and an inability to consume fluids after the first few feedings. Generally speaking, most runners prefer to consume solutions containing 5-20 grams of sugar per 100 milliliters of water. Although saline is rapidly emptied from the stomach (25 milliliters per minute), the addition of even small amounts of sugar can drastically impair the rate of gastric emptying. As carbohydrate supplementation is of secondary importance during exercise in the heat, the sugar content of the oral feeding should be minimized.

In light of the preceding discussion it seems logical to propose the following changes for the management of heat stress during distance running:

1. Rules that prohibit the administration of fluids during the first seven miles of a marathon race must be amended to permit fluid ingestion at frequent intervals along the race course. In view of the high sweating rates and body temperatures during distance running in the heat, race sponsors should provide "watering stations" at 2-2½-mile intervals for all races of 10 miles or longer.

2. Both competitors and sponsors of distance races must be informed of the importance of consuming large amounts of fluid during long races in the heat. Since thirst can be an inaccurate estimate of body water needs, runners must learn to consume fluids (200 milliliters or more) at regular intervals (every 2-2½ miles). In order to prevent gastric filling and to promote maximal absorption, the solutions ingested should contain minimal amounts of sugar (less than 2½ grams per 100 milliliters). To minimize dehydration, competitors must be encouraged to consume 400-500 milliliters of fluid 10 minutes before competition.

3. Promoters of distance races should refrain from scheduling long races (longer than 20 kilometers) during the hot summer months. During this period, all distance races, regardless of length, should be conducted during the coolest part of the day.

Race sponsors and runners must realize that efforts to reduce dehydration via fluid ingestion will not eliminate the risks of overheating. Runners must learn to reduce their running speed and energy expenditure during warm weather races. In addition, runners must learn to recognize the early signs of "critical" hyperthermia. Our experiences indicate that most highly trained runners sense pilo-erection over the trunk and a throbbing pressure in the head when their rectal temperatures reach 103.5-104.5 degrees F. When temperatures approach or exceed 105.5, all men experience extreme muscle weakness, involuntarily reduce their running speed and may demonstrate a reduction in sweating.

HOT-WEATHER MARATHONS

BY T.D. NOAKES

At the time he wrote this following article, Tim Noakes was a South African medical student.

Marathon running is, from a medical point of view, one of the finest sports. At a time when the Western way of life is increasingly incriminated as the cause of a number of diseases, particularly heart disease, it is becoming evident that the health of marathon runners of all ages is better than the normal—often better than individuals 10-20 years younger.

However, two potentially fatal conditions—heat stroke and kidney failure—are associated with marathon running. Exercise-induced kidney failure occurs more commonly than classical heat stroke in athletes, but both conditions are preventable. By understanding what occurs when severe exercise is undertaken in heat, the athlete is able to aid his body in overcoming this dual stress.

While running, the human body acts as a machine converting chemical energy (glycogen and fats) into mechanical energy in the muscles. As in any machine, this conversion is incomplete and energy in the form of heat is liberated. However, at excessive temperatures certain of the body's regulatory mechanisms break down, blood fails to circulate adequately, and—because of both an inadequate blood supply and a direct effect of the heat—the major organs of the body (brain, heart, liver, kidney and muscle) are severely damaged. This condition is known as heat stroke.

We see, then, that it is important for the body to be able to control the heat rise associated with exercise, preferably at as a low a value as possible. How is this achieved?

As exercise begins, the muscles demand and receive more blood. Not only does the heart pump more blood, but blood is preferentially diverted away from other organs towards the working muscles and skin. As it passes through the muscles, this blood is heated up and it distributes this heat throughout the body—but particularly to the skin. In this manner, as well as by a direct transfer from muscles lying close to the skin, heat is conducted to the skin surface. Here circulating air currents convect this heat away, while any nearby objects whose surface temperature is lower than the skin temperature attracts this heat, which travels by electromagnetic waves in a form of energy transfer known as radiation.

The above methods of heat loss are only effective when the environmental temperature is less than about 90 degrees. Above this, the direction of heat transfer is reversed, and the superficial tissues gain heat from the environment. Sweating then becomes the only method of heat loss. However, as the humidity of the air increases, the evaporation of sweat diminishes. When the stress of exercise is added to that of heat and humidity, the athlete's ability to achieve heat balance will be limited.

Dr. Griffith Pugh has shown that at environmental temperatures above 68 degrees athletes running at world-class marathon pace sweat maximally. Because of decreased skin blood flow, they are no longer able to lose heat adequately. They thus run the risk of developing heat stroke, the supreme danger of which is that it gives no warning of its imminence. An athlete will continue to run with a rising body temperature until collapse from heat stroke occurs.

Probably of more importance to marathon runners is the understanding that dehydration (which is caused predominantly by sweat loss but may be compounded by vomiting or diarrhea), also causes the body temperature to rise and is commonly found in victims of heat stroke. The prime object of the marathon runner must be to avoid dehydration by drinking adequately during a run. My experience is that very few runners know what is adequate. This problem arises because of the international ruling that stipulates when an athlete can drink or be sponged during a marathon, and is compounded by the practice of many world-class marathon runners *not* to drink during a race.

Ron Hill ran the world's third-fastest marathon without drinking any fluid. This practice is to be condemned as it sets an example for less-gifted runners, whose bodies are not capable of withstanding the heat stress as well as those of world-class runners. It also makes runners careless in their attitude towards the longer races. In these races, very severe dehydration will occur, and the danger of heat injury is increased immeasurably. Five cases of heat-induced kidney failure occurred in the Comrades 57-miler in the years 1968-72.

This article opened with the suggestion that heat injury should not occur in marathon running. If the following practical considerations were enforced by the three groups mentioned below, this ideal would be realized.

• **The race organizers.** (1) The international ruling that restricts the athlete from choosing when he wishes to drink or be sponged off

During long distance races such as this one in tropical Puerto Rico, heat stress is always a threat. (Roso Sabalones photo)

must be ignored or abolished. (2) No marathons should be run in severe environmental conditions (certainly a temperature of 85 degrees represents the uppermost limit, while the dangers of any temperature above 68 degrees must be clearly understood by all).

• **The medical profession.** (1) I.A.A.F. Rule 165:2 states that all marathon entrants must have a physical examination by a qualified doctor before the race. Unfortunately, it is not possible at the present time for any doctor to pick out the "at-risk" athletes. Although almost all cases of heat injury have certain characteristics —tendency to obesity, lack of heat acclimatization, recent illness— these factors by themselves are not sufficiently selective. (2) Anyone who has in the past suffered from heat injury should never again be allowed to compete. (3) Athletes who have passed an abnormally dark urine following exercise should be thoroughly investigated as they may be particularly susceptible to kidney failure.

• **The athletes.** (1) Heat-acclimatized athletes lose 1-2 liters of sweat every hour, with the heavier athletes losing the higher values. However, it appears that even under ideal conditions, the human body is capable of absorbing only one liter of fluid every hour. This absorption is maximal if the fluid is cooled to about 40 degrees. All athletes must drink at least one liter of fluid every hour (250 milliliters every 15 minutes) and should start drinking *immediately* because intestinal absorption carries on at a constant rate and it is not possible to "catch up" once a water deficit has occurred. A good guide to the adequacy of fluid replacement during a run is to assess one's post-race weight loss, which should not exceed 3% of body weight. A further guide is offered by the time interval between completing the run and passing the first urine. This should not exceed one hour.

(2) String (fishnet) vests aid convection, T-shirts hinder it— particularly when soggy with sweat, as a layer of air is captured next to the body. This rapidly heats to skin temperature and effectively *insulates* the body.

(3) Sponge frequently. Both by a direct cooling effect and by acting as an "artificial" sweat, frequent sponging aids the body's cooling system.

(4) Although heat acclimatization is beneficial to performance in races of any length, it becomes imperative to be adequately heat acclimatized if one is to run a race lasting more than two hours. It is only after this period of time that the difference be-

tween two equally fit but not equally heat acclimatized athletes
becomes evident. The problem is that heat acclimatization is specific
as regards the environmental conditions and the intensity and duration of the exercise. Thus, to acclimatize to run a particular race
one has to simulate race conditions very accurately (running speed,
distance and/or environmental temperature). Empirically, it has
been found that eight days of repeating this will heat acclimatize
and that this will be retained for 2-4 weeks.

(5) In the past, the salt tablet has been held in mystical es-
teem by marathon runners, but considerable doubt now exists as
to its real value. The problem has arisen because of a physiological
paradox in the functioning of the human kidney. Stated simply,
it is this: without adequate salt (sodium chloride) in the body, the
kidney is unable to conserve water and dehydration occurs. However, the converse—that plenty of salt alone *without water* will prevent dehydration—does not apply. Taking salt tablets alone removes water from the body. Thus, if you wish to take salt, it must
be as a dilute solution, less than 0.3% (three grams sodium chloride
per liter).

There is also some doubt as to whether it is necessary to add
salt to your food during periods of heavy training as the average
Western diet contains considerable amounts. However, a continuous slow loss of weight coupled with a feeling of lassitude, giddi-
ness and muscular cramps is a strong indication that a chronic salt
deficit is developing, and under these conditions it is imperative
to increase one's salt and water intake. Potassium depletion can be
caused by taking too much salt, particularly in a diet that is defi-
cient in the potassium-rich foods such as citrus, bananas and toma-
toes.

(6) Mention was made that heat stroke occurs with tragic rapidity, giving little warning. However, severe vomiting, diarrhea, confusion (irritability and aggressiveness) or a dry skin, particularly under the armpits, are serious signs. The wise athlete will quit at this
stage rather than run the risk of never being allowed to run again.

*I would like to express my appreciation to Professors Wynd-
ham and Strydom of the Human Science Laboratories, Johannes-
burg, South Africa, whose inquisitive research has supplied most of
our knowledge concerning exercise in the heat.*

TRAINING AT ALTITUDE

BY E.C. FREDERICK

E. C. Frederick, a doctoral candidate at Northern Arizona University, wrote this article for his scientifically-oriented publication, "Running."

Few people realize the effect that training at altitude has had on modern distance running performance. Altitude training first gained widespread attention before and during the 1968 Olympics held in 7500 foot Mexico City. In the years since, altitude training has gradually become a basic ingredient of success for many world-class runners. Frank Shorter, Jeff Galloway and Jack Bacheler trained in 8000-foot Vail, Colo., previous to their outstanding performances during the summer of 1972. Even more interesting is the fact that *all* of the Munich gold medalists from 1500 meters through the marathon were altitude trained.

The circumstantial evidence is overwhelming. These are just a few examples of the many cases where altitude training has presumably contributed to the success of a distance runner in international or national competition. This wealth of positive testimony is not without opposition, however. Many runners and scientists feel that altitude training contributes nothing special to a runner's performance capacity. Indeed, altitude training is not a "sure fire" success formula. Many runners have poor performances following altitude training. And at least two scientific investigations could find no improvement due to training at altitude (Grover, 1966; Buskirk, 1967).

These data raise certain questions about the effectiveness of altitude training. Does it in fact enhance performance? Or is it just another fad training technique? Is it simply coincidence that so many altitude trained runners lead the world today? These questions are difficult to impossible to answer. The infinite complexity of the physiology of conditioning and the multifarious aspects of individual training regimes make it difficult to evaluate the role of altitude training (as separate from training at lower elevations).

It is possible, however, to eliminate some of the variables and take a cold, logical look at some of the physiologic changes brought about by living and training at altitude. A knowledge of these special adaptations is helpful in understanding the potential role of altitude training in performance enhancement. In fact, they make it hard to believe that altitude training *could not* cause some improvement.

PHYSIOLOGICAL ADJUSTMENTS TO ALTITUDE

Despite the apparent contradictions, one thing is certain. Living at altitude does bring about a number of fundamental changes in the structure and function of several tissues and organs. These changes, curiously enough, are identical to many of the physiologic changes which result from distance running training at any altitude. But then this is not so remarkable when you consider that both conditions involve a "struggle for oxygen" as a major stressor.

At altitudes significantly above sea level (5000 feet and up), the atmospheric pressure is low enough that the partial pressure of oxygen (the gas oxygen is responsible for 20% of the total atmospheric pressure regardless of altitude) is not adequate to allow enough oxygen to be absorbed into the blood. At 7000 feet, the hemoglobin can only be saturated to 93% of its total. The result of this hypoxia (deficiency of oxygen) is that not enough oxygen is transported to the tissues during normal breathing to provide an adequate amount for maintenance of aerobic metabolism. So begins the struggle for oxygen.

In order to meet the demands of the tissues for oxygen, the body increases respiration and heart rate. This increases the volume of blood reaching any tissue during a given time. In this way, the body compensates for the inadequate oxygen supply. This immediate reaction is not sufficient for long periods of time. The extra work load imposed by the increases in heart and respiration rates detracts from the energy requirements of other systems. Thus, the body seeks more basic, longer lasting adaptations to provide the much needed oxygen.

These longer lasting adaptations constitute what is called *acclimatization*. This acclimatization can be broken down into two basic categories: (1) changes increasing the flow of oxygen from the atmosphere to the tissues, and (2) changes increasing the diffusion and utilization of oxygen in the tissues.

The alveoli of the lungs provide an area where the blood can come in close contact with the atmosphere. One of the primary adaptations to hypoxia is an increase in the alveolar space accompanied by a permanent dilation of the alveolar capillaries. These changes increase the diffusing surface of the lungs and thus allow a greater volume of air to come in contact with a greater volume of blood.

This increased diffusing capacity is of little benefit, however, if the capacity of the blood to carry oxygen is not also increased. As you would expect, this capacity does increase. The volume of the oxygen-carrying red blood cells increases, and the concentration of hemoglobin in the red cells also shows a significant increase.

Again, this is obviously not enough. Despite the fact that the diffusing capacity of the lungs and the oxygen-carrying capacity of the blood are increased, the adaptation sequence is not complete unless we can efficiently deliver this oxygenated blood to the tissues. To accomplish this, the heart enlarges, and the density of the capillaries in the tissues themselves increases. The whole effect thus far is a more efficient and rapid movement of oxygen from inspired air to the tissues.

At sea level, there is sufficent oxygen so that the problem of hemoglobin releasing oxygen to the tissues is insignificant. Under normal conditions, hemoglobin will release only a portion of its oxygen. At altitude, where this kind of inefficiency cannot be tolerated, we see an increase in the oxygen releasing capacity of hemoglobin.

So far, altitude adaptations have increased the flow of oxygen from the atmosphere to the tissues. This leads us naturally into a discussion of the second aspect of altitude acclimatization: increasing the diffusion and utilization of oxygen in the tissues.

The mitochondria of the cell are organelles in which oxidative metabolism takes place. It is the mitochondria that need oxygen for energy transformation. A substance called *myoglobin* facilitates the movement of oxygen from the capillaries into the mitochondria. Thus, it is not surprising that myoglobin levels in muscle tissue are shown to increase with prolonged altitude exposure.

With the increased myoglobin concentration the oxygen has arrived at its destination, the mitochondria. It is here that the oxygen is utilized in aerobic or oxidative metabolism. The capacity of the tissues themselves to utilize oxygen is enhanced in altitude adaptation. Not only do we find this increase in aerobic capacity but also we see an increase in anaerobic capacity. The total picture is one of increased capacity for the uptake, transport and utilization of

Steeplechaser Bob
Price competing in
the 1968 Olympic
Trials 7500 feet up
in the California
mountains. The
site was chosen to
simulate the alti-
tude of Mexico
City. (Steve
Murdock photo)

oxygen. Also, the altitude adapted body is capable of greater energy transformation both aerobically and anaerobically.

PHYSIOLOGICAL ADJUSTMENTS TO TRAINING

Virtually all of the physiologic changes found in an altitude
acclimatized individual are also shown to occur following a program
of distance running training. Increased lung volume, blood volume,
heart size, vascularization, myoglobin content, and enzymes of aerobic and anaerobic metabolism are all shown in endurance trained individuals. The notable exception to this parallel situation is that
the concentration of hemoglobin is not shown to increase following endurance training.

From a purely physiologic point of view, it is obvious that both
endurance training and altitude adaptation produce similar changes.
These changes involve broad increases in the aerobic capacity and,
to some degree, enhancement of the anaerobic capacity. But what
of the combination of the two?

Training produced a 50% greater increase in myoglobin content
in rats trained at altitude than not trained. Numerous studies done
on altitude trained individuals all showed increase in the *maximum*

oxygen consumption rate upon return to sea level. In addition, the performance of these individuals as a whole was greatly improved by their training at altitude. These studies along with the well documented physiologic changes mentioned above lead us to the conclusion that the combination of endurance training and altitude acclimatization can produce "super-normal" performance.

Beyond the purely physiologic benefits of compounding these two stresses, there are certain other benefits concurrent with altitude training. Because of the low oxygen pressure, training mileage is "worth more" at altitude. For example, 80 miles a week at 7000 feet is considered roughly equivalent to 100 miles at sea level. More is accomplished in a shorter time. Another advantage is that, try as you may, you *have* to run slower. This should result in fewer injuries and, thus, less lost time. A further little appreciated benefit is increased *resistance*. Adaptation to altitude has been shown to increase resistance to influenza and other viruses. Again, the resultant effect on training volume is obvious.

THE "HOW'S" OF ALTITUDE TRAINING

How High? Recommendations vary as to what altitude is best. An altitude of 5000 feet is considered minimal for the effect to be significant. Practical considerations make 10,000 feet about the highest one can live in any sort of comfort and maintain high mileage. Since it is obvious that the higher you go the more dramatic are the effects, athletes should seek training sites as close to 10,000 feet as possible. The majority of altitude trained runners, however, live between 5000 and 8000 feet.

How Long? It takes at least 4-6 weeks to acclimatize to moderate altitude. This should be considered as the minimum stay. However, many of the adaptations will take as long as a year to maximize. So it is advisable to stay as long as possible.

How far? It is advisable to cut back training mileage as much as 50% upon arrival from sea level. This may not seem necessary during the first few days, but within the week the reason will become obvious. Mileage can then be gradually increased to former levels at a rate dependent on the progress of *your* adaptation.

Racing at Sea Level: It is advisable to either race within 24 hours of arrival at sea level or to train for 10 days to two weeks at sea level before racing. You will slowly lose your altitude adaptations over many weeks, but it will take as long as a year to return to pre-altitude levels. The 10-day to two-week period will not significantly detract from gains made at altitude.

REFERENCES

1. Balke, B., and J. G. Wells, and J. P. Ellis. 1956. "Effects of Altitude Acclimatization on Work Capacity," *Fed. Proc.* 15:7.

2. Barbashova, Z. I. 1964. "Cellular Level of Adaptation" in Dill, Adolp & Wilber (eds.). *Handbook of Physiology: Adaptation to the Environment,* Section 4, Washington, D.C.: Amer. Physiol. Society, pp. 37-54.

3. Berry, L. J., R. B. Mitchell, and D. Rugenstein. 1955. "Effect of Acclimatization to Altitude on Susceptibility of Mice to Influenza A Infection." *Proc. Soc. Exptl. Biol. Med.* 88:543.

4. Buskirk, E. R., J. Kollias, R. I. Akers, E. K. Prokop. E. R. Reategut. 1967. "Maximal Performance at Altitude and on Return from Altitude in Conditioned Runners." *J. Appl. Physiol.* 23:259.

5. Clark, R. T., D. Criscurao, and C.K. Coulson. 1952. "Effect of 20,000-foot simulated altitude on myoglobin content of animals with and without exercise." *Fed. Proc.* 11:25.

6. Faulkner, J. A., J. T. Daniels, B. Balke. 1967. Effects of Training at Moderate Altitude on Physical Performance Capacity. *J. Appl. Physio.* 23:85.

7. Frederick, E. C. 1973. *The Running Body.* World Publications, Mountain View, CA.

8. Grover, R.F. and J. T. Reeves. 1966. "Exercise Performance in Athletes at Sea Level and at 3,000 Meters Altitude. *Med. Thorac.* 23:169.

9. Hurtado, A. 1964. "Animals in High Altitudes: Resident Man." in *Handbook of Physiology:Adaptation to the Environment.* Sec. 4. Washington D.C. *Amer. Physiol. Soc.* pp. 843-860.

10. Hurtado, A., A. Rotto, C. Merino, and J. Pons. 1937. 'Myoglobin at High Altitudes." *Amer. J. Med. Sci.* 194:708.

11. Klausen, K., S. Robinson, E. D., Michael and L. G. Myhre. 1966. "Effect of High Altitude on Maximal Work Capacity." *J. Appl. Physiol.* 21:1191.

12. Lenfant, C., J. Torrance, E. English, C. A. Finch, C. Reynafarje, J. Ramos and J. Faura. 1968. *J. Clin. Invest.* 47: 2652.

13. Loeppky, J. A., and W. A. Bynum. 1970. "The Effects of Periodic Exposure to Hypobaria and Exercise on Physical Work Capacity." *J. Sports Med.* 10:238.

STRAINING UP HILLS

BY DR. GEORGE SHEEHAN

Dr. Sheehan's articles appear regularly in "Runner's World" and other publications.

Hills are great levelers. If there is anything that can cut a runner down to size it is a reasonably long hill with a fairly steep grade— and particularly if it is placed near the end of a race. Hills make all men brothers. Coaches who use them for training swear by them. Runners who find them sources of pain and suffering swear at them.

The runner's world, you see, is divided into two worlds: the world of hills and the world of the flats. The hills are an entirely different world from any other.

In the hills, the runner must move vertically as well as horizontally. It is a simple matter of physics: a body of known weight moving at a certain speed up a specific grade for a given distance. A simple matter of physics, it seems to be, but it is one that causes physiological results that can be close to unendurable. Quite suddenly, this simple equation in physics transforms the pay-as-you-go effort of the flat into the I'll-pay-you-later-if-I-only-survive struggle of climbing the hill. The runner, working on oxygen he has not yet received, arrives at the summit, his lungs bursting like a swimmer who has been held underwater, his leg muscles filled with lactic acid and screaming for him to stop, his entire body becoming a dead weight.

Such tortures are common. If the ecstasy of distance running is felt in those periods of rhythm and grace when everything is easy and flowing and natural, then certainly the agony of the sport is in the dysrhythmic, graceless, tortured movement up the hills. If the heaven of this distance running is in the moments when the runner and his running seem to reach toward infinity, then assuredly its hell or Purgatory is in the hills that expose him as failing and inadequate and finite. And if running on the flat is the world of those

Runners in the IC4A cross-country championship climb infamous "Cemetery Hill" in Van Cortlandt Park. (Steve Sutton photo)

optimists that William James called the once-born, running the hills
is for the twice-born—those of morbid mind who see and accept
the evil in the world.

Chris Haines leads Alaska's rugged Equinox marathon, which features several hundred feet of climbing. (Kathleen Schedler)

Most runners have felt this. They have gone from sailing along
serenely until the first unseen but already felt grade. Then the hill,
and the pace gets slower and slower. The breathing becomes more
and more labored, the legs more and more difficult to move, then
finally moving hardly at all. The head almost touches the knees
in a futile attempt to use gravity to go uphill. And all the while you
accept pain that could be terminated in a second by stopping.

Some hills are, of course, worse than others. On the east coast,
we have some well known monsters. Heartbreak Hill in the Boston
marathon, Cemetery Hill at the four-mile mark of the five-mile
course at Van Cortlandt Park. There is hardly a major race that
doesn't have a strategic hill to make the event memorable for the
runner. I have run all of these, and on them reached areas of pain
unmatched at any other time in racing—even in flat-out finishes or
in marathons where I had to quit from exhaustion.

But the worst hill of all was in a 15-mile race one August.

The heat and mileage had taken a toll, and I was nearing the finish line when I reached this hill, which seemed the longest and steepest I have ever had to climb in a race. Going into the hill, I was some 10 yards behind another competitor and well ahead of any pursuer.

Up on top of the hill, a teammate yelled encouragingly to me, "Go get him, you can get him." Twenty yards up the hill I had slowed perceptably. The runner in front began to pull away.

"Pick it up, pick it up," came the cry from the top. By now, I was leaning forward, making groping movements with my hands but very little forward progress. My friend would not give up.

"Keep moving," he yelled. "Keep moving." It was no use. And now the others behind me were catching and passing me. The runner who was ahead of me had reached the crest and disappeared.

Then from the top of the hill came the best advice of the day. "Walk fast," he shouted. "Walk fast." I did and I passed two men who were running.

DANGERS OF HIGHWAYS

BY HAL HIGDON

Hal Higdon, masters champion and for more than a quarter-century a runner, has contributed many articles to Runner's World. This one first came out in the RW of May 1972.

A running companion of mine named Ralph has no respect for the dangers of this automotive age.

Ralph might most charitably be described as a long distance jogger, not runner, a Volkswagen in a world where laurels go to Ferraris. As I write this, he has failed again to meet the qualifying standards for Boston and alas, barring some sudden surge of dedication, he never will.

He lives on the south end of town, across the street from some woods, a minute's jog away from a cinder track, not far from some back country roads. Yet Ralph insists on tempting death by running his workouts through the heart of town, sometimes late at night, along an unlit two-lane street.

Even when he comes out to run on the lakeshore near my home, he often shuns the beach (except on days when girls in bikinis are present) and trundles along the road above.

You can go two directions from my house: west into town and east out of town. West into town isn't bad except between 3:00 and 6:00 in the afternoon when people in cars returning from school or work clog the road. By big city standards, the traffic hardly rates as "heavy"—but why encounter any traffic at all when there are alternative routes? I tell Ralph this, but like Horace Greeley, he says: "Go west, young man."

Ralph also complains of backaches and when I suggest that he move off the hard pavements in favor of the many softer nearby paths through woods and over golf courses, he sneers. He fails to see the connection between physical injuries and his methods of training. Several years ago we convinced Ralph to run in a cross-country meet when we needed a fifth man, but he got lost and failed to finish.

Ralph also suffers another ailment common with many run-

In the heat of a race, runners don't realize it. But they themselves are a traffic hazard as they force cars off the road and
slow the ones stuck behind them. (George Beinhorn)

ners today: marathon mania. Any distance below or above the
tradtional 26 miles 385 yards is beneath (or maybe above) his dig-
nity. Yet he will climb in his car and drive night and day to attend
a marathon 1000 miles away.

That is another hazard for runners in the automotive age.
Many years ago I belonged to a ski club in Chicago, an equally peripatetic breed who would rush off in their cars on Friday evenings,
ski and party for two consecutive days, then drive home late on Sunday evenings to be home in time for work the next morning. In the
three years I belonged to the club I only recall one broken leg on
the slopes but two people hospitalized and one dead in separate
automobile accidents. The only thing that saves long distance runners on their equally peripatetic weekend jaunts is that during our
season there is seldom snow or ice on the roads.

But consider the dangers of automobiles, both when you are
in them and when they are coming at you. Dogs may not be runners' best friends, but they certainly aren't runners' worst threat
That dubious honor belongs to the automobile.

During the '60s, Ralph Nader effectively pushed Detroit to
the point where cars are made considerably more safe than those
of a decade before. But that's on the inside. For the runner, it

matters little whether he gets hit by a 1962 or 1972 car. Datsuns can inflict the same damage as Cadillacs.

Recently I have read of several runners who have been killed by automobiles. We probably are fortunate that the toll has not grown larger.

Several years ago on a wintry afternoon with snow flakes falling, I ran with another training companion called Steve toward the town of New Buffalo north of my home. We ran on the shoulder of a four-lane highway.

I looked ahead and perhaps 200 yards away a passenger car started to pass a semi-truck. But the roads were slick and the rear end of the car began to break loose. The car spun and slid across the highway into the ditch, hitting with a dull cru-umpp! The semi drove on, its driver possibly unaware of the accident in its wake.

Steve and I reached the car quickly and found the driver more embarrassed than hurt, so we continued our run. But I couldn't help but think that mere chance had prevented us from being at the point on the highway where we would have been clipped by that spinning car.

It is the chance we all take when we leave the relative security of the running track to share the hazardous environment of the automobile. Sometimes there is no alternative. Not to run on the roads for some runners means not to run. But that doesn't mean

"It is the chance we all take when we leave the relative security of the running track to share the hazardous environment of the automobile." (Andy Warren)

that we can't become defensive runners just as the National Safety Council urges people to be defensive drivers.

Long distance runners are a singular, testy breed. We are individualists. Under stress, any person's judgment can become impaired. When it comes down to those last few miles of a long distance workout, it becomes irritating to have to move over when approached by a speeding car. Yet consider the alternative if you don't move.

I know many runners take the position that it is they, not the drivers, who should possess the right-of-way. They run into traffic as though daring drivers to hit them, forcing cars to swerve across the center line to pass.

I consider this an act of arrogance.

More than that, I consider it an act of suicide. The next time you are behind the wheel of a car look ahead and imagine a runner in your path. Consider the maneuver you would have to make to avoid him. Then consider that another car was coming toward you, preventing you from moving wide. Finally, consider the consequences if you happened to be daydreaming, or drunk, or maybe were mad at the world.

That imaginary runner you would have hit might have been Ralph.

Page 204: Photo by George Beinhorn

FOOTWEAR

EXAMINING YOUR SHOES

Desmond O'Neill, an attorney from California and an experienced distance runner, contributed the lead article to this series on the running shoe. The collection originally appeared in Runner's World, January 1973.

Imperfect Shoes and Feet

BY DESMOND O'NEILL

It might as well be stated at the outset that the human body wasn't built for road-running. Primitive man may very well have loped barefoot over the veldt in pursuit of his dinner, but he did his loping on soft surfaces, with only occasional high-speed bursts. Certainly he rarely had to run long distances at a fast steady pace on hard road surfaces, and therefore never evolved the body necessary for that sort of activity. That leaves us, his descendents, ill-equipped for our own self-appointed tasks, which we perform without even the reward of a meal.

Granted that we really aren't made for that sort of running. Does this mean that we can't run? Of course not. Regular training can inure the body to many of the stresses of this sort of activity. Through gradual and careful stressing in workouts we can prepare for the demands of racing, whipping our hearts, lungs, circulatory systems and muscles into shape for the miles which lie ahead.

Unfortunately, the benefits of training pretty well stop with the bodily bits and pieces listed above. We can go on battering ourselves until we become fit up to a point. However, nothing we can do, in training or in racing, will have much positive effect upon our basic skeletal structures—the bones, joints, ligaments, tendons which also have to be considered. More and more of us are finding that hard training can have quite serious effects upon our skeletal apparatus. What is happening is that we're literally overpowering the frame, pushing it to carry very high, unnaturally high stresses over long periods of time, without realizing that the skeleton can't benefit from or adapt to this sort of running.

What you have, skeletally, is what you'll have a 1000 or 5000 miles from now. You'd better learn to accept that and take care of yourself. Repairs and replacements, for all the modern wonders of medicine, still don't work too well.

There isn't much question that skeletal moans and groans are on the increase. Read any of George Sheehan's columns in *Runner's World*, or listen to the locker-room conversation at the next race. Few of us pull muscles, but sooner or later we'll all have sore feet, ankles, tendons and whatever. Injuries to these parts, some of them serious, are already numerous, and will become more and more common in the future. Our first generation of high-mileage runners is now getting into its 30s, some runners having averaged better than 100 miles a week for 15 years or more. Their juniors on the way up are exceeding those mileages already, seeing in quantity at least part of the secret to success. Indeed, it is, but there are a lot of risks involved also.

I am particularly concerned with the relationships between feet, shoes and injuries. There are a few Abebe Bikilas in this world, and most of us wear shoes, of necessity. A lot of injuries are direct results of failure to use proper footwear and to take proper care of our feet. It may be a personal idiosyncrasy, but I suspect that many injuries to upper legs, hips and backs begin with neglected foot problems. The body is a very delicately balanced and integrated mechanism and a slight impairment of proper function in the foot will throw everything else out of balance and out of line—often with the most catastrophic consequences. Favoring a sore heel may put extra pressure on a knee, or pull the back out of line, and then it'll take six weeks, or six months, to recover. So take care of yourselves, take care of your feet, make sure that you give them all the help that they need by giving them good shoes to operate in and on.

Well, then, what *is* a good shoe? First of all, it appears that few shoes are built for high-mileage runners. Some look good, some are heavily advertised, but only a couple offer much protection for the working foot. Hell, most of them don't even fit the foot at rest, much less in motion—a point which you may easily prove to yourself by tracing an outline of the sole of your shoe on paper, and then superimposing upon it an outline of your own foot.

Most shoes are too pointy, low and narrow in the toes. Several are too narrow in the ball of the foot or at the heel. And this doesn't even take into account all the blister problems you can get over the top of the shoe.

The forward part of the shoe, if ill-fitting, can be uncomfortable. An ill-fitting or badly designed heel, however, can be downright dangerous, due to the loads on the heel, and few shoes are more than barely adequate there.

Most of us run with a fairly flat foot placement. The foot approaches the ground heel down but lands more or less flat, from the ball of the foot back to the heel, initially on the outside edge and then taking weight as the foot rolls over towards the inner edge and into a flat position. Due to the construction of the body, however, most of the body weight lands on the heel, with the rest of the foot serving as either balance or, on takeoff, as a lever for the application of power in the push-off.

In the case of an average 150-pound runner, the bearing surface of the foot (that portion actually in contact with the ground at some point in the stride) will be about 12 square inches, but upwards of 80% of that 150 pounds (120 pounds) will land on the four or five square inches of heel surface. The load is 24 pounds per square inch at rest, actually somewhat higher due to the impact forces on landing. That's a lot of weight and a lot of shock. That's what does most of the damage and causes most of the injuries, yet there is very little recognition of these forces and stresses in running, and of the need to adequately cushion the foot, particularly the heel, to guard against injury.

Regardless of advertising claims, no shoes cushion the heel adequately. What looks like nice, soft, comfortable sponge rubber when squeezed between thumb and forefinger will distort almost flat, almost simultaneously, under full body weight. That fast distortion of the rubber means that almost all the shock is transmitted through your foot, all the way up to the top of your head. It hurts, and the more you run the more you'll hurt, depending upon body weight and individual variations in stride. That shock hurts, not just in making you tired, bruised all over the legs (the heavy thigh muscles in particular—remember your last marathon?), but also hurting pressure points and bearing surfaces in the joints as well—until eventually these become inflamed and painful, or even chipped and fractured.

Most sponge rubber in shoes isn't absorbing much shock. It's too soft. Worse, it tends to flex unevenly (outer edge to inner) under the normal action of the foot. That quite natural landing becomes unnatural and exaggerated due to the action of the rubber, applying sideways force to ankle, knee and hip. Most sponge lay-

ers should be replaced with crepe or gum rubber, which does provide cushioning when body-weight is applied to it, and is also much
more durable. Hard nylon or composition rubber, except for stick-
on tips, should be avoided; it wears well and is stable under the
foot, but does not cushion at all.

Another desirable feature in a shoe, notably absent in most,
is a strong heel cup to hold the foot stable laterally—eliminating
side-to-side roll which can cause trouble in the achilles tendon.
When I speak of a heel cup, I don't mean the "counter," a stiffened
leather strip at the back of the heel, but a genuine cup extending
from the bottom to the top of the shoe for the insertion of the achilles,
the ankle, and downward as far as three inches. This cup should be

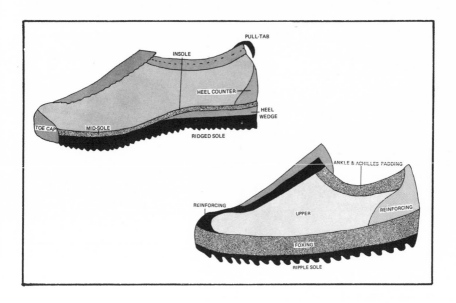

of reinforced leather, a really honest piece of work rather than an
ornament.

The last nice feature of a good heel would be some protection
at the top of the shoe for the insertion of the achilles, that very
tender point where the tendon starts into the groove of the heel-
bone. There is considerable movement here, one to two inches per
stride. Over the course of a long run the tendon can get pretty
sore at that point, with inflammation of the tendon and bursae and
the formation of calcium deposits. Using a tight shoe-back which
forces the tendon hard against the bone is asking for trouble. Within the last couple of years all shoe manufacturers have recognized

this and begun raising and padding the back of the heel. Unfortunately, there has to be some contact between shoe and foot here,
to hold the shoe on, so the problem hasn't been completely solved.

Going forward in the shoe and on the foot to a couple of
other possible problem areas: Is an arch-support necessary? Whether it is or not can't really be determined from experience with the
factory-installed supports, particularly the Japanese. They're too
light and insubstantial to support anything, and really serve as filler
material. You may feel them there, but they aren't doing you very
much good. If you really need arch supports your feet will tell you
so by letting down, hard and painfully, along the inside edge, and
the arch will hurt like hell. If that happens, get a decent leather
arch support. A shoemaker can build one up, out of several thicknesses of leather, and cut it to fit inside your shoe under the inner-
sole, replacing the soft rubber one already there. Commercially-
made supports are probably too big for your shoe, and also tend to
slide back and forth, causing blisters.

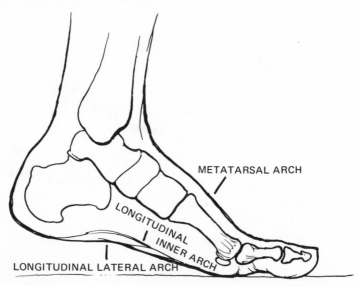

Really severe arch trouble may need more than half measures.
Professionally fitted and custom-made supports, wedging the foot
all the way from the ball to the heel, may be necessary, but I suggest that you take the time and trouble to consult someone who
has real experience with runners' feet. Most doctors don't, and
conventional wisdom isn't applicable to an activity as unconvention-
al as marathon running.

Forward from the arch, under the ball of the foot, the main consideration again is proper cushioning. Most of the remarks already made about the heel are applicable here, although a little less so since the loading is less, and only about half the rubber needed under the heel is required under the ball.

The upper of the shoe should be fairly tight from the front of the ankle to the ball—again a feature difficult to find. The reason for this is that the footbones, the metatarsals running fore and aft, are held together by ligaments, rather like a bunch of five sticks held together by rubber bands. A long run, with the metatarsals spreading each time the foot lands, causes the ligaments to stretch until they become very painful—not sharply so, but as a generalized footsore ache. A good shoe should give the ligaments some support. Since the foot and shoe move very little if at all in relation to each other at this point, the shoe can be tighter here without much risk of blistering. Lacing the shoe tightly may do some good, but is only a partial solution.

The toes on most shoes are, as noted previously, pretty bad. They should be much wider, with higher toecaps to allow the toes full flex. Most shoes are built too narrow and too low. Only one shoe now available in this country has a really sensible toe design, almost flat across the front, like a flipper viewed from above. It's an ugly shape, but functional.

One last point: A frequently ignored source of trouble is poor repairs, either do-it-yourself or shoemakers'. Few runners or shoemakers seem to realize that repairs have to be carefully done so that thicknesses of soles and heels of both shoes of a pair are identical, assuming that most of us have legs of equal length. A slight difference in height, less than an eighth of an inch, may be enough to unbalance the stride, so slightly as to be imperceptible to the runner but nevertheless enough to throw that extra and usually sideways thrust into the joints. Unevenly worn heels and soles can do the same, comfortable as that old pair of shoes may feel.

We often neglect such factors in running, and our neglect is compounded by poor shoes. Take good care of your feet. Avoid trouble there, and the rest of the body will probably get along quite well also. Hurt a foot, and expect to hurt a lot more besides.

Home Remedies

At the risk of raising false hopes among desperate sufferers, we have to mention that relief may be as close as a slab of rubber. Two race walkers have found this for themselves, curing serious and long-standing ailments with appliances they discovered themselves.

In 1972, Bill Weigle had shin splints so bad he was almost incapacitated. He found, among other things, that one leg is shorter than the other—a surprisingly common affliction. He added a strip of rubber to the sole of his left shoe. The shin splints cleared up quickly. Bill made the Olympic team that summer in the 50-kilometer walk, and later won the AAU championship at that distance.

Tom Knatt race walks long distances too, and like Weigle he is a converted runner. Knatt's trouble was achilles tendinitis. He lived with it for months before accidently finding the source of the injury was in his weak arches. He added supports, and both the achilles and arch soreness went away. Tom walked in the US Olympic 20-kilometer trials in July '72.

Simple do-it-yourself shoe modifications aren't going to eliminate all foot and lower leg complaints. Some of them need professional help, as described in "More Support for Sore Feet" (September '72 *RW*). There are some things even the pros can't fix. But before spending all that money on them, make your own experiments.

Weigle and Knatt describe theirs.

Bill Weigle: I went for a long easy training walk on Aug. 8, 1971, and noticed a little soreness in my left ankle. Since I had gone 10 miles farther than ever before, I wasn't too surprised. The next day I race walked up into the mountains about 7-8 miles and ran back. The shin area in the lower third of my left leg was very sore, and the next day I couldn't train. I had to baby it for the next few weeks.

Although I soon got back to doing long workouts, the shin pain continued on and off through November. It seemed to be getting no better and was unpredictable. One day I'd make it through a workout, but on another day the pain would be so acute I could only go a mile or two.

After reading an article in *Runner's World* about appliances in the shoes to correct foot problems, I visited a podiatrist. He found two things wrong with my feet and legs. First, my left tibia (lower leg bone) is twisted. Second, my toes and heel don't land in the same plane. When my heel is flat, the line formed by my toes is at a 10-11 degree angle so that the big toe is raised off the floor. The podiatrist took molds of my feet and had plastic inserts made for the rear two-thirds of my shoes.

The next three months were very depressing. The appliances, which originally were comfortable, had a plastic bar added to the front bottom of them to correct the 10-11 degree angle my toes made with the ground. I could only get them in one pair of street shoes (no training shoes) and they were very uncomfortable. Each step was like walking off a ledge. Also the heel was raised a bit, making the shin muscle sore every time I walked. In February I walked a 25-kilometer race in them and hurt badly. I could hardly break 2:30 (I have averaged 2:11 for the halves of 50-kilometers since then).

Scott Eden's bloodly sock and flap of skin tell a story. (P. Crowell)

In the meantime, we discovered that my left leg was about one-half inch shorter than my right leg. This shortness was accentuated by walking on the left side of crowned roads. Finally I realized that four things—short leg, twisted tibia, crowned roads, toes

Cooling feet which have taken a pounding. (Jay McNally photo)

not in proper plane—were all working *together* to cause my leg to roll inward as I walked from heel to toe. I could actually see it and feel it. This apparently was irritating the tendons in the lower shin area of the left leg. I guess it's also why I got sore knees and horrible pain in my calves whenever I extended myself.

After talking it over with the doctor, I decided to simply add a complete half-inch sole to my left shoe to see if it would eliminate the symptoms caused by inward roll. I used Tiger marathons since they were the lightest shoe and I would be adding a lot of extra weight.

It worked! I immediately found I could train 70-plus miles a week.

I could see that as the left shoe wore, the front of it was wearing only on the outside and was more or less performing the same corrective action that the plastic insert had been. When I looked over the other old shoes I could see that they had all worn the same way. All along, the shoe wear pattern was telling me something and I hadn't realized what. I'd just patched the shoes and created more stress on the shins.

Once I tried to put a new sole on my left shoe and sand it down the way another shoe had worn. But it didn't work. In fact, it was no better than not having that extra half-inch at all. The best thing seemed to be to let the extra sole wear itself into the correct mold.

On one pair of shoes, I put a second layer of very thin, tough material after the shoe had worn into shape, to keep it from wearing too much. That seemed to work. The idea is to replace only the thin piece when it wears through and always to have a shoe with the right correction.

Tom Knatt: In the summer of 1970, I walked in a race from Lawrence to Lowell, Mass. I was still struggling to get proper walking style, and was hitting quite hard on my heels. I came away from that 12-miler with a slightly swollen and very painful right achilles tendon.

Needless to say, I abandoned this style of walking, but I couldn't get rid of that pain in the tendon. It persisted through the winter, would sometimes feel better but then would get worse if I ran a hard workout. I tried heat, leaving a heating pad on my ankles while I slept. I tried stretching by standing on the edge of a stair and dropping my heel below the level of the step. And I tried some rest, going two or three days without workouts. Nothing worked.

In March 1971, I raced again and came away with a pulled left longitudinal arch. Feeling very discouraged, I mentioned the arch problem to a woman at the New Balance Athletic Shoe Company. She suggested I try her "cookies". These are arch supports made of semi-hard sponge runner and shaped like a flying saucer with one edge cut off. (The square edge fits against the side of the shoe. The rounded part supports the arch itself.)

I tried a pair, wearing one in my left shoe only to help that arch. That trouble cleared up shortly, but I kept wearing the support. I added one in the other shoe, only to keep a feeling of symmetry. To my great surprise and pleasure, the achilles tendon pain cleared up in about a week. After the winter of injuries, I ran the Boston marathon in 2:39:21—my best time. I had no problems with the arch or the tendon, during or after the race.

That's the history of the injuries. Neither has recurred. My observations are these. An examination of the muscle structure of the foot and lower leg shows very clearly that the arch muscles are connected to the muscles at the back of the leg. A breakdown of a muscle often results in the more serious strain of a nearby tendon because the tendon absorbs some of the pull that the muscle is supposed to handle. It is no mystery why an arch problem can result in other complications.

I've tried other kinds of shoes with so-called arch supports inside. I find that these aren't enough, so I use the "cookies" instead. I have very high arches. At first the cookies felt like lumps under my arches, but soon they went unnoticed.

I often make the supports myself now. I use a piece of sponge rubber that does not compress easily, and carve it to shape. Anyone interested can buy a pair of the cookie supports for $1.00 a pair (plus postage) from the New Balance Athletic Shoe Company, 176 Belmont St., Watertown, Mass. 02172. These will give you an idea what they look like. You then use them as a pattern for making your own.

I prefer having several sets of supports because I stick them in each pair of shoes with two-sided tape. If not stuck down, they slip and end up under my heel—particularly when running.

If anyone is having the slightest bit of trouble, with achilles tendons, arches or muscles in the backs of the legs, the cookie supports are worth trying. I know of no way they can hurt, and they certainly helped me.

Effects of Weight

Instincts serve a runner fairly well. Common sense tells him
to wear solidly-built (and therefore heavy) shoes when he's going
long and slow distances, and to switch to light ones when he wants
to go shorter and faster. He wears the shoes that fit his needs for
either support or speed. Few shoes offer one without sacrificing
the other.

When it comes to racing, shoe weight is a vital consideration.
But how vital? How much difference does an ounce of weight here
or there make? Ed Winrow, track coach at Valparaiso University
in Indiana, made this the subject of his master's thesis.

Winrow devised tests to determine the energy required to carry shoes of various weights at various speeds. He evaluated five
well-trained runners in a series of half-hour runs on a treadmill.
They ran at three different pace levels—about 10, seven and 5½
minutes per mile—in three different weights of shoes. The lightest
flats averaged 13.9 ounces per pair, the weight of typical road racing shoes. The medium weight shoes, warmup flats, weighted 22.3
ounces. The heaviest were low-cut sneakers lined with a weighted
insole. They weighed 34.5 ounces.

Winrow measured the runners for three factors: (1) exercise
heart rates; (2) caloric expenditures; (3) expired air volumes.
Rises in any of these indicate increased energy cost in running.

The tests, according to his *Track Technique* report, showed:

● Added shoe weight slightly boosted heart rates at all pace
levels. Pulse counts with the heaviest shoes were about five beats
higher per minute than with the lightest shoes.

● Calories cost per minute wasn't much different for any of
the three shoe weights. However, the discrepancy grows with pace,
and this is significant.

● Expired air volume tells how heavily the runner is having
to breathe to keep going. The demand increases markedly at faster
paces, and also according to shoe weights: 10-minute pace—1.2
liters per minute difference between the volumes while wearing
heavy and light shoes; 7-minute pace—4.4 liter difference; 5½-
minute pace—11.4 liters.

Winrow concludes that weight difference really only becomes
important at high speeds. At low-stress paces, the body apparently
adapts easily to the slight extra load. But when the runner starts

pushing his limits, the weight begins to tell.

Ed puts this in marathon terms: "The total energy costs for the full marathon at six miles per hour (10 min. per mile) for light (13.9 oz.) and heavy (34.5 oz.) shoes respectively would be 2594 and 2673 calories, and at 11 miles per hour (about 5:30/mile) would be 2286 and 2686 calories. This predicted increase in total energy costs of 400 calories for the full marathon appears large enough to affect the runner's energy stores and performance.

"In practice the increase in total energy expenditure is not of primary concern, but in competiton the athlete must utilize more oxygen due to the increase in energy costs. Therefore, increases in energy requirements caused by added shoe weights must be accounted for by the distance runner."

Where speed and lightness count most... (Tony Duffy photo)

Is Barefoot Still Best?

Distance runners go barefoot from time to time—in cross-country races on the grass mostly. There are a few iron-men like Abebe Bikila, who won the 1960 Olympic marathon over Rome's cobblestone streets in his bare feet. But that could be explained by saying Bikila was used to it; he had run that way all his life.

Several American distance runners haven't run that way all
their lives but prefer it even in road races. Ray Darwin, a Californ-
ian, started running barefoot because he couldn't find shoes that
fit comfortably over his deformed toes. He ran a sub-2:30 marathon without shoes. In 1972, Carrol Sternberg of Milwaukee
found his feet were heating up halfway through the Boston marathon. He shed his shoes and went on to run 2:38, finishing close
to the front in the 40-plus age class.

These things happen on cross-country and roads, but rarely
on the track. Several British runners have risked it, though. Bruce
Tulloh ran that way when he set European records back in the early 60s. Jim Hogan preferred to go shoeless. And Ron Hill didn't
wear any in the 1968 Olympic 10,000. The results were good in
every case.

Hogan said, "When I put spikes on, I feel I am tied to the
ground." He ran his six-mile over 40 seconds slower with shoes.

Shoes have two purposes: speed (in the form of better grip-
ping power) and safety (by protecting against pounding, brusing,
cutting, etc.). Track runners are most interested in the first factor,
long distance runners in the second. Distance men occasionally
don't wear any, but when was the last time you saw a barefoot
sprinter?

A South African researcher, Danie Burger, thinks there should
be more of the latter—especially now that all-weather tracks are
so common. These tracks are kinder to feet and more slip-proof
than old cinder types.

Burger made a case against spiked shoes for sprinters in the
March 1972 issue of *Track Technique.* He said, "Despite weighing
little, (wearing spikes in sprints) means that extra weight must be
carried during the race. The protective plate in the running shoe...
together with the sole of the shoe and the shoe itself limits toe-
drive very drastically. The toes in a running shoe can only move
minimally up and down past the plane of the ball of the foot. An
analogy is a shot putter who is prevented from giving a final finger-
flick before the shot leaves the hand."

He lists three other disadvantages: (1) a "drag" as the spikes
enter and leave the track at different angles; (2) loss of leg "im-
pact-energy" and speed while driving the spikes into the track; (3)
adhesion between the track material and the spikes ("where long
spikes are used on a dry rubber track," he says, "adhesion will
tend to be maximum").

Burger felt that each of these admittedly small speed limits added up to a major time loss over even the shortest sprint distances. So he tested the theory with trained sprinters. He started by applying thin layers of rubber solutions to their feet for protection and grip. After test runs in spikes and warmups barefoot, the sprinters tried barefoot time-trials from the blocks.

Burger reported these results: "A slight variation in sprinting rhythm due to the absence of running spikes was observed. Stride frequency was greater throughout. Even the initial time-trials without spikes proves to be as fast or faster than with spikes. After five runs there was an average improvement of 0.12 seconds over 40 meters." He tried the same tests with hurdlers: "Although it was expected that hurdle fear due to unprotected barefoot running would affect time-trials, there was a general speed-up of 0.1 seconds in times taken after the third hurdle."

RW surveyed its readers in 1971 asking about their shoe wear. One of the questions was do you ever run barefoot. One runner answered, "If the price of shoes keeps going up, I may be forced to." It may not be such a sacrifice to go without them after all.

GET A SHOE THAT FITS

BY DR. GABE MIRKIN

Dr. Mirkin, an experienced long distance runner, advises a great number of runner-patients at his office near Washington, D.C.

A review of chronic leg injuries in runners seen during one year revealed that 82% had an "inverted" (commonly called "flat") foot and 60% had a B or narrower width yet were not wearing narrow shoes. More than half of the injuries were in runners with *both* an inverted foot and a shoe that did not fit. And a signficant percentage came from an unstable or inadequate heel. Most of these problems could have been prevented with proper shoe choice and fit.

Inverted foot: The name "flat foot" implies that the longitudinal arch is flat. This is virtually never the case. The entire foot is rolled inward and gives the appearance that the arch is flat. Cup your hand and place it on the table. Now roll the hand inward. The "arch" will seem to disappear. This is what happens in "flat feet."

Because the foot is rolled inward, an abnormal force is transmitted to the inturned side of the ankle, and pain frequently occurs at that site. To compensate for the pressure on the inner ankle, an opposite stress is transmitted to the outer, lower border of the kneecap and the outside ligaments of the knee. Ailments known as patella chondromalacia and lateral band syndrome may result. Force is additionally transmitted to the hamstring and to the ligaments around the hip, predisposing the runner to injury there. Pain can also occur in the small of the back.

A simple yet effective self-treatment for inverted foot is the use of a "cookie" type of arch support. These supports made of hard rubber can be obtained from a cobbler, or, if not available locally, can be ordered from the New Balance Athletic Shoe Company in Watertown, Mass.

As everyone's arch is different, it will take some manipulation to fit the cookie to your foot. Do not glue in the cookie until you have found your fit. The cookies are best kept in place with two-sided adhesive tape. If the cookies feel too high, they may need to be filed down. With experimentation, most people can quickly find a fit that is comfortable.

If inverted feet are the cause of your trouble, your problem should improve within a few days.

Shoe width: Running high mileage in shoes that are too wide or too narrow eventually results in foot, ankle, knee and/or hip pain. In the many years I have treated athletic injuries, I have repeatedly noticed chronic injuries occurring in runners who wear shoes that are either too narrow or too wide.

Most running shoe manufacturers have ignored the narrow and wide foot. Instead of having widths, they prefer to confuse the runner with hundreds of different shoes which vary only slightly. I would prefer that they make one training shoe, one racing flat and one spike, all three coming in widths. New Balance, however, is the only company making a serious effort to help the runner who doesn't have average feet. Most other brands come only in a standard C or D width.

When shoes are being fitted, the big toe should be about three-fourths of an inch back from the end of the shoe. If it has to be much closer or much farther than that to insure proper width, then the shoes are too narrow or wide for your feet.

Width is absolutely critical. Make sure to have your width measured in a shoe store. If you have a B width, you can use a Spenco insole to reduce the width of the shoe by one letter (a C width with a Spenco becomes a B).

If you do not have a B-C-D width, you should not use most conventional shoes. You should either have yours specially made, or get the proper width from a manufacturer which pays attention to this important detail.

Heels: If the heel of your training shoe is lower than the heel of your walking shoe, you are putting additional stretch on your achilles tendon at a time when it already is under maximum stress. Too low heels are a frequent cause of achilles injuries, as are heels which are too narrow, badly run-over, loose fitting or which rub on the tendon. Although most street shoes have adequate heels, only recently have running shoes been equipped with substantial ones.

If the heel wedge in your shoe is not adequate, either replace the shoe or have an additional wedge built in by a cobbler. Do not put pads in the shoe under your heel. This tends to raise your heel out of the shoe and make the heel less stable.

A heel that fits loosely into the shoe will wobble with each plant and put undue strain on the achilles. Even runners with proper fit in the front of the foot sometimes have narrow heels. No running shoes come in variable heel widths. Since the shoe manufacturers ignore this problem, the athlete must become his own manufacturer.

You can correct this problem by putting moleskin on the sides of the shoe's heel and covering the moleskin with rubber tape. Be careful not to run the moleskin around the back of the shoe, as it will shorten it and push the foot too far forward.

SHOE-SHOPPER'S GUIDE

This article first was published in the booklet "Shoes for Runners."

Each shoe is going to strike the ground some 800 times a mile, each step almost exactly like the one before. Think about what each small flaw may mean, of each extra ounce of weight that has to be lifted, when it is multiplied by 800, 80,000 or 800,000. Choose your shoes with that in mind.

Obviously, the best way to choose shoes is to examine them yourself, to try them on and run in them before any money changes hands. This is the ideal situation, to fit running shoes with almost as much care as eyeglasses. It isn't always possible to be so careful, though, since running shoe dealers aren't as accessible as optometrists.

So runners often find their own best shoes through trial and error. Nearly every runner's closet is littered with erroneous trials. Once they find their own best brand, model and size, mail-ordering will do. But on the first trial, a trip to the nearest running shoe store is a good investment no matter what the expense in time and money. This trip could save trouble later on.

Once in the shop, don't be overwhelmed by the displays and by the salesman. There'll be lots of models on the shelves, and the salesman will be anxious to put a pair on your feet right away and send you down the street.

Take your time. It's your money and your feet. Sort through the models. Squeeze them. Bend them. Feel every inch of them, inside and out. Try on as many pairs as you need to find the right one. When you find that one, at least walk in it. If the office space and the salesman allow, run in it.

What do you look for in a good running shoe? At least eight things. Taken together, they can be called the "Guide to Shoe-Shopping."

1. **Needs**—How will the shoe be used? Racing or training? Road, track or cross-country? Hard or easy running? Shoe needs, of course, vary from running type to running type. In general, run-

ners in the shortest and fastest activities wear the flimsiest shoes, and long slow distance runners use the most substantial shoes. This is because protection gets progressively more important than speed as distance grows. Fit shoes to the activity.

2. **Price**—Get the best ones you can afford. The runners we surveyed go through an average of two pairs of shoes a year. That's $30-50 at today's prices. Few are willing to spend much more than $25 for a single pair, no matter how special they look. They shouldn't be expected to pay more when adequate shoes are available for less. On the other hand, avoid bargain-basement specials. The true bill for them comes due later.

That takes care of the visual screening. You've seen the models the store has and you can use, the ones that look good and have the right price. Don't be swayed yet by appearance and fad before making a closer inspection.

3. **Weight**—Pick up each shoe. Weigh it in your mind. Lightness is a virtue, but only to a point. You obviously can run a bit faster in light shoes like the nylon racing flats. But in doing so you give up the support features of the thick "stone-crushers." You may be willing to sacrifice support in races, where efforts are relatively short. In prolonged training, though, a little extra well-placed weight won't hurt.

Just make sure the shoes are worth their weight.

4. **Last**—The last is one of the first things to examine. This is the shape of the shoe when you look at it from the bottom. Ideally, it should be the same basic shape as the foot. Unfortunately, most running shoes aren't.

Arthur Lydiard, a running coach and shoemaker from New Zealand, said several years ago in a *RW* interview, "The worst feature of most of the shoes sold in this country (the US) is that the lasts are wrong. They don't comform to the shape of your foot. The lasts are straight, so your big toe is in the wrong place, forcing you to run on the side of your foot."

When the lasts are wrong, the foot constantly fights the shoe, trying to make it conform to the foot structure. The shoe is less pliable than the foot, so the shoe has its way.

Other problems: German and Japanese shoes are made for the German and Japanese feet, and they come in only one width. The shoe is less pliable than the foot, so the shoe has its way.

Most of these shoes, says Desmond O'Neill, "don't even fit the

foot at rest, much less in motion—a point which you may easily
prove by tracing an outline of the sole of your shoe on paper, and
then superimposing an outline of your own foot."

Chances are, the forefoot won't line up with the shoe's last,
and the toes will either be lost in the front of the shoe or will lap
over the edges. It doesn't take a podiatrist to guess what happens
when you start running: twisting, cramping, slipping, all of which
are most unsettling.

5. **Cushion**— Squeeze and bend the sole. This is what the shoe
is all about. The rest of it just holds the sole—either rubber or spikes
—in place.

In flats, you're looking for a sole that makes you feel like
you're crossing a bed of marshmallows, right? Not exactly. Remember you're running on your feet with full body weight on them—
not on your hands. So the pinch test isn't entirely reliable.

Most sponge rubber in shoes doesn't absorb much shock, its
intended role, because it's too soft. Higher-density rubber may do
a better job of neutralizing shock, to say nothing of lasting longer.
Yet it can't be so hard that it's wood-like. If that is the case, shock
again radiates from toe to head.

A second sole factor to check is flexibility. The shoes should
bend, but only selectively. Noted sports podiatrist Richard Schuster of New York recommends that all distance runners have shoes
with "rigid shanks." By this he means limited flexibility from the
heel to the back of the ball of the foot—the metatarsal heads. The
rigid shank, Schuster says, reduces strain on the arches.

From the metatarsal heads forward, though, the shoe must
have good flexibility. This area, the front one-third of the foot, is
where the roll of toe-off occurs. If the shoe doesn't bend here, the
leg takes the stress.

The bending shouldn't take any unusual effort.

Now slip inside, wearing the socks you use when you run. If
you don't use socks, don't wear them. Test the feel and the fit of
the shoes—both of them. Stomp on the heels and soles. Spring off
the toes. Jog around the shop if you have the nerve.

The shoes, if they're good ones, should immediately feel comfortable. If they don't feel right in this limited test, think how
they'll feel when they start hitting the ground 800 times a mile.

Give special attention to three more areas while you're inside:

6. **Upper**—Wiggle your heels, arches and toes, feeling out irri-

The choice of running shoes has never been greater. (S. Pantovic)

tating breaks or seams in the material. Think of each one as a potential blister.

The upper should be snug from one end to the other, but not
overly tight. If you feel cramped, go to a larger size. If you still feel
too tight in some places, yet too loose in others, go to another model. This one will never fit properly.

Nylon or leather? Both have advantages and disadvantages. Nylon is lighter, softer and washable. But leather is more rugged and offers better support. Good shoes are made of both materials —also bad ones. You have to look at other factors.

7. **Heel**—This can cause trouble in any number of ways, because about 80% of the runner's weight comes down on a few square inches of heel on each step.

Look for the following in heels:

● Slightly higher than the ball of foot, but not so high that it throws the weight too far forward.

● Wide enough to prevent instability, a rolling motion on foot-plant.

● Rigid counter on back and sides of upper, to stabilize heel.

● No "bite" into heel bone and achilles tendon on top of heel.

Look for moderate elevation and a feeling of snug stability in the entire heel area.

8. **Arch**—An arch is something like a fingerprint. It's personal. It's doubtful whether the arch supports built into running shoes do much good. Many shoemakers add these supports almost as an afterthought, and many runners immediately rip out the form rubber cookies.

Some runners don't need arch supports. Those who do need them need more than half-measures. A more substantial slip-in support (such as Dr. Scholl's) may do the trick, or perhaps a custom-molded insert from a doctor.

The shoe should have nothing inside that isn't needed, and room for what is.

All this examining takes time, both your's and the shop's. But this isn't an impulse item. If the shoes you finally decide on are good ones, they'll be part of you—the very important part that contacts the ground—for the next million footsteps or so.

TECHNIQUE

RUNNING WITH STYLE

This collection of articles was first published in November 1973 Runner's World.

It is dusk, and you're running home into the lingering glow of the western sky. Up ahead, a quarter-mile away on the crest of a hill, another runner cuts across your path. He's silhouetted against the reds and golds of early evening.

From this distance and with this backlighting, you can't see the runner's face. But you recognize him immediately. You know him by the way he runs. His identity is in his style of movement— his stride, his trunk, arm and head carriage.

Style is a personal trademark as different from runner to runner as are their fingerprints. The way one runs is partly hereditary, partly learned while growing up, and only slightly changed through running training. A runner looks much the same after a year or five or 10 years of serious work as he did when he started. He's more efficient, perhaps, but the basic habits are still there.

Some glide over the ground like deer, barely seeming to touch down. Others pound the earth like angry rhinos. There are "striders" who gobble up the earth in great gulps, and "choppers" who take it in jerky little bites. There are "windmills" who flail their arms like propellers, and "boxers" who run as if they were protecting their faces from attack. There are "head-rollers," "star-gazers" and "ground-watchers" who all look everywhere but ahead. Their individual styles identify them.

The style variations aren't necessarily wrong or in need of change. In fact, more harm may come from treating insignificant personal quirks as problems than from ignoring them.

Ken Doherty, a leading American technical track writer, says in his *Track and Field Omnibook* that "running technique is primarily an individual matter. It began when the athlete was two years or so of age, and over the course of a dozen or a score of years it had become so 'natural'—or at least so firmly established —as not to be changed without disturbing a man's inner as well as outer balance and relaxation. A sound rule of thumb when it comes to running technique is to leave it alone."

Doherty isn't saying that obvious and easily-corrected form faults don't warrant correcting when they slow a runner down. He's saying that more effort is wasted in trying to produce picture-perfect form than in running the familiar less-than-perfect way.

Viljo Heino (left) was known in the 1940s—the latter days of the first Finnish Golden Age of running—as an exceptional stylist.

"The technique of some men can and should be improved," Doherty says, "as long as we remember that improvement is related to a man's competitive performances—not to whether his technique is aesthetically pleasing."

There are no prizes for form. Otherwise, people the caliber of Jim Ryun, Emil Zatopek, Murray Halberg and Bruce Kidd would have been left out.

Ryun, one of history's fastest middle distance men, always has been a "head-roller." Four-time Olympic winner Zatopek "boxed" his way through his races. Former two- and three-mile record holder Halberg all but lost the use of one arm in an accident, yet compensated nicely. Kidd, onetime boy-wonder of distance running, threw his arms every way but the "right" way when he raced.

Normal and acceptable running style covers a great range of individual quirks, even at world-class level. And only a very few of these quirks need to be—or even can be—changed.

Pekka Vasala (l)
and Kip Keino,
stride for stride
in the 1972
Olympic 1500-
meter final.
(Presse Sports)

Ken Doherty advises, "Do what comes naturally, as long as 'naturally' is mechanically sound. If it isn't, do what is mechanically sound until it comes naturally."

He says the focus should be on "the overall action rather than the details of technique. To focus attention on one part is to upset the vital balance. And man is not likely to run economically until that vital balance is restored."

Economical running springs from the unconscious mind. A runner who focuses too strongly on single steps may change his overall flow so much that he trips over his own feet. These are Ken Doherty's views.

Percy Cerutty would scoff at this appraisal of running technique. Doherty has built his reputation by reporting the accumulated wisdom of track. His writing reflects well-founded, conventional approaches.

Cerutty is not conventional. The Australian made his name in the late '50s through the tradition-challenging training he gave miler Herb Elliot. Elliott stayed away from the track and the stopwatch—a radical departure in the 1950s—and instead charged up

sandhills, lifted heavy weights and tried to adopt the unorthodox
style Cerutty was teaching.

Doherty and Cerutty agree on one thing. They both say that
running habits are learned in the early years. But Doherty says
they're permanent and therefore should be left alone. Cerutty ar-
gues that these are bad habits that must be torn down and rebuilt.

Cerutty claims that "homo sapiens have lost most of the ability—through separation from natural and primitive living—to move
as an animal." He teaches his athletes to run like horses. This, he
says, "requires re-education as to movement, posture and relaxation."

Doherty and Cerutty represent extremes of thought on this
running form question. Doherty warns not to think much about it.
At best, this preoccupation is a waste of time, he says. At worst,
it is damaging to overall running performance. Cerutty says go
primitive. There's no better way to spend effort than in breaking
sloppy human running habits.

Between the two extremes stand Bud Winter and Bill Bowerman. Both have now retired from college coaching, but still are
known as the most successful American men in their events.

Winter is a sprint master. Three of his runners—John Carlos
(100y), Tommie Smith (220y and 200m) and Lee Evans (400m)—
have held world records. Smith and Evans won Olympic titles at
Mexico City.

Bowerman works his magic with distance runners. Two of
his pupils—Steve Prefontaine (5000) and Kenny Moore (marathon)
—placed fourth in the '72 Olympics. Two of Bowerman's steeple-
chasers—Mike Manley and Steve Savage—also ran in Munich.

While Winter and Bowerman don't go to Cerutty-like lengths
to remake a runner's style, they do feel that emphasis on this trait
is well-placed. They tend to agree with *Sports Illustrated* writer
Gwilym Brown, who says, "The answer to the question of why
one man can run fast while another of similar physique seems forever destined to be slow is more often that the slow fellow is running incorrectly than he was born that way."

These four coaches, and writer-runner Brown, are dealing in
areas of speculation. Toni Nett doesn't speculate. He deals with
the blacks and whites of statistics and photo images on paper. Nett,
a West German, specializes in technical analysis of track and field
athletes, using sequence photography as his main tool.

Nett and the four coaches all look at running technique from different viewpoints. All speak with authority, and a composite of their views gives a clearer picture of what this technique is or should be.

They seem to say:

• Foot-fall and stride length are functions of running speed, and must shift to fit that speed.

• Erect body carriage gives maximum power and efficiency at least among distance runners.

• Arms aren't just along for the ride, but have important balancing and driving functions.

• Stride, stance and arm action are the keys to improving technique if it can be improved.

Where Feet Meet Earth

"Foot-fall and stride length are functions of running speed, and must shift to fit that speed."

Toni Nett has verified part of this from photographic evidence. In his technical track studies, Nett has shot hundreds of top runners and has checked their styles. The only "universally applicable technique," he says, is the foot-planting pattern.

Nett states that all good runners plant the same way at a particular pace, and shift only as speed picks up or slows down. He finds that a sprinter running long runs like a distance man, and that a distance runner kicking at the end of his race plants his feet like a sprinter.

Nett's slow-motion and sequence films show an increasingly flat-footed landing as distances go up from the sprints and speed drops. He lists his conclusions in *Track Technique* ("Foot Plant in Running," March 1964):

1. Runners at all distances land first on the outside edge of the foot then roll inward. This has a "shock-absorber" effect.

2. The precise point of contact along the outside edge varies with speed.

3. In the 100- and 200-meter sprints, the landing is high on the ball of the foot, near the joints of the little toe. In the 400, it is a bit farther back.

4. In the 800 and 1500, the contact point is the metatarsal arch area. The landing looks nearly flat.

5. In longer distances, there is heel-first contact.

The West German says no such universal pattern shows up in the carriage of the arms, trunk and head, or in the length and number of strides. These are questions of "individual style," though somewhat related to pace as well.

Stride length, like foot-plant, shifts with pace. It shortens as the runner slows and stretches out as he speeds up, like a car shifting gears. "Overstriding" and "understriding" imply running in the wrong gears for the circumstances at hand.

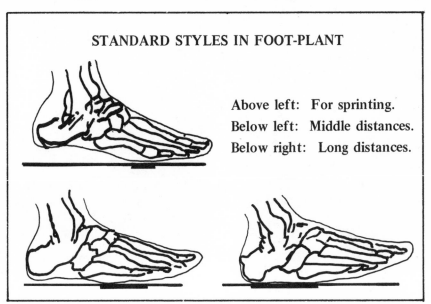

STANDARD STYLES IN FOOT-PLANT

Above left: For sprinting.
Below left: Middle distances.
Below right: Long distances.

Bill Bowerman lists two fundamental rules for controlling stride length ("The Secrets of Speed," *Sports Illustrated*, Aug. 2, 1971):

● First, your foot should strike *after* it has reached the farthest point of advance and has actually started to swing back."

● "Second, when your foot first strikes, the point of contact should be directly under your knee, not out in front of it, and as nearly as possible squarely beneath your center of gravity."

"Fortunately, " Bowerman adds, "both fundamentals are easy enough to comply with by keeping your knees slightly bent at all times and by not overstriding. If the foot hits the ground

ahead of the knee, the leg will be too straight and will act as a brake instead of an accelerator."

In short, keep your legs under you and stay with the pace they're setting.

"Lean" Years Have Passed

"Erect body carriage gives maximum power and efficiency."

Percy Cerutty says we run *on* the legs rather than *with* them. He points out that most of the body's weight is centered above the hip sockets. Using the upper body properly is as important as balancing the load on the back of a pack mule.

Both Bill Bowerman and Bud Winter are advocates of running erect. They make their points with graphic illustrations.

Bowerman says in his *SI* article, "A forward lean might be useful for someone trying to bash down a wall with his head. But in running it merely gives the leg muscles a lot of unnecessary work."

Winter talks of sprint form in the *Track and Field Quarterly* (Vol. 72, No. 1), and some of his comments are in the *Guide to Sprinting* booklet. The retired San Jose State coach says, "In the old days, we used to think that an exaggerated (forward) lean was necessary, which meant running with head down and the caboose sticking way out in back.

"We know now that sprinters have to 'run tall.' To do this, they must push the chest out, pull the caboose in and run high on their toes. The position is similar to that of a soldier standing at attention."

The most vital element in smooth and efficient running style, according to Bowerman, is an upright posture. George Sheehan comments, "Bowerman's prescription for perfect running could already have been deduced from watching his men in action. In more exaggerated form, it would be a Groucho Marx walk—a semi-sitting position with the shoulders kept level at all times, but easy and relaxed. That's the Oregon style. The straight back is a Bowerman trademark."

Bowerman himself says the posture should be so erect that you could drop a plumb-line from ear level and it would fall "straight

The form of Frank Shorter. (Mark Shearman photo)

down through the line of the shoulder, the line of the hip and then on to the ground."

The way to accomplish this is to pull back the shoulders and pull in the buttocks. Balance the trunk over the legs and the head over the trunk.

In Bud Winter's words, get a proud look on your face. "Run tall!" Winter tells a sprinter. "Keep the eyes right on the finish line all the way."

Run *on* the legs.

Value of Hand-Holding

"Arms aren't just along for the ride, but have important balancing and driving functions."

Three of the coaches agree here.

Bill Bowerman: "The faster you swing your arms—so long as the action is rhythmic—the faster you will be able to move your legs."

Bud Winter: "The arms are a source of speed and power. The faster the arms go, the faster the legs will have to go."

Percy Cerutty: "According to my ideas, all running starts with the thumbs and ends on the feet... When all the upper body and arm movements are correct, the legs will function properly."

Hands and arms influence the movement of the legs and the body carriage. Seemingly insignificant details of fist and wrist position, elbow angle and shoulder sway can set off a chain-reaction of form faults.

Run with the fist loosely cupped, the wrist fixed, the elbow unlocked and at an angle, the shoulders so level you can balance chips on them. In summary, this is the advice of the three coaches.

Again, these are slight differences between sprinters and distance runners. But most of the principles carry through from event to event.

Winter's technique for the sprints: "Hold the hands cupped and relaxed. Now bring the arms up to almost 90 degrees, palms upward a bit to keep the elbows close to the sides. Swing the arms parallel to each other, not across the chest. By pumping the arms parallel, you can gain some inches."

Bowerman concurs: "While sprinting, keep your arms low and pump them hard and rapidly."

The arms are a driving, pumping force in the sprints. In longer runs, with more of a coasting action, the arms are more of a balance mechanism. They swing somewhat across the chest, but not excessively so.

Cerutty: "The hands never pass a center line projected out in front of the chest, but always work in toward that center line."

Bowerman: "For slower running, hold your arms in a comfortable, restful position and keep their action to a minimum. Your hands should be fairly close to your chest, at about the height of pectoral muscles... Lower each hand and arm no more than a foot or so as the leg on the opposite side goes back."

The arms work gently in the distances, in a state of poised relaxation. They are neither rigid nor flaccid, but are somewhat in between. They're in a position to fight off tension.

Tension begins in the hands and arms, and tension is lowered when the hands are cupped and arms are flexed. Try this. Straighten the fingers and the forearm, and note the feeling of rigidity. Now pull in the fingers and bend the elbow, and feel the muscles relax. Flap the wrists up and down a half-dozen times, then think how tired they'd get if they kept this up for miles.

Fist loosely clenched, wrist rigid, elbow unlocked and angled... This is what Percy Cerutty means when he talks of running starting from the thumbs and moving up from there. The outspoken Australian coach says that unclenched hands and limp wrists are signs not only of weakness in running form but also weakness of character.

But the worst of faults, according to Cerutty, is the unmoving elbow. In his book *Middle Distance Running*, he says, "Above all else, the elbows must be unlocked. The most common fault of all is the locked elbow." Cerutty has found that when the elbow is locked, the shoulders sway and dip wastefully.

It takes just that much to destroy a delicate balance.

Getting Your Racing Kicks

Practice makes perfect?

Ken Doherty thinks not. He says technique is so ground into a runner by heredity and early environment that it can't be changed much.

Percy Cerutty says yes, technique is learned. If learned improperly, it must be unlearned and relearned to make it right.

The two of them argued this out earlier, and this much is clear from what was said there and since. If practice doesn't make perfect, it at least (a) compensates for some weaknesses by creating new strengths; (b) chips off the rough edges to produce a smoother and more efficient running, and (c) removes self-consciousness from the form and pushes it back into the unconscious—a kind of "automatic pilot."

This is *general* form we're talking about—the kind of action that takes us through 99% of our running and racing miles. There are also *specialized* kinds of running form, and these without doubt are perfected in practice.

Starting, running hills, finishing—all are special techniques. We've talked about the mechanics of sprint starts and methods of climbing and descending hills in *Runner's World*. ("Standing in the Blocks," May 73, and "Try This for a Start," Oct. 73, cover starting. "Gearing Yourself for Hills," Oct. 73, covers hill running.) Refer to those for details.

Finishing needs more discussion. Finishing a distance race can be the best or the worst of experiences. It can be a powerful acceleration or a "survival shuffle," depending on the kind of background a runner has. That's where learning comes in. Repeated experience tells a runner how much and what kind of training he needs, how to pace himself, and how, when or if he can kick.

Tony Benson is a master kicker. The Australian (featured in the Sept. 73 *RW* "Profiles") has run the last lap of a 5000-meter race in under 52 seconds. In his career, he has lost only once when he was with the field at the bell.

Benson says, "I believe the possession of the big kick is partly a mental faith, partly (pace) judgment, partly will to win and, most importantly, the result of the correct combination of cardiovascular efficiency, basic speed capability and power training designed to allow fast changes of momentum."

Benson trains for endurance and the speed needed to hold the pace. All runners do that. But he goes an extra step into special "kick" work.

"Kick," he says, "relies specifically on the ability to open an unbridgeable gap of 15-20 meters, and is usually executed within the final 300 meters. Obviously, practice is necessary."

Tony practices fast uphill sprints, with accelerations at the crest. "oxygen-debt work," over the race distance (for instance, 5000 meters of 100 sprinting, 100 striding) and acceleration over 150-300 meters. This, of course, comes on top of endurance and pace-speed training. Without them, there'd be no base to kick from.

He says that "merely recording faster underdistance times than one's rivals is no guarantee of success, and may in fact mean the opposite because of the emphasis (on speed) needed to achieve these times. The Munich 5000 was a classic example in that Lasse Viren and Mohamed Gammoudi outkicked the much faster Ian Stewart, Steve Prefontaine and Emiel Puttemans."

Kick isn't so much a matter of speed as being able to shift suddenly into a higher gear at a point where the natural urge is to shift the other way. This ability to kick is a fortunate combination of learning and emotion.

The full-speed form of sprinters Larry Black (left) and Willie Deckard in the 220. (Stan Pantovic photo)

TRY THIS FOR A START

BY BROOKS JOHNSON

Brooks Johnson, who once had a share of the world indoor 60-yard record, coaches at the Sports International track club in Washington, D.C. These articles first appeared in Runner's World, October 1973 and February 1974.

As I watched a taped version of the 1973 US vs. USSR meet on television, I saw and heard something that at first gave me some satisfaction. But this initial sentiment quickly turned to concern. Let me give the background.

The picture was of Steve Williams getting off to a very good start in the 100 meters. The announcer was commenting on how good Williams' start was, after having noted in his introductory remarks that Steve was usually a very bad starter. In fact, in track circles Steve was noted for his wretched start, despite the fact that he was the fastest man in the world this year.

Now let's go back a couple of weeks before the meet. Steve was the premier runner on the US national team headed for Europe in early July. I was the coach of the women's team. Steve and other athletes were laughing and commenting on their performances at the Nationals. Since their mere presence on the plane was manifestation of them having done well, the mood was light, with a warm give-and-take, with just a little bit of bragging thrown in for good measure.

Williams happened to be talking to Maurice Peoples about how much faster he, Steve, could go if he had a "good start." Maurice suggested that he talk to me. Steve approached me and said, "I want you to help me with my start when we get to Germany." To have the fastest person in the world come up to you and ask you for help with his start is an interesting experience. But again the initial twinge had barely been experienced when concern came to my mind that here is the world's fastest human feeling uncomfortable about his start.

I told him the way to develop a good start is to start with a philosophy. I'm not going to say there is *a* philosophy, but I do maintain that to get a consistently good start there must be some kind of rationale involved which is understood by the athlete himself.

First, I asked Steve what bothered him about his start. He stated that he was always last out of the blocks. I related to him that being last out of the blocks is not necessarily an indication of a bad start. Sound strange? Williams thought so, too. I pointed out to

"The way to develop a good start is to start with a philosophy. . . I maintain that to get a consistently good start there must be some kind of rationale involved which is understood by the athlete himself. " (photo left by John Marconi; below by Ed Lacey)

him another "world's fastest human" was also supposed to have a "bad start," yet he won the 1964 Olympics and held virtually every sprint record of significance.

Despite the fact that Bob Hayes was rarely out first, he was always in command of the race by 25 or 30 yards, and this was most important. His rate of acceleration was superior to everyone else's, and this was the crucial criterion. Bob would get up to maximum

The first steps. . . (Ed Lacey photo)

speed before anyone else, and could hold it longer than anyone else. There was something in his start that allowed him to do this despite the fact that people like Charles Greene, Mel Pender and almost any other quality sprinter would have the first few steps on Hayes.

I also mentioned to Steve that the role of the start is to get the runner into the running rhythm that he desires as soon as it is feasible. Breaking it down further, I explained that the start is simply a technique used for overcoming inertia of one sort, and generating inertia of another sort. The law of inertia states that an object in motion tends to stay in motion and an object at rest tends to stay at rest. Thus, the start is supposed to overcome the inertia of being stationary and get you into the inertia as it applies to movement, as soon and as efficiently as possible.

The key word is "efficiently." It's possible to sacrifice too much effort and concentration trying to "get out," and in doing so expending an inordinate amount of effort in this task, almost defeating the purpose of the start itself. Too much energy expended at the blocks takes its toll elsewhere in the race. Often this kind of "rocketing" creates tension and contracting of the muscles that is detrimental to getting the maximum use and extension of the legs—ultimately causing a level of performance lower than possible.

I pointed out to Steve that there are two crucial aspects of running. The first is leg speed—the rate at which one leg passes the other. The second is leg *span*—the distance in between each stride. There are some sprinters who depend upon leg speed to get the job done (Pender, Greene, Jean-Louis Ravelomanantsoa, etc.). This is particularly the case in smaller sprinters. Taller sprinters (Tommie Smith, John Carlos, Henry Carr) rely more upon leg span to get them through. Valeriy Borzov is perhaps the best example of a balanced mixture of the two. Most other sprinters tend to rely on one aspect or the other, depending upon size. But the Russians, through their scientific approach, were able to get the optimum utilization of both leg speed and leg span from Borzov.

Williams, tall as he is (6'3½") and with an extremely high split, should not sacrifice his long suit in an effort to match the rhythm with the shorter men—especially at the start. His start should simply allow him to get out under control and provide him with the basis for getting his legs up to their fullest extension as soon as possible.

Another aspect of starting we delved into was the psychological end. Starting, because of he extraordinary focus most sprinters and coaches place on it (not to mention the inherent pressures of the exercise iteself), requires a certain psychological preparedness. Most simply put, it requires confidence. In order to accomplish what the start is supposed to do, one must have confidence in the fact that his start is doing what it should for him.

I pointed out that Steve, like Hayes, was being victimized by the press because he was not the quickest out of the blocks—that a constant bombardment in the press and by others about how bad his start was, was not going to serve any purpose. He should not allow himself to be conditioned and influenced by what he read and heard, but rather should look to the objective results. They showed that he was the fastest man being timed over his chosen distance. He must be doing a hell of a lot more things right than wrong, and his start, while it may not appear to be an asset, certainly didn't appear to be that much of a handicap. Being so far back simply forced him to be competitive for a greater part of the race.

Once in Europe, we continued our talks about starting. During one practice session in Germany, Steve was taking gun starts with the other sprinters and was getting out so badly that he came over to me and said, "Hey, man, this is ridiculous. What's happening?" I mentioned a couple of very simple things, like his hand placement was not allowing him much room to move. In a word, he was too jammed up in the blocks.

Now you have to understand the petty jealousies that exist between coaches on these teams. Being the women's coach, I wasn't supposed to have much to do with the men, even if they sought me out. It was in this light that Steve said, "I'm going inside away from these people. Will you come in and work with me for a while?"

Once inside the indoor warmup area adjacent to Olympic Stadium in Munich, Steve and I began to work. We were joined by Roy Griak, one of the men's coaches who watched and commented as we analyzed Steve's starting technique. (Griak obviously had no objection to my helping.) The first thing we did was to move his blocks farther back from the line, allowing his legs more room and ease to move as they came out. The other thing we did was to have him lift his head up to the angle he used when he came up and out of the blocks.

There was an immediate improvement. The action was easier, more fluid, and most of all Steve was more under control when he came out. The look of relief on his face was warming to both Griak and me as we left. Steve's start in Munich was not spectacular, but he reported that he later felt good and that he was sure it would get better as he gained confidence in it.

But perhaps the greatest single element, responsible for the kind of start he got in Minsk, was something that happened almost by accident. In Italy, we were supplied with blocks that were not attached to each other. They were not attached on a common shaft as most blocks were, but were capable of being placed where the athlete wanted them to be. This was especially important because

I encouraged Steve to put the blocks "where they feel most natural." To our mutual surprise, they were placed several inches farther apart than ordinary blocks would allow. Being further back in the blocks, he did not feel cramped. Having them farther apart, he was able to come out with a wide stance, giving him greater balance. Having his head at the proper angle for his ascent out of the blocks, he was able to move right up into that natural, long, powerfully fluid stride of his with a minimum of balance difficulties. We "borrowed" the Italian blocks and things kept getting better.

But my concern emanates from the fact that I know there are other sprinters, perhaps not as gifted as Steve, who are right now being victimized and handicapped unnecessarily because they are not sure of the philosophy employed in their starting techniques. I should hasten to point out that the same person who now coaches Steve Williams, coached Bob Hayes. That's Dick Hill. So I'm not for one instant being critical of Steve's handling, but simply pointing out the fact that he, Steve Williams, did not understand fully what he was doing or supposed to do. Once he did, the result was just like it would be with nay intelligent, gifted, competitive athlete... success.

Starts, Step-by-Step

After the previous article appeared in *Runner's World*, a number of runners and coaches have asked me to elaborate on my ideas about starting. Essentially, they want a specific, detailed explanation of my approach to sprint starting. Before I undertake this, let me briefly review some of the basic concepts touched upon in the other piece:

First, starting is basically the vehicle used to overcome the inertia of being at rest, to get into the inertia of movement. Second, have a technique of starting that is known to the athlete, that he understands and in which he has confidence. Third, don't misplace the emphasis on starting so it takes away an inordinate amount of energy that might be better expended elsewhere in the race. Finally, remember that sprinting is essentially a matter of who can get up to maximum speed the earliest and hold that maximum the longest.

I think that coaching runners as young as five or six years old has helped me come up with a simple, practical and effective method of starting and teaching the start. At this level, everything has to be simple and basic. I try to break the start down into its component parts and put them together in the most natural way possible.

We start with three relatively simple theories:

• Even a very young mind can grasp the idea that an object in motion tends to stay in motion and an object at rest tends to stay at rest. How? Simply point out to him his experience with his bike or a pedal car. I explain how it is harder for him to get it started when it is stopped than to keep it going when he has it moving. I also point out what happens to him when he hits an object and is suddenly jerked foreward.

• For every action there is an equal and opposite reaction. This can be easily shown through the simple act of walking and the opposing efforts necessary for locomotion.

• A third concept is balance. I show how the mind and body combine to instinctively keep the body in a balanced position, demonstrating by simulating tightrope walking along a crack in the floor or a line on the field with arms extended to help maintain balance. It is easily seen that the mind and body naturally combine to try and offset any tendency toward imbalance.

Armed with these three principles, the runner begins to learn the art of starting. There has been discussion of late on the crouch start vs. the standing start. For most sprinters, I feel the crouch is better, and I'll limit the discussion here to that style.

1. Begin by placing the hands (bridged) slightly behind the starting line, hands set in a position slightly wider than the shoulders so they can pass by the hips and legs without danger of contact.

2. The second concern is the placement of the feet. If right-handed, place the right foot farthest back in the blocks. This becomes the "quick side". The left side is the "power side" because it is going to produce the major thrust forward at the start.

3. Next, find the leg angle in the "set" position that allows the most powerful push. A relatively simple way of finding this approximate position is to bend the knee so as to get the most push upwards as in a lay-up in basketball. This angle will likely be close to a 90-degree bend. Once the angle has been determined, simply place the foot as far back in the blocks as necessary to achieve that angle. This angle is used in the "set" position, with the hips slightly higher than the shoulders in most cases. The "quick" foot, or

right foot in the example we are using, should be about 7-10 inches farther back as a rule.

4. Back into the blocks by getting down on all fours in front of the starting line and move toward the blocks, carefully placing the feet in the blocks so only the toe of each foot (barely) touches the track.

5. Turn the heels in just a little bit so the toes point slightly out.

6. Head and shoulders at this point are as far forward as they are ever going to be in the "set" position. If this is the case, the sprinter need only make one movement at the command "set."

7. Bring the hips up to a position where the surge of power comes to its height in the "power side" leg, about in the middle of the thigh. After many experiments, the athlete will be able to determine just where this maximum power feeling comes in. He stops there. At different times, the angle will vary slightly.

8. The head is at an angle it naturally assumes in everyday activity. In other words, the head should not be down in a relaxed position. The body will inevitably follow the head. If the head is down, then the body will go forward *and down* on takeoff. Sprinters who start this way make an adjustment to compensate. They usually snap their heads up quickly. Their bodies come up prematurely, and they lose some of their power and thrust. Stumbling may also result from erratic, jerky, almost uncontrolled first efforts.

9. In the "set" position, think principally about snapping the "quick side" hand back at the sound of the gun. This equal and opposite reaction (between hand and the leg) and the desire to remain in balance should facilitate a quick, controlled start, putting the runner in a natural position of ascent out of the blocks. The greatest difficulty is in getting the athlete to snap the quick hand very fast.

10. You are in the final starting position. Now what? Some people are advised at this point to "concentrate." But the problem is, what does one concentrate on? My own advice depends on the sophistication of the athlete involved. For the beginner, the suggestion to concentrate on the gun is good. For the more advanced sprinter, I suggest certain gimmicks that will allow them the millisecond advantages that sprinters so desperately crave.

The most consistent advantage in starting comes in a basic understanding of what you are trying to do and how. Then you have to know how to do it and have confidence in what you are doing. The final bits of confidence come from knowing when the gun is going to be fired. Now there is no exact way of knowing this, but there is a method that is the next best thing. It requires some knowledge about the person who is actually firing the gun. My experience has been that all such people have habits and idiosyncrasies. Many of the poorer ones have a rhythm they use between "set" and firing the gun.

The ability of the person to react to the gun is in some degree native. Some people simply appear to be born with better reflexes than others. On the other hand, reaction to the gun can be improved, and a person with only average reflexes can become an excellent starter with attention to common sense and proper mechanics.

Too often we in the US have accepted the fallacious idea that sprinters are born. Sprinters, like many other athletes, are born with certain gifts. But these gifts are useless unless they are developed and utllized. Over and above the physical gifts are certain mental or psychological gifts that need to be refined and honed as well. In any and all cases, what nature gave us can still be extended through intelligent handling.

Our basic problem in sprinting in the US is that we often neglect sprinters because we feel sprinting is "natural" talent. We have not begun to tap the real depth of potential that man has for running extremely fast over relatively short distances.

A few men have taken an intelligent and scientific look at this fact and realize that we are only scratching the surface. One is Wilbur Ross. Ross has known for years that a 12.5 120-yard hurdle race is possible, and long overdue. Rod Milburn gave us an inkling that sub-13-flat was possible. Yet it has taken people far removed from the American scene and its influences to come up with proof that we are neglecting hurdlers and sprinters in the US. Valeriy Borzov is an excellent example.

I was not so much impressed with Borzov's physical gifts and mechanics as I was the fact that here was a sprinter who was *totally* prepared and developed. It was this *totality* of preparation that made him so superior to Munich. Whatever his gifts were, he was primed to get the most from them. Had the American sprinters, Rey Robinson and Eddie Hart, made the 100-meter final, the winner would have been the same because Borzov was most ready for the task at hand.

LEARNING HURDLING

BY DR. JOHN T. POWELL

Dr. Powell, an acknowledged expert in the technical aspects of track and field, wrote this introduction to hurdling for "Modern Athlete and Coach" magazine in May 1969.

Hurdling is sprinting with a number of nuisances in the way. It is the fast and economical negotiation of these obstacles which allows speed to be gained over the ground. When teaching, one should never use the expressions "jump," "glide," or "float" over the hurdles. The best way is to assume that everyone will *run* over the hurdles.

Equipment necessary:

- 18 dowel rods or bamboo canes 4 feet long.
- 54 bricks or 18 hurdle stands.
- 10 or more low hurdles.
- An area 27 yards wide by 60 yards in length, preferably on a straightaway of a track.

Place low hurdles 2½ feet in batches of three, but not touching, and stand astride of the hurdle. Very few will touch the hurdle. Have those who do stand on tiptoe see how little it requires for them to clear the hurdle. It is important to start the lesson this way to convince beginners that they will not have to jump to clear the hurdle, will not hit themselves on it, and can run over it.

Scratch a starting line across the track and at 15 yards scratch another. If no marks can be made on the track, simply place metal high jump bars on the ground. Grade the class according to height, and place them in groups of tallest, medium and shortest. Use six lanes so that running can be performed down one and the return made up the other.

From a standing start (with the foot from which the drive over the hurdle is to be made to the rear), check how many paces were taken to the 15-yard scratch line. It will be either seven or eight paces. If it is over eight paces, it is obvious that the approach run was simply not fast enough. If seven paces are taken and the athlete

Leading British high hurdler Berwyn Price. (Tony Duffy photo)

strides over the mark on the eighth stride, the approach is suitable for that individual and the takeoff foot is the one to the rear at the start. If eight paces are taken and the performer crosses over the line on the ninth stride, it appears that the takeoff has been attempted from the wrong foot. This will necessitate a change of the feet in the start. However, it could also happen that the athlete simply cannot make an approach in seven paces because of lack of speed or leg length, and must change the position of feet at the start to create an eight-stride approach to the first hurdle.

Have a partner place a stick on the ground between the 11th and 12th stride (or 12th or 13th), depending on a seven- or eight-stride approach to the 15-yard line). Sprint over the marks. It will be observed that the sticks will be farther apart in the lane where the tallest participants run, and some will not be able to "fit in" their strides to the marks which are suitable to others in their lanes. Either move the participants to another lane to try new marks, or have a vacant lane set aside to create a suitable new stride pattern.

Now place a stick on a brick or the first peg (four inches above ground) on the hurdle stand at the 15-yard and at the next mark. Ask the participants to run over the sticks fast and note that: (1) there should be no attempt to hurdle the bar; (2) each leads with the same leg over both bars (not alternate legs); (3) no exaggerated movements are made over the sticks; (4) there is no "dwelling" in the air.

After this, raise the sticks to eight inches and have the running repeated twice. Insist on very fast sprinting before introducing a third "hurdle" at the above height by placing it between the 15th and and 16th strides (or 16th and 17th). Check that each performer uses the correct lead leg over all three barriers.

It may not become necessary to reduce the seven- or eight-pace approach because of the tiredness of the group. Do it by adjusting the first barrier to a position between the fourth and fifth stride. Lack of momentum makes it a little more difficult to clear the next two hurdles, but this gives the teacher the opportunity to stress "putting the foot down" over the hurdle and will cut down the time in the air. Do not say "stamp" the foot down as this causes more arrestation than progression.

Next, raise the sticks on bricks placed on a T-position or on the third peg of the hurdle stand and ask the class to run over the new barriers. A positive inclination to "hurdle" will now be observed. There will also be a "pause" in the air over each obstacle. Were the teacher to turn his back, he would hear "ta, ta, ta—ta, ta, ta." The change in the thythmic beat is when a hurdle is negotiated.

The time is now right to introduce the arm action—a sharp stabbing action of the opposite arm to the instep of the lead leg, forward and down. As a potential hurdler runs over the obstacles, have his lane-mates hold a stick at the height of about five feet. and one foot in front of each hurdle with the athlete going over one stick and under the other. Stress: (1) lead hand fast forward and down; (2) getting lead foot down to ground; (3) keeping shoulders square to front; (4) an attempt to run over the hurdles.

As a final aspect of this learning stage, raise the sticks to 1'6" or place it on top of two end-on bricks and have the partners hold sticks at five feet in front of the hurdle. Now stress: (1) pick-up of the knee of the lead leg (as in sprinting); (2) eyes looking forward at the next obstacle; (3) driving at the hurdle; (4) no change of rhythm prior to, during and after hurdle negotiation.

This covers a full lesson. Subsequent periods should cover raising the canes, increasing the distances between hurdles, the action of the trailing leg, the action of the arms, the introduction of the "change step" and hurdling exercises.

Hurdling Exercises: These should be introduced with the hurdle at 2'6" with later practices at 3'0" and 3'6", when and if considered necessary.

1. Rhythmic pressing (hurdle at 2'6"): The wrists are draped over the hurdle top (do not grip the hurdle), trunk lowered until shoulders are in line with the hands, with the seat back from the firmly planted feet. Looking at the bottom of the hurdle, rhythmically press shoulders forward, keeping arms straight at all times.

2. Trail-leg action: Walk down a row of hurdles, placed about 12 inches apart. As each hurdle is approached the lead foot steps to the side but forward of the hurdle. The body is lowered towards the thigh and the knee of the trailing leg leads over the hurdle. Insist that: (a) the shoulders are square to the front; (b) the eyes are directed at the next hurdle; (c) the leg of the trailing limb swings forward into the next stride. After three paces the next hurdle is negotiated. Performers travel down one side of the hurdles, turn and travel back, doing the same exercise on the other side. Change direction to allow both legs to be exercised.

3. Angle sit: Sit in the hurdle position. Correct the position as much as reasonable. Then raise the arms sideways and keep them up. Change the position of the legs without the hands touching the ground. This exercise test hip mobility.

4. Two to a hurdle: Stand with lead leg (which should be bent at all times) over the hurdle. Place hands on hurdle, one hand on each side of the thigh. Rock body back and forth over the hurdle without touching it, except with the hands. Allow the lead foot to come to ground close to the hurdle. Take hands off the hurdle, forcing the body forward and the trail knee close to the chest to clear the obstacle and swing into next stride. Repeat this exercise from a three-pace walk.

5. Two to a hurdle: Stand with the inner knee, side of shin and ankle on the hurdle top. The supporting leg is straight, directly beneath the hip, hands by the sides. The trunk is lowered and both hands are placed to the ground on the inside of the instep of the supporting leg. There should be no pressing of the trunk downwards. Neither should there be any pressing forward in the hip region when the body is returned to the stretched position. Insist that the knee on the hurdle is directly opposite the hip at all times. This exercise should be performed on both sides.

6. Hurdle sit: Clasp the hand of the arm on the same side of

US international hurdler Deanne Carlson. (John Marconi)

the trail leg. Place the elbow to the ground and circle it out and
around the bent knee, keeping it on the ground all the time. Use
the trunk powerfully. Repeat this exercise on the opposite side.

7. The change-step: Stand about five yards from a hurdle. Take several small steps with a high knee lift. When close to the obstacle change step in the air, lift one knee high and *step* over the hurdle, dropping body forward to bring trail leg through economically into next stride.

Hurdle Clearance: The high point of an athlete's movement in hurdle clearance, in any hurdle race, is prior to the hurdle. The athlete comes down over the obstacle. The greater the speed, the greater the take-off distance. However, the faster the hurdler, the more important it is to spend time on the ground rather than in hurdle negotiation. So the takeoff to landing position must be adjusted.

The lead leg should be "picked up" smartly with the knee leading. The lead leg is never completely stretched. Otherwise, it would have to be bent again on landing, thus wasting time.

The lead arm should remain low and (in the process of the takeoff at the hurdle) should be reaching forward. The position of this arm may determine the opposition of the body in clearance and plays a vital role in the trail leg action. It circles out and around the bent knee as it is pulled through into the next stride, absorbing rotation caused by the shortening of its lever and its consequent speed. The other arm acts as in sprinting. Its action is slowed, but it is brought back to the hip ready to be driven forward.

The position of the trunk determines how soon the athlete will be able to continue efficient running. Directly from the takeoff, the trunk should be driven at the hurdle and never be lowered to the thigh. A common fault, which should be corrected immediately, if it occurs, is standing up after hurdle clearance. The trunk should be kept forward, enabling a drive into the next stride.

The trail leg's work is to ensure an efficient and exceedingly powerful drive at and over the hurdle top. At the takeoff, it creates a good "split" at the hurdle. On the way down, it acts very fast. The higher the hurdle, the higher does the knee of the trail leg come to the chest.

RACE WALK TECHNIQUE

BY ANATOLIY FRUKTOV

At the time this article appeared in "Modern Athlete and Coach," Fruktov was coach of the Soviet national walking team.

Outstanding performances in walking, as in other athletic events, can be achieved only through regular and systematic all-year-round training. The training for a beginner is broadly planned three or four years in advance before a change to a more individual approach takes place. However, a gradual but constant increase in the training load and intensity is observed right from the beginning.

Technique training at the early stages has a number of major tasks in attempting to establish a correct walking action at various speeds and in developing an optimal stride frequency and length:

● **Introduction to Walking Technique:** Walking technique is usually introduced by a demonstration by a coach or screening slow motion walking films. At the same time, the major points in walking mechanics are explained to the beginner before he is asked to use the basic elements in practice. The demonstration by the coach, an advanced walker, is is repeated several times at normal speed (170-190 strides a minute) and also at a deliberately slow pace. The first attempts of the novice, carefully observed and corrected, are over 50-60 meters distance.

● **Correct Leg and Hip Action:** Leg and hip action is developed at slow and slightly accelerated speeds, concentrating on the placement of a straight leg on the ground to be kept in this position until it has passed the vertical line of the body. The hip action around the vertical axis is stressed by using very long strides. Hip action is also improved by walking on the spot with alternate shifting of the body weight from one leg to the other.

All these exercises are executed over distances ranging from 50-100 meters and are repeated until each element of the technique has been mastered. As soon as the athlete is capable of shifting his body weight correctly, the last two exercises are eliminated from the teaching program. It is important to observe that the feet are always placed straight and not with the toes pointing outwards.

• **Correct Arm and Shoulder Action**: The following exercises are recommended to learn the correct arm and shoulder movement: (1) Correct arm movement on the spot; (2) Walking with arms behind the back; (3) Walking with arms swinging fully stretched; (4) Competitive arm and shoulder action combined with the correct walking movements.

In the first exercise, it must be observed that the novice avoids any arm movement across the body. The other two exercises stress the need for an active shoulder movement to accompany the arm action, especially when walking with arms behind the back is used. In all exercises, a wide and relaxed motion is emphasized over distances up to 100 meters.

Olympic champion Vladimir Golubnichiy of the Soviet Union leads Paul Nihill (72) and Ron Laird (22). (Jeff Johnson photo)

- **Development of the Technique:** After the basic action has been satisfactorily established, emphasis shifts to correct upper body posture and relaxation of arm and leg action. Distances ranging from 200-400 meters are now used. The walking speed is constantly changed, and walking up and down hills, on roads and around the curve on the track is introduced. Correct rotations of the shoulder and hip girdle in opposite directions is given special attention before the walker attempts with the assistance of his coach to establish an optimal cadence which depends largely on the developed stride length.

Common faults to be carefully corrected at this stage are:

1. Insufficient straightening of the leg in the supporting phase.

2. Sideways movement of the trunk, usually caused by a wide placement of the feet.

3. Noticeable drop in the shoulders towards the supporting leg side which leads to an out of line hip movement.

4. Arm action across the body, too high in the forward and too high in the backward movement.

5. Bending of the trunk and an out-of-line head position.

6. General lack of relaxation.

7. Walking with the right leg crossing to the left and the left leg to the right of the straight line.

To correct these common faults there are several recommended exercises. These include:

1. Walking with a bent trunk so that the forward moving leg is touched by the opposite hand.

2. Walking with a bent trunk with hands on the knees to assist with an emphasized straightening of the knee joint.

3. Walking with a flexible forward plunge in each stride, emphasizing the driving action

4. Straightening of legs from a crouch position without removing the hands from the ground.

5. Legs wide apart, the back foot on the full sole, the front foot on the heel. Change the load and position 30-40 times.

6. Legs about a foot astride arms across the chest. Repeated performance of rotating the shoulders and hips in opposite directions.

7. Walking with short strides, legs crossing in front of the body.

8. Walking with the left side leading and the right leg crossing the left alternately backwards and forwards to establish an emphasized hip rotation.

9. Walking with toes pointing inwards, using a stride length of less than two feet and stressing hip rotation.

10. Walking a "snake path," swinging two to four yards to left and right.

11. Walking with a stressed hip rotation with arms hanging relaxed on the sides of the trunk.

• **Training:** The preparation phase is used for solid all-around conditioning to develop endurance, strength, mobility and speed. Emphasis at this stage is on the development of general endurance (aerobic capacity). To avoid staleness through monotony, the program is varied in the methods employed as well as training loads and intensities. In addition to walking, it is recommended to use general and specific morning exercises, walking in sand, dunes, runs over 5-6 kilometers (3-4 miles), and workouts in the gymnasium. Training should be carried out daily and could include five days outdoor work and two or three days in the gymnasium. Many walkers combine indoor and outdoor work every day of the week.

The outdoor training is directed towards the development of general endurance by long marches, race walking-type walks, long cross-country runs and skiing. At the same time, speed is not neglected and fast walks are regularly in the program. These should include occasional walking with very short and fast strides to develop cadence and workouts on the track even if covered with snow. Competitions are important to check the progress made, and it is advisable to participate in contests regularly.

The gymnasium workouts, dropped to only once a week towards the end of the preparation phase and eliminated in the spring, include gymnastic exercises, medicine ball work and weight training. For variation and agility, it is recommended to include occasional games such as volleyball and basketball. Specific exercises to improve joint mobility take a very important place at this stage of the training and should be included in the morning exercise program as well as gymnasium workouts.

During the spring, a gradual change in the training program towards more specific work takes place. More walking is included, and the amount of running is reduced but not completely eliminated. It is expected for a walker to cover at least 2000 kilometers in walking, running and skiing during the preparation phase. In case of a 50-kilometer exponent, the mileage would be much higher and well over 3000 kilometers.

During the competitive phase, the walker continues to develop his general endurance. But the bulk of his training now aims to improve walking techniques, maximum speed and pace judgment. The main training methods used are exercises during the warmup, special exercises to improve walking technique, the development of speed and running to maintain the general endurance level. The emphasis simply shifts from general to specific endurance to allow for the maximum expected and planned walking speed over the full competitive distance.

The judgment of pace is very important and must be carefully developed. An experienced walker must know his average speed so his pace judgment doesn't differ from the stopwatch more than a second or two for a lap. At the same time, technique should not be overlooked. It is constantly developed during practice walks and by the employment of special exercises.

During the competitive phase, the walker trains usually five days a week in forests, parks, roads and on the track. His training load and intensity increase constantly, and the recoveries take the form of easy running and walking. Occasionally, the training load is slightly dropped. For example, before an important competition or after three weeks of relatively hard training, the program includes a relatively easy week. Some experienced walkers allow up to three days rest before a significant contest.

At the end of the competitive phase, the walker reduces his training load and starts a short "active rest." A complete rest from physical activities at this stage is not recommended because it would mean a drastic drop in the level of fitness reached during the year. The main task during the active rest phase is to correct technique faults which occurred during the competitive season, and conduct long marches and long, slow runs to avoid any noticeable reductions in general endurance capacity.

Page 262: Photo by Mary Rosenfeld

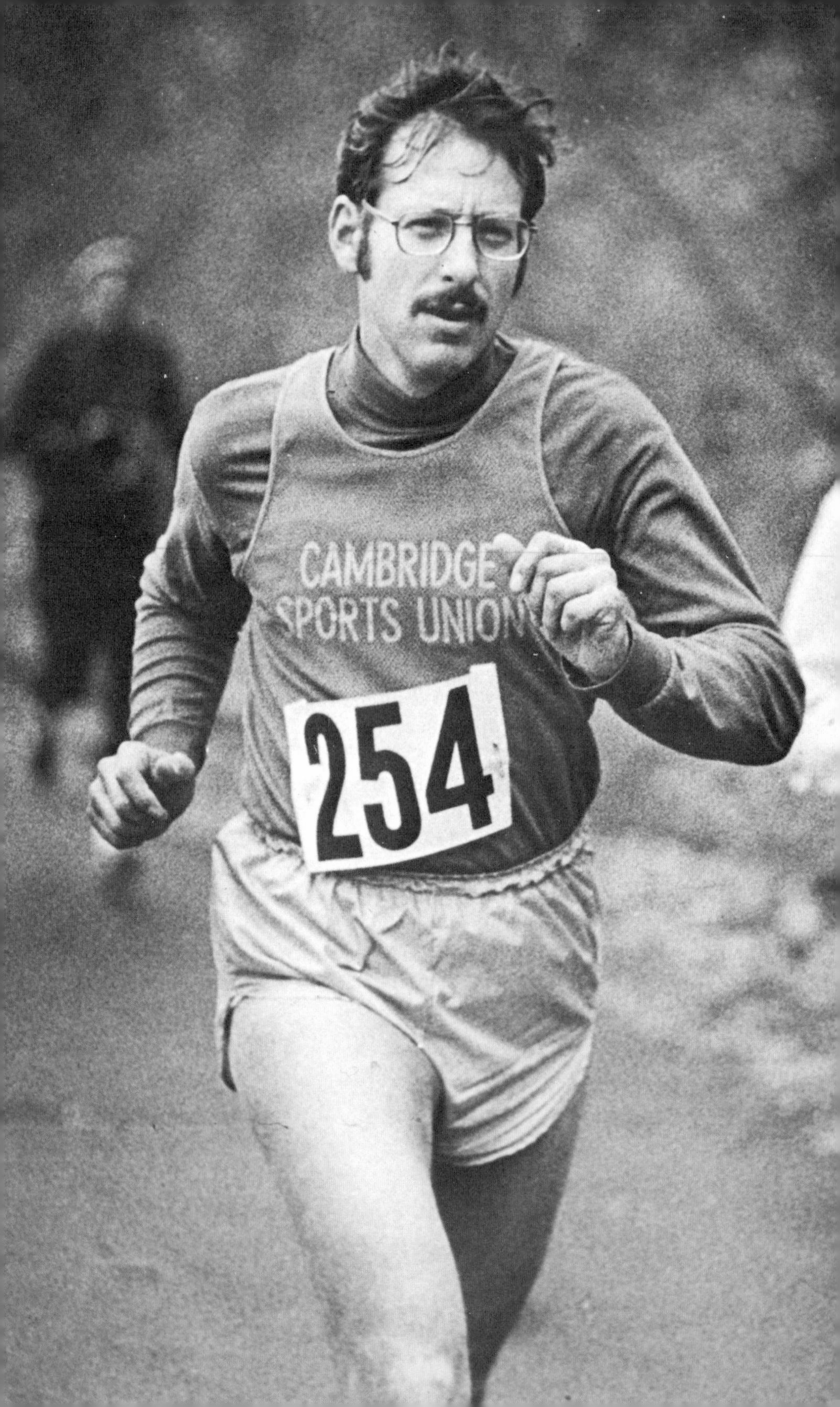
CAMBRIDGE
SPORTS UNION
254

10

EXERCISE

BEYOND EXTRA MILEAGE

BY DR. GEORGE SHEEHAN

Dr. George Sheehan, a New Jersey physician, is one of the world's all-time best runners in the over-50 age group, as well as a recognized authority on running medicine.

In 1964, Tony Ward, one of Great Britain's best known track and field authorities, wrote, "I firmly believe that weight training will play a significant part in the training program of the great distance runners of the future."

It was a radical statement at the time. Hadn't Roger Bannister gone through the four-minute barrier with ony five carefully planned 30-minute workouts a week? And didn't this mean that increasing practice mileage would eventually bring every record to the the physiological limits?

It seemed so. And then Lydiard and his New Zealanders made it so, breaking records and dominating the Olympics. Lydiard himself said, "My athletes never do weight training. They don't need big muscles, only supple, strong muscles."

Lydiard opened the door for the enormous mileage logged in our current distance runners, although not without opposition. Bannister in 1966 said that he still thought the optimum training for a mile might well be a judicious one hour a day. But he could foresee the day when schedules involving eight hours of training a day would be devised. Bannister rejected these long daily training periods on a philosophic basis. The runner, he said, would be little more than a machine, but he conceded that he would improve in performance.

But will he? Have we reached the ultimate in performance from current training methods, from extrapolating them to the absurdity of Gerry Lindgren's Dare-To-Be-Great program of 50 miles a a day?

I think so. And so does John Jesse, the author of *Strength, Power and Muscular Endurance for Runners and Hurdlers.*

Jesse says that for a mere 45 minutes three times a week you could become the distance runner coaches dream about. And those

45 minutes can be used at home after supper (although Jesse cautions that it should be at least 1½ hours after the meal).

The secret ingredient here is the low energy cost of weight training. It is minimal compared to running. Pinpointing the particular muscles to be developed (Jesse has a smorgasbord of 46 different exercises according to the runner's event and his particular needs) allows the athlete to budget this energy outlay, guard against overtraining and prevent staleness.

That weight training alone can produce excellent performances was proven by Marty Liquori, who had been kept off the track for six weeks with a heel spur and a foot strain. During that time, he had worked only with weights (adding three inches on his chest) and had done some swimming. Despite this, he was able to come back with a 4:00 mile and followed with an 8:31 two-mile.

We can now speculate as to what a continuing weight-lifting program done in conjunction with his regular workouts could do for him. Jesse sees no need to speculate. He is sure that weight training is the answer.

"(It is) the most effective method to use in the development of dynamic strength," he says. And dynamic strength is the element that produces speed and stamina." The athlete who lacks this, says Jesse, will often experience great fatigue in his back, arm, leg, and hip muscles long before the maximum demands have been made on his heart and lungs.

Thre are other ways besides weights to build up dynamic strength: running up hills and stairs or in sand, surf, or snow, for instance. You can also climb ropes or use a rowing machine. These are all okay as far as they go, says Jesse, but they fail in one requirement: progressive overload—the addition of load after load applied selectively to the specific muscles for the runner's event.

This could be the answer for runners who've reached their mileage ceiling and are wondering, "Where do I go from here?"

"YOGAROBIC" RUNNING

BY IAN JACKSON

Ian Jackson is a staff writer at World Publications.

"Iyengar is a terror," they had told me. I sat silent and nervous as his bare feet resounded on the hardwood floor. His dark eyes scrutinized us, one by one—three rows of motionless, cross-legged figures. When he was finished with his inspection, he leaped up on the stage and turned to face us. He looked displeased.

B.K.S. Iyengar, master teacher and author of Light on Yoga. Brilliant, witty, energetic and controversial— his art offers much to runners.

When you have this kind of flexibility, injuries become a rarity. It brings a feeling of "weightlessness" and leads to smooth, fluid, and effortless "floating" running.

(Photos courtesy of David Hall)

Virabhadrasana–the front leg is too far forward so as to demonstrate one of the mistakes described on page 281. Only if the leg is at a right angle can the muscles work economically. Only then can the true "laziness" of yoga be realized. (George Beinhorn photo)

"What am I doing here," I thought. "I should be ambling down some country lane."

"You are supposed to be teachers," he said. "But I can tell from the way you are sitting that you know little about yoga. Yoga is one, and yet your postures tell me that you believe in different yogas–bakti yoga, jnana yoga, karma yoga and the yoga that you hope to learn from me, hatha yoga.

"Teachers become so intoxicated with ego that it is difficult to teach them anything," he went on. "Nevertheless, I will do my best. In the next three days, I want to show you how to become students of yoga once again. Let us begin. Stand up. Tadasana."

Tadasana is the basic standing pose: feet together, spine stretched up, body weight evenly distributed, arms and legs symmetrically aligned. Iyengar jumped down from the stage and began pacing the rows again. I noted with relief that I would be last. That would give me plenty of time to learn from the mistakes of others.

"What I say for one, I say for all," he said. "No one here is standing correctly."

As he went down the far row, I noticed how physical he was– not in the least bit shy about roughly grabbing a shoulder or pushing a hip to adjust alignment. He stopped beside a tall man and stared at him coldly. The hall was thick with silent tension. I

could see fear in the man's eyes, and feel it in the pit of my
stomach.

"Sir! Wake up! Watch when I adjust others! Listen to what
I say!" He kicked his ankles and slapped him sharply on the upper
back.

"Feet together. Adjust the shoulder blades."

The violence shocked us awake. From that moment on, I observed as closely as I could, hoping to perfect my stance by the
time he reached me so as to avoid his anger. I had a feeling that he
was going to be especially hard on me.

If it hadn't been for my running, I would have been somewhere else, far from this frightening man. But running had led me
to yoga and yoga had led me to Iyengar, and now there was no
running away.

As I explained in "Yoga for the Runner," I took up yoga as a
way to undo the damage when overenthusiasm and overambition
had seduced me into overtraining. A couple of years of casual running had led to a series of fast races capped by a 2:33 marathon.
So fantastic were these performances (by my standards) that they
led to some tempting dreams.

"If you can just take off three minutes, you'll qualify for the
Olympic Trials. You're in this kind of shape on casual running—
what will happen if you really get down to it?"

That was the beginning of the end. Casual running became
serious training; long slow distance became longer, faster distance.
My log notations changed from qualities to quantities. Comments
on the pride of a soaring eagle, the grace of a deer on the trail, or
the smoothness of the fog blanket on the bay gave way to notes on
hill efforts, pace, recovery rates, weight fluctuations and other
details.

The first few months of serious training brought improvements beyond my wildest dreams. Sometimes my training runs
were faster than I had ever expected my races to be. I had no idea
that I had developed so much strength. My running future looked
bright.

But instead of breakthrough, I met breakdown, which over-
took me slowly, insidiously and mercilessly. The first signs were
minor leg pains; they were just vague irritations, the kind that can
usually be run through as a matter of routine. My legs became
generally tight, and my hamstrings were slightly sore from day to
day. It was easy enough to stop the pain by trying a different foot

placement, a higher knee lift, or a more erect body carriage. I got into the habit of living with the minor pains, and I learned to live with them as they became major.

Along with these physical problems developed psychological problems: loss of enthusiasm, irritability, insecurity, and a sense of aimlessness.

Finally, I reached the end of my tether. I could live with the pain and depression no longer. My legs hurt even when I was just sitting at the table. Sometimes the dull ache was so persistent that I couldn't get to sleep. I was sick at heart. Instead of rising to glorious heights, my running was going under and dragging the rest of my life with it.

I was extremely fortunate in discovering Hans Selye's *The Stress of Life* at this time. Through it, I came to see the obvious with blinding clarity: I was simply grossly overstressed. By cutting down on my running, I began to regain my sense of proportion and my enthusiasm for life. As would be expected, all my stress symptoms slowly evaporated.

All except the leg problems, that is. The less I ran, the more my legs hurt. It was as if they were getting back at me for ignoring their cries of abuse for so long. Friends suggested that I might have sciatica, which worried me enough to threaten my returning optimism.

They say that drowning men will clutch at straws, which is exactly what I did when *Runner's World* floated one my way. On reading Joe Henderson's "The Runner's Final Stretch" (Jan. 1973), I clutched at the idea that yoga might solve my leg problems. According to Joe, my chronic pains were caused by muscular imbalance. In opening up the cardiovascular system, those daily miles, with thousands of identical steps per mile, were closing down certain parts of the muscular system. Certain muscles were being overdeveloped at the expense of others. The solution—simple and straightforward—is to work for muscular balance and flexibility through yoga-type stretching exercises.

The article included some simple positions that Robert Bahr, editor of *Fitness for Living*, had found helpful in his own daily program. They looked easy enough, but when I tried them I failed miserably. There is something cruelly decisive about those tests of flexibility—once you are at your limit, you know it in a very painful way. I felt repelled at the prospect of a daily struggle with Bahr's exercises. Besides, I thought, better to go to the source— the ancient science of hatha yoga.

But now my problem was learning how to do yoga. Like many road runners, I have an ingrained aversion to coaches, and I saw no reason to change my attitude with yoga teachers. There are plenty of books on yoga. Since I can follow written instructions (or so I thought), and since I don't need the motivation of a teacher, I saw no reason to consult one.

So I bought a wide selection of books on yoga, and within a few days of fascinating reading I had acquired some basic knowledge about the science. I was surprised by the parallels between yoga philosophy and the discoveries of modern science, and was impressed by the benefits that practice could bring. "What yoga can do for you" includes such promises as robust health, increased vitality, relief from the stress of anxiety, youthful flexibility, better muscle tone and greater adaptive resilience.

The yoga approach to exercise is almost diametrically opposed to the approach we have taken here in the West. Rather than strenuous, exhausting calisthenics and competitive sports, yoga exercise is composed of a series of "asanas," or postures, which systematically stretch all the muscles of the body. The individual postures are taken up with slow precision and then held without movement for a period ranging from a few seconds to several minutes. Each session is designed to be a relaxing and pleasurable experience.

At first, I was very skeptical about the claims. How can you be really healthy without aerobic exercise? The foundation of health is the supply of oxygen to the cells, and I didn't see how yoga postures could increase the efficiency of the heart-lung system, without which it is impossible to get oxygen to the cells. Then it occurred to me that the ancient yogis must have done far more walking than modern man does, so their needs for aerobic exercise were naturally filled. If they enjoyed far more energy and vitality than their contemporaries, who also walked a lot, then it must have been a result of adding the yoga practices to the high level of aerobic fitness already existing. Since this would be essentially the same situation I was in, I was eager to get started.

Of all the books I had read, I settled on Richard Hittleman's *Be Young with Yoga*. Most books were illustrated with photos of dark, intense Indians doing asanas that were obviously out of the question for me, but Hittleman's was illustrated with photos of average people with whom I could identify—students, teachers, housewives and businessmen. If they could do it, I could do it.

Paschimottanasana—a good hamstring stretch. (Jan Herhold photo)

Besides, Hittleman's course covered a manageable seven weeks, and he made a golden promise: "Once you have started yoga, you will never want to give it up."

It sounded too good to be true. Could the solution to my muscle problems really be all that enjoyable? The first week of practice seemed to prove Hittleman wrong. Not only did I want to give yoga up, I was so stiff and sore that I had to. My muscle pains were aggravated, not alleviated.

When I had first discovered how stiff I had become, I had eased the sting a little by convincing myself that it was just a superficial problem. I imagined the stiffness as a layer of mud encrusted on a running shoe. All that would be necessary to work it out was a few judicious flexes and twists.

With this image in mind, I attacked the asanas with brute force, trying to agonize my body into the correct position. I wanted so badly to be free of my chronic pains that I tried to remedy overnight a condition that had taken months to develop. Looking back on it now, I can see that I was transferring my obsessive striving from running to yoga.

How else can I account for the way I completely ignored Hittleman's cautions: "Remember that you must never strain, jerk or fight to achieve a more extreme position. Just go as far as you can, regardless of where it may be, and have the patience to hold [the posture] as indicated. The 'hold' will gradually impart the elasticity that is needed to accomplish the most extreme positions."

One of the extreme positions is Paschimottanasana, which I am demonstrating in the photo above. On the first day of the first week of Hittleman's course, I was determined to reach the extreme position. I sat on the floor with my legs stretched straight out, and reached forward to grab my legs as far down as I could (only about midway between my knees and ankles—I was *really* stiff).

I'm sure my face must have shown a comical mixture of bafflement and consternation. This just wouldn't do. I took a breath, gritted my teeth and then forced my head down as far as it would go. In spite of the excruciating pain, I managed to gain only an inch or two. Nevertheless, I forced myself to bear it because I hoped it would take me on a shortcut to recovery.

Of course, by the end of the first week of that desperate insanity, I could do no more. With my legs in worse condition than ever, I had to take a week off to recover. Before trying yoga again, I reread the instructions. "Yoga is slow and gentle," I told myself. "Slow and gentle."

What a difference that made! When I did the asanas with measured deliberation and calm attention, I discovered that yoga was indeed a pleasurable experience. My leg pains began to recede, and before long I felt good enough to increase my mileage and work myself back into racing shape again. But, ironically, I found that I now preferred yoga to running. For a while I continued to run a token amount each day, but eventually I dropped it altogether and concentrated on yoga alone.

Having called me away from running for a while, yoga soon coaxed me right back into it. As I progressed, I freed not only my legs from soreness and stiffness, but also my entire body. I realized a new-found pleasure in simple movement. I was light on my feet. My limbs swung freely and easily. I had an incredible feeling of weightlessness and vitality, much like the "high" that comes when switching from base training to sharpening training.

Before long, I was back into running again, with that same casual attitude that had prevailed before the dream of success spoiled everything.

After five months of daily practice, I felt that I had mastered Hittleman's seven-week course, so I searched the bookstores for something more challenging, something that I could really sink my teeth into. That's when I discovered B.K.S. Iyengar's *Light on Yoga.*

I could tell at a glance that it was far superior to anything I had seen before. Most authors take an apologetic attitude about yoga. There are so many bizarre misconceptions about it that they spend 90% of their books in "selling" yoga and only 10% in giving directions for proper practice. Iyengar, on the other hand, takes it for granted that anyone working with his book will be far beyond the need to be "sold."

His book is almost solid instruction, with more than 600 photos showing not only the final position of each asana, but also the proper steps to be taken in reaching it.

In the appendix, for the intensive student, there is a 300-week course designed to lead to mastery of the heights of the science. For the less highly motivated, there is a beginner's course (the first 30 weeks) and an intermediate course (the first 78 weeks). The course starts with a series of basic standing asanas. As it progresses, the asanas in the series are changed. More challenging asanas are added and easier ones are dropped.

Iyengar advises against trying to hold rigidly to the time schedule: "Most people...take far longer than I have stipulated to master all these asanas with comfort and ease." However, it is important to stick to the sequence he has outlined, because this has been very carefully adjusted to the natural development of structural flexibility. According to my calculations, it will take me at least 500 weeks to master the course at my present rate of progress.

Before I got into running, anything as drawn out as this would have seemed preposterous to me, but now I realize that health is not a matter of a seven-week course, or even a 300-week course. It is a way of life that must be followed year in, year out. If you want to be healthy, you have to work at it every day.

When I first switched over to Iyengar's course, it was an entirely different experience from the Hittleman course. In *Exercises for Runners*, I compared my yoga beginnings to a YMCA jogging program, and Iyengar's course to having the personal attention of a Bill Bowerman or an Arthur Lydiard.

The popular books describe the "classical" asanas, like the headstand, the shoulder stand, the plough, the cobra, and the locust. The student is advised to work on these classics with relaxed, slow deliberation. In Iyengar's course, the classics are buried among other asanas. The plough is introduced in the third week, the cobra in the fourteenth week, and the headstand in the sixteenth week. The wisdom of this arrangement is that it helps to avoid bad habits in practice. Each asana is a technique of precision and control. Unless the student has developed sufficient flexibility and strength, he will be unable to execute it properly. Since these are powerful stretches, incorrect technique can cause problems. Iyengar's step-by-step arrangement ensures orderly progress. For instance, the standing asanas, with which the course begins, prepare the student for the forward bending asanas "which can then be acquired with ease."

The standing asanas, by the way, are far more specifically beneficial to the runner than the classical poses: they stretch the very muscles that usually get shortened, tightened and stiffened in training, and they help balance the muscles that are neglected and underdeveloped. I chose several of them for the *Exercises* booklet.

When I wrote the article for the booklet, the benefits that I emphasized were fluidity, ease and economy of movement, and the prevention of injuries. Since then, my awareness of benefits has expanded considerably.

The first benefit is increase in cardio-vascular efficiency. I expect this to be met with disbelief, so I will explain at some length.

Most runners are familiar with the distinction between aerobic and anaerobic exercise. Aerobic exercise demands a continuous supply of oxygen and thus develops the heart-lung system, which delivers oxygen to the tissues by way of the bloodstream. Some of the best forms of aerobic exercise are running, swimming, cycling and cross-country skiing.

The anaerobic exercises do not require a continuous supply of oxygen, and so they are useless as conditioners of the heart-lung system. This means that such mainstays as weightlifting, calisthenics, and isometrics are a complete waste as far as basic conditioning is concerned.

Yoga asanas, which are static stretches of the muscles, apparently share the same drawbacks as weightlifting and isometrics, but when you consider the "yogarobic effect," the picture changes. The "yogarobic effect" is speculation on my part, just the guesswork of a runner. However, there is enough evidence to make it a definite possibility.

Here is an intriguing item from *Medical World News* (Feb. 1, 1974, page 11).

"Would yoga be a safe way for cardiac patients to exercise? If findings in normal individuals hold true for persons with heart problems, the answer may well be yes. Studies carried out by two sophomore medical students, Steve Warres and Steve Anton of

Emory University in Atlanta, under the direction of cardiologist Charles Gilbert, show yoga exercise brings about improved utilization of oxygen equal to or slightly better than that obtained by jogging and running. In addition, post-yoga blood lactate levels, pulse rates and blood pressure readings are much lower than those after jogging and running."

Dr. Gilbert gave me a polite but firm refusal when I asked him for further information. He pointed out that it was too early to make any firm evaluations: "I am afraid that it will take many years to evaluate in a scientific manner the effects of yoga...I think your own experiences with yoga are fascinating, and, like our preliminary work, suggest some possibility of 'training' the heart and circulation without, or apart from, large muscle endurance activity."

While the effects of yoga have yet to be evaluated "in a scientific manner," they have been proved time and time again, over thousands of years, by practicing adepts. The aerobic dogma about the uselessness of yoga postures is due for a review.

To get a feeling for my theory, try a little experiment. Get down on the floor with your legs stretched out in front. Without straining, see how close you can come to reaching the posture in the photo (see photo p. 271). Keeping your knees down, try to bury your chin between your shins while resting your chest solidly on your thighs. Unless you have been doing some regular stretching, you'll probably find yourself in much the same condition I did when I first started—stiff and immobile.

I can't help feeling that there must be a great circulatory difference in my muscles now that they have become relaxed and loose. When I was running 15-20 miles a day, with my muscles stiff and getting progressively stiffer, surely they were more resistant to blood flow than they are now.

I believe that there was a vicious circle at work. As the muscles became progressively tighter and more contracted, blood flow must have been ever more restricted. The chronic contraction may have been closing down large areas of arterioles and capillary beds. So just when they needed more blood in order to make repairs, they were getting less.

In other words, running without stretching is working at cross purposes. By forcing a greater supply of blood to the tissues, it opens up supply lines, but by causing chronic stiffening and tightening of the muscles it closes down supply lines.

Let me remind you that this is just the speculation of a runner, not the experimentally validated conclusion of a scientist. However, if it has any merit at all, then it might have far-reaching implications for runners. If we assume for the sake of argument that tight muscles do indeed suffer reduced blood supply, and that yoga, by stretching and relaxing the muscles, can open up chronically contracted areas, then maybe it can go beyond that. It might be able tó open up further supply lines—to free areas of tissue that would never yield to straightforward running.

We could define the "yogarobic effect" as follows: "A phenomenon observed in muscular tissues, whereby regular stretching releases areas of chronic contraction, and produces increased blood supply above and beyond that which can be accomplished by aerobic activity."

Perhaps a description of what happens in the stretched muscle will make this seem more plausible. In *Yoga Self-Taught*, Andre Van Lysbeth points out that muscles are usually found in three differing states:

• The state of contraction, in which the muscle "by shortening itself, acts upon the skeleton...It is almost the sole basis of gymnastic exercise and sport."

• The state of tone, "the normal state of the 'awakened' muscle—latent but nevertheless prepared to contract as soon as some order reaches it through an impulse of the nerve."

• The state of relaxation, which occurs during sleep.

There is also a fourth state, "exceptional in everyday life"— the state of stretch. One of the effects of stretching "is that blood, especially when venous, is squeezed out. The circulation of venous blood does not depend on cardiac impulses, but on the alternate contraction and relaxation of the muscles, which, by compressing the veins, expel the blood in the direction of the heart. But it is only by the action of stretching that the muscle can be properly emptied. As soon as the stretch is released the muscle returns to its normal size and 'breathes in' fresh blood which serves to bathe, cleanse and nourish it."

You have no doubt seen water pouring into an obstructed channel. It is always the first shock of water that breaks down the most obstructions. Maybe the initial rush of blood, the first irrigation of the released muscle, does something in opening up capillary beds that the normal flow of blood in the exercising muscle cannot do.

Besides the "yogarobic effect," I have become aware of other benefits that should be interesting to runners. Briefly, they are better breathing, better posture and better concentration.

My breathing became better as my chest and abdominal areas relaxed. We are led to believe that the ideal posture, for both males and females, is "chest out, belly in." If we buy this non-sense, we tend to go around with chest expanded and rigidly held out, and with stomach muscles chronically tightened and held in. But for free and easy breathing, the whole front of the trunk, from the upper chest to the pubic region, should be completely mobile.

Like most runners, I am proud of my physical condition. I like to think that my flat stomach is an outward sign of inward ef-ficiency. No beer belly on this body! So I was a bit put out when my wife started kidding me about my stomach.

"You're getting a belly," she laughed. "Is this what your yoga does for you?"

She was right. I looked down and saw that what had been a hard, flat stomach was now much softer. It did not sag or form a "pot" by any means, but it certainly showed a gentle curve. This was at first puzzling as well as disconcerting. After all, my abdo-minal muscles were far stronger than they had ever been before. Why were they so loose? Then I recalled several examples of the relaxed outward curve in physically well-developed people. The statues of the ancient Greeks show heavily muscled but relaxed ab-dominal areas. Photos of superbly healthy primitives often show a relaxed abdominal curve.

Distance running lore also attests to the superiority of relaxed abdominal muscles. How many times have you reminded yourself to "belly breathe" when struggling at the end of a race? Rather than having to concentrate on freeing the breathing when it is too late, why not free that uptight "belly in" so that you breathe fully at all times?

Yoga asanas also helped by changing the tilt of my pelvis. As Bill Bowerman points out in the chapter on running technique, an erect body carriage is far more economical than a forward body lean. If you lean forward, your butt sticks out, and with your butt sticking out it is difficult to lift your knees. (Try it.) If the body is held erect and the butt tucked in, it is easier to lift the knees and easier to run. Through the asanas, I found that I could keep an erect posture with comfort. This did not happen quickly, but over several months.

The ability to concentrate has obvious advantages, especially for distance runners. I have often thought that my best races were those in which I maintained the best concentration. Yoga is extremely effective in developing the ability to concentrate. The very way in which the asanas are practiced makes it impossible not to concentrate. When you are dealing with muscle stretches that must be held precisely on the comfort side of the pain line, your full attention is engaged at all times. This is why yoga can never become a dead, mechanical repetition. By its very nature it is always alive and engrossing.

As I worked with Iyengar's program and became more and more impressed with the resources of yoga, I began thinking about getting in touch with him. I hoped to get his opinion of my yoga article and some suggestions about running applications.

The publishers would not condescend to answer my letters, so I called the yoga centers listed in the Yellow Pages. Although everyone seemed to know of Iyengar, no one knew how to get in touch with him.

"Iyengar is a notoriously hard taskmaster," one teacher told me. "He is a terror. I understand that he is training teachers for the school system at his institute in London. People are shocked by his methods—shouting at students and knocking them around. But he is really in a class by himself. He is an absolute genius. If I had the money, I'd be in England with him right now."

("People like you give yoga a bad name," he said to a frightened girl. "Have you not yet learned? Your stance is dead. Wake up. You must feel each individual toe." He slapped her a few times. She was obviously fighting back tears.

"You see," he said, "Her bodily imbalance is in her emotions, too. How can an unstable person like this teach yoga? Do not venture to teach until you have attained maturity, or you will not be able to bear the consequences.")

This news about his work in London frustrated and intrigued me. I wanted more than ever to get in touch with him, but it seemed impossible. Several weeks later, when I had all but given up hope, I heard of a South African couple living in nearby Palo Alto—Felicity and David Hall. I was told that David was a research engineer in computer science. He had traveled to India to give a paper on computer science and yoga, and was now practising structural integration. This method, better known as "Rolfing" (after the originator, Ida Rolf), is a yoga-related way of realigning the body

masses so that they relate functionally to gravity. Correct alignment can improve both physical and psychological functioning.

According to Ida Rolf, "...the release of such masses permits
the emergence of a more sensitive being... Ancient mystery schools
apparently understood this...among their teachers were men expert
in refining the body for the express purpose of furthering individual psychic progression...witness the branch of Yoga sometimes
misnamed "Hatha."

But Felicity's background was more immediately interesting
to me, because she taught the Iyengar methods of yoga. Here I had
been searching high and low, even contemplating writing to the
London school system, and she had been nearby all the time. Con-
tacting her was as easy as consulting the phone book. The accent
told me that I had the right number

"Yes, I teach Iyengar's methods...I learned from one of his
star pupils—J.B. Rishi of France...I've been teaching for five years...
You're on the 30th week of his course? In that case, I don't know
if I can teach you anything. If you're interested, you're welcome
to come to the class tonight. We meet at seven."

I was really excited. With a copy of the exercise booklet in
hand, I arrived at the class early. I was sure that she would be interested to learn that Iyengar was getting some exposure to a potentially receptive audience. I was also hungry for approval.

She looked at the photos closely. I didn't know what she was
looking for, but I hoped that everything was all right.

"We-ell," (long pause for suspense) "These are not too bad.
You are making some mistakes, but they are not likely to mislead
your readers. This booklet is quite a surprise. Since you're so interested in Iyengar, you'll be glad to hear that he's coming to the
Bay area in about a month to hold a teacher training course."

Iyengar himself? Right here in the Bay area? Could I possibly
attend the course?

"The class was full long ago, and there is already a waiting list.
But I'll see what I can do for you."

By now the other yoga students had arrived, and it was time
to start the class. Felicity took us through the poses in the booklet, and I learned, to my embarrassment, that there was far more
to them than I had assumed. My weight distribution was wrong, or
my foot placement or my spinal stretch. By the time the class was
over, I felt very guilty about having written on yoga with so little
understanding.

"Don't worry," Felicity said. "If you waited until you were absolutely sure of yourself, you would probably never write anything. I know how you feel, though. I have been teaching for five years, and the last time I saw Rishi, he told me that I was only just beginning to get an idea of what the standing poses are all about."

Next week, at the class, Felicity told me that she had secured a place for me in the Iyengar seminar. I couldn't believe my luck. Only a year ago, I had started yoga in a very crude and clumsy way, and now I was going to be getting the attention of the master himself. In the next three weeks, I worked hard on the standing poses, because I knew that he was very particular about them.

Finally, the seminar was on us. The schedule included a dinner in Iyengar's honor on Thursday night. (Someone joked that if we got to know him first, we wouldn't feel so bad when he knocked us around in class.) On Friday, Saturday and Sunday there were to be concentrated sessions of asanas and pranayama. As I realized that I was really in the seminar, I had last minute butterfly feelings in my stomach—was I biting off more than I could chew?

After the dinner, I made the mistake of showing Iyengar the exercise booklet. He barely glanced at it, but it seemed really to provoke him.

"What do you know about yoga?" he asked me angrily. "What right have you to write about it?"

I was unable to defend myself. As a matter of fact, I didn't have the nerve to try. Luckily, someone had set up a slide projector to show pictures of Iyengar and his daughter doing asanas. That diverted his attention somewhat, because he had to answer questions and point out technical features in the asanas. Perhaps he sensed that I was upset by his abrupt criticism. He occasionally remarked on asanas that would be especially good for runners.

"Look at this," he said. "You see, you have to stretch the hinges. All this is in my book...You must learn one thing. It is easy to write, but then you must understand what you have written.

Now here I was in the first asana class, worried that he was really going to let me have it for presuming to write on yoga. He was working his way towards me. Every time he slapped a student I grew more apprehensive.

I heard his footsteps right behind me. He stopped. Thwack! Thwack! Thwack!—right on the back of the neck.

"Sir! Are you asleep? By now you should have learned. What I say for one I say for all. Relax your neck. Relax your

throat. Relax your tongue...Stiff neck, sore brain. How can you
think with a stiff neck? How can you run?"

He slapped me a few more times for good measure, and then
jumped up on the stage. The blows sounded much worse than they
actually were. They didn't really hurt, but they made an unfor-
gettable impression. Now I realize that I have had chronically tight
neck muscles for who knows how long. As I write this, I can feel
that I have to consciously relax that area. Without his cuffs and
slaps (of which I got more than my share in those three days), I
would probably still be unaware of the tightness. As it is, I at least
have a chance to try to work it out. I occasionally catch myself
tightening up, and then I consciously relax. When I run, I find that
relaxing my neck area seems to loosen up my entire body.

Standing on the stage, Iyengar looked up and down the rows
to make sure that none of us had slipped back into old bad habits
of standing.

"They say that bakti yoga is different from hatha yoga. But
look at yourselves now. Notice your awareness. Are you not doing
bakti yoga right now? Are you not showing your devotion by the
way your feet kiss the ground?"

His remark shocked me, because just at that moment it had
occurred to me how marvelously alert I felt, how securely rooted,
how solidly balanced. The soles of my feet seemed alive. I was
glad to be standing there, in spite of my fear of Iyengar.

This was only the beginning. As the class progressed, he showed us again and again how closely related the body and the mind
are. Indeed, he demonstrated that they are inseparable. He showed us the profundity of yoga: he led us to appreciate our bodies
as fantastic instruments of sensitive awareness.

For instance, while teaching us parshvakonasana, he gave a
dramatic demonstration of the "intelligence" of muscles. The forward leg must be bent at an exact right angle, so that the weight
rests precisely on the shin bone. The weight should be transmitted
down to the feet in a line that goes directly through the center of
the bone. If there is the slightest deviation, the muscles have to
make numerous compensations, and work far harder than is really
necessary.

"Watch the mistakes," he said, brushing the hair smooth on
the thigh of the forward leg. He went down into the pose, with
the front foot too close in (bending the knee too much). The hairs
on the top of his thigh stood on end. He smoothed the hairs and

went down into the pose again, this time with the front foot too far forward (not bending the knee enough). Just as before, the hairs stood on end. Finally, he smoothed the hairs and executed the pose correctly. This time the hairs remained smooth.

"Your books tell you that yoga should be gentle and easy," he said. "Those writers do not understand what they have written. This is a strenuous pose, is it not? Yet look how my muscles are at ease. This is the art of laziness in yoga. This is what you must strive for—complete laziness."

That made an especially deep impression on me because I had just read about similar muscular "laziness." Karlfried Durckheim, in *Hara: The Vital Center of Man*, gives this example:

"Kenran Uneji, the archery master, bade his pupils test his arm muscles at the moment when his bow was drawn to its fullest extent—a bow which nobody but himself was able to draw. His muscles were completely relaxed. He laughed and said, 'Only beginners use muscle power—I draw simply with the spirit.'"

Whether you call it "complete laziness" or "working with the spirit," the fact remains that some people have learned how to use their muscles with incredible efficiency. If we could learn how to do it, we could eliminate all "muscular static" (unnecessary disturbance) and our running would approach an effortless "float."

Yoga seems to offer a method for achieving remarkable states of high function, both physical and psychological. Iyengar didn't propagandize about this. His method was subtle demonstration. He never warned us or prepared us for special experiences. He simply led us, all unawares, into an altered state of consciousness, and then called our attention to it *when we were already there*. Had he announced his intentions, we would undoubtedly have tensed up: "That sounds fantastic. I hope I can follow instructions properly, I hope I don't miss this."

At the end of the first session, he had us relax in a certain variation of the plough posture. For 10 mintues, he held us there, directing our attention to muscle effort, skin tension, breathing and other details. Every now and then he would correct someone's posture (no blows this time). I remember noting to myself that I seemed to be in good tune with his voice. Rather than going through my ears to the brain and then to some area of the body, his instructions went straight to the body. It was as if my muscles had ears of their own. Aside from this, which was only mildly intriguing at the time, I wasn't aware of anything special.

"Enough!" shouted Iyengar. "No more. I can't take the responsibility. If you get any more, the men will be leaving their wives and the women will be leaving their husbands—all to practice yoga."

Of course, this was in the spirit of witty exaggeration (he often poked fun at grandiose claims about yoga), but nevertheless, there was some truth to it. It was only then that I realized I had been blessed, for the last few minutes of the relaxation, with a blissfully restful cessation of the background static in my mind.

My mind had been like a deep pool, unruffled by random thoughts and fancies. If I had had the slightest expectation that he was going to lead us into that sort of an experience, I would have been so greedy for it that I would have missed it altogether.

The best way to experience the fragrance of a flower is to be surprised by it, to catch it on the wind as you run by a garden. If you get greedy and try to snort it in like a pig rooting in the ground, you miss it completely.

The same is true of the fragrance of yoga. It is a subtle thing that cannot be taken by force. You cannot go to it with expectations and demands, because you will be trapped in your own tightness and thus unable to receive it.

Considering the dynamic, even violent, way that Iyengar teaches, the idea of fragrance may seem too fragile and ethereal for his yoga. Nevertheless, it is there. His methods are controversial, but they reflect his deep concern with his art and his students. Perhaps he has found that the best way to give students the fragrance is to shock them out of the ego traps of their preconceptions.

The essence of yoga is joy, vitality, courage and spirit. As Iyengar said to us after one of the sessions:

"When I die, I want the coffin to know it carries Iyengar. I want even the wood to feel the joy of my back." At age 56, Iyengar makes the vitality of our outstanding senior runners seem pallid by comparison. There is joy in the soles of his feet, in his eyes, in his whole body. We cannot expect to reach his level, but we can at least hope that the practice of his art will teach the ground to feel the joy of *our* feet.

PERSONAL OBSTACLES

BY RICHARD BORKOWSKI

Borkowski coaches at the Episcopal Academy in Philadelphia.

The next time you're looking for a change of pace in your running program, give this idea a try. It's challenging, different, able to fit your specific needs and is a lot of fun. Half the fun, in fact, is that you design the program. The idea can be very formalized, and used by a track squad, geared for the evening jogging club, or completely individualized for just you. I call it "personalized obstacle-course running."

This can be done anywhere: at the local high school track, the playground, the neighborhood park or any other place where you now run. You can even do it at home—if you have an understanding family.

The basic concept is a combination of the formalized English-born conditioning program called "circuit training" that has grown in popularity for the past decade, and the old obstacle-course idea. While many variations of circuit training have developed since its introduction, its basic objective is still to try and perform a designated number of activities in continually less and less time.

For example, let's say you design a course and run through it in 20 minutes. the next time you run the course, performing the various activities you selected, you try to break your 20 minute mark. When you can knock off a pre-determined amount of time from your original time on subsequent trials, thus achieving your goal, you can readjust the course.

Say your goal was to do the course in 18 minutes. When you reach this target, you can do one of several things: continue to try and lower your time; add an additional obstacle or obstacles; increase the repetitions at each obstacle, or increase the overall distance of the course. By making one more of these adjustments, you establish a new, more challenging obstacle course tailored for your needs and interests.

Let's use the local high school track or playground and lay out our sample course offering a number of "obstacles":

Pick a starting point, start a stopwatch, and start *running (1)*. When you complete a certain distance of your choosing, find a nice soft spot and perform a set of conditioning exercises. Let's say you do *10 jumping jacks (2)*. Keep that watch going. As soon as you complete the last jumping jack, *sprint (3)* a designed distance and perform another exercise. Maybe this time, it is *10 push-ups (4)* for arm strength. Take off again to another landmark, such as a tree or building. Perhaps this time, however, it's a *backward run (5)*. At this place, you might do some *sit-ups or leg-raisers (6)* for abdominal strength. Remember, design a program to work all areas of the body.

If some type of incline is available, like a hill or steps, this would be a good activity at this point. Run the *incline (7)* and move on to the next point. This station, or obastacle might be to *lift a light log or rock (8)* you've previously placed there. Lift it over your head as many times as your level of fitness dictates. Continue on to the next obstacle, in a *hop-straddle fashion (9)*, perform the activity, which might be *squat thrusts (10)*, and end your course with a run to the spot where you started. Check your time.

Remember to record your course, how many repetitions you are doing and the time it takes you to get through it each time. Can you beat yourself?

Some additional obstacle ideas for your consideration could be: (1) carrying a weight from one obstacle to another; (2) running sideways; (3) running in place, with knees high; (4) move from one place to another on your hands and feet; (5) skip rope at a station; (6) perform some isometric exercises; (7) do some neck bridges, usually called "wrestler's bridge"; (8) perform any conditioning exercise of your choice.

You can also use any special terrain features for your personalized course, such as vaulting over fallen branches, climbing over rocks, in and around trees or buildings.

These same principles can be applied to any area. You can develop a course at the shore, in the woods, or on a city street. On rainy days, set a course in your house. Perform an activity in the basement, run upstairs to the den, into the living room, up to the second floor and continue through each room. As said earlier, you'll need an understanding household for this one.

Reviewing the sequence of developing your course:
1. Look over your regular running area and plan your obstacles.
2. Jog through it once to make sure it works.

3. Decide on the number of repetitions you'll do at each obstacle station. Keep the number of repetitions the same whenever possible for each station, for convenience. Most important, start with a limited amount of repititions and work upward from there.

4. Go through the course once and record the time. If, because of area limitations, you feel the course is too short, go through the course two or three times, and record that time.

5. Decide on a time you'd like to aim for in future course runs.

6. Adjust the obstacles, distances and repititions as you achieve your various goals.

11

TRAINING

ROOT OF ALL TRAINING

BY IAN JACKSON

Ian Jackson, editor of Soccer World, takes a special interest in what he calls "natural running" and "natural diet." This article first appeared in the May 1973 issue of Runner's World.

Since the prospect of turning into a middle-aged fat slob revolted me, I decided, many years after my undistinguished track career, that I'd better take up running again. Not knowing any better, I resumed the kind of training that I had been so fruitlessly coached in: hard intervals. I was so thoroughly indoctrinated with the "pain is gain" dogma that hard interval training was the only form of running that I considered real running. The slow dawdlers that I was repeatedly streaking past were doing something entirely different.

If pain were really gain, then I should have gained enormously during that misguided period. I seemed to be in pain all the time. I was in pain while running the intervals; I was in pain for the rest of the day; I was even in pain through the weekends, when I vainly tried to recuperate. The only reason I tolerated all this pain was that the fear of turning into a fat slob was even more painful.

Luckily, when compound injuries, aches and soreness had me seriously weighing which of the two evils was the lesser, I was saved by some sensible guidance. I read a quotation from Arthur Newton, one of the greatest ultra-marathoners of his day. Newton wrote:

"Every man-jack of us, like every other animal, is born with all the speed he is likely to require. It has been built up through all the countless centuries of our evolution. Just consider wild animals, which on the whole are certainly much healthier than the average modern man. They run plenty, but never at any time for all they are worth unless obliged to by absolute fear. Even then it is only being scared stiff that will make them extend to their utmost.

"So if you take this lesson to heart, you will know that sheer racing should be kept within distinctly restricted limits. Set about running, then, to run in an easy and serene manner, knowing that once learned—and even during the learning—you can thoroughly enjoy every bit of the exercise."

When I analyzed my training in Newton's terms, I saw that it consisted entirely of "running for all I was worth," and artificially induced "fear" which came at the end of each recovery jog and always lasted for exactly one lap. There was no doubt in my mind: I was going to make an immediate changeover to this attractive new method.

What a relief! What a change! The easy running became a new pleasure in my life, a wonderful recreation, an eagerly anticipated part of every day. My injuries evaporated, and I soon found myself covering enormous distances in complete comfort. A few months later, I entered a marathon, which I managed to finish in 3:14.

I was hooked. I had found a sport that would keep me in top condition and was enjoyable too. When I found out that the *Marathon Handbook* publishes the name of every marathoner under three hours, I began to entertain myself with the fond dream of taking 14 minutes off my time. Getting my name in a running book, even as a 2:59 marathoner, would mean recognized membership in the distance running fraternity and a symbol of triumph over "fat slob-dom." I didn't think there was any real possibility of my realizing the dream. And yet, after nine more months of easy training, I ran 2:33—a hard effort but comfortable.

Since I knew, from personal experience, the power of "natural training," I was eager to extend my experiment to "natural foods." I knew nothing at all about the subject, so I read everything I could find. The first few books I read seemed to be a lot of faddist nonsense. But soon I came across some well-written, well-documented material, from which I learned that the natural diet, is based on solid physiological foundations.

Once I was assured that natural foods and fasting are both soundly based, I did some experimentation. Although I had great success with fasting, my trial of natural foods was faltering badly until I discovered the Waerland diet. (I described how all this came about in the booklet *The Runner's Diet*.)

It took me several weeks to make the complete transition to the Waerland diet, but the results when I began to feel them were electric. Many months of natural training had produced such a high level of fitness that it seemed unrealistic to expect anything more than marginal improvement. Yet I soon found that my concept of fitness would need to be considerably expanded. I slowly

developed what can best be described as a natural high, a steady
wave of exuberance and vitality that buoyed me up both psychologically and physically.

**"The wave broke—not with an abrupt collapse of a wave on the
shore, but with the slow crumbling erosion of a wave far out at
sea."** (Doug Schwab photo)

I noticed the difference particularly on marathon-distance runs.
When I was on a conventional diet, I would be quite tired when I
finished them—not exhausted by any means, but definitely tired.
After a few weeks on the natural diet, I was finishing the same distance at the same pace with plenty of energy to spare, far more
than could be explained by the training effect alone.

I was functioning at such a high level in all ways that I had to
laugh when I remembered my casual daydreams about breaking
three hours. Now, with a solid 2:33 under my belt, and my recent
surge of energy, I could get serious and work for some worthwhile
goal—like a sub-2:30.

About this time, I learned a little of Hans Selye's stress theories, and I used them to explain my increased energy and to justify
my expectations of further improvement.

Briefly, Dr. Selye believes that every disease is a symptom, in part, at least, of too much stress. If we are burdened beyond our stress tolerance we become ill, or we develop emotional problems, or we run into the physical breakdowns that hard-working athletes are prone to.

I had been free of injuries since switching to natural training. The stress theory explained the additional energy from the new diet in two ways: first, superior nutrition had increased my general stress tolerance; second, the elimination of foods containing unphysiological chemical additives and insecticide residues had decreased my overall stress burden. With these two factors in my favor, I decided that I could take on greater training stress without having to worry about physical breakdown.

When I began this program, I had a period of exhilarating success, and my faith in catering to the body's natural physiologic needs grew even stronger. Everything responded beautifully to the increased mileage and the faster pace. My energies seemed to be part of a mounting wave of organic power.

Unfortunately, the wave broke—not with the abrupt collapse of a wave on the shore, but with the slow crumbling erosion of a wave far out at sea. There's no need for me to go into details about it.

Looking back now, I still find it hard to understand how I let it happen to me. I knew the signs of overstress. Why didn't I ease up when they first appeared? How could I have been so foolish? What is it in ambition that can blind us to the obvious?

I know that I'm not alone in my foolishness. Since going through the traumatic experience, I have become aware of far too many runners making exactly the same kinds of mistakes. I realize now that it does no good merely to know the danger signs of overstress. We must also have the clear vision to recognize them in ourselves. I suspect that this clear vision is only possible if we can maintain a steady sense of proportion about our lives. We must be both well-informed and wise.

I was fortunate. I was made to see what I was doing to myself before I suffered serious damage. I shall be eternally thankful to the great man who brushed the scales from my eyes, because he did so much more than re-order my running. He brought about a profound revolution in my entire way of life. It was not easy for for him. I was blinded by self-congratulation about natural training, and by self-congratulation over combining natural training with natural diet, and by ambition. Yet at one stroke he brushed away all my illusions and set me free from their limitations.

It happened when, on a chance impulse, I read Hans Selye's book, *The Stress of Life*. Suddenly I realized how absurdly superficial my understanding of his ideas had been, and I was ashamed at the way I had trivialized them. My only excuse is that I had no conception of the tremendous significance of his work.

When I first met Selye, he was just an unfamiliar name in Joe Henderson's *LSD* book—a "scientific authority" whose theories were said to support the practice of endurance training. My wide readings in the field of diet had shown me, often in amusing ways, that a "scientific authority" can be dug up to support virtually any belief. For all I knew, Selye could have been a backwater crackpot with no standing whatsoever in medical science. Even later, when I was using his ideas to justify a heavier training load, I had no idea of his stature.

Now I know that he is one of the key figures in the field. Medical authorities routinely class him with such brilliant innovators as Claud Bernard, Louis Pasteur, Paul Ehrlich, Walter Cannon and Sigmund Freud.

I met Selye recently, during a visit he made to the University of California at Berkeley. I was deeply impressed by Selye's personality. You'd never guess that he is 66 years old. He is warm, witty and enthusiastic. Far from being a typically sterile academic, he is one of those rare men who radiates love of life, of his work, and of other people.

During the informal discussion, which focused on the relationship between stress and longevity, Selye showed that he combines the qualities of both the sage and the scientist. He is at the forefront of the search for knowledge, but he also possesses the sage's intuitive wisdom about the practical application of knowledge. It occurred to me that I was basking in the presence of a master, that we were like a small group of disciples, learning the path of enlightenment at the feet of our guru.

I bring up this sage/guru identity not casually, but because it is an important element in the way I see Selye's book. I believe that the intelligent runner will take it as a kind of modern Bible, based not on divine revelation but on the insights of modern science. Selye would probably be shocked by this suggestion, because he obviously has deep respect for scripture and genuine humility about his own work. Nevertheless, he does acknowledge a relationship.

He writes: "In an age so largely governed by intellect as ours, it is gratifying to learn that what religion and philosophies have taught as doctrines to guide our conduct is based on scientifically understandable biologic truths."

The Stress of Life is divided into five parts, the first four of which describe what has been discovered about stress and how it was discovered, and the last a brilliant and inspiring illustration of how we can use these discoveries to guide us.

As Selye points out at the beginning of the last part, "When we finished our laborious analysis of its nature, stress turned out to be something quite simple to understand. It is essentially the *wear and tear* in the body caused by life at any one time." This simple understanding is all that is necessary to follow his suggestions on finding "the natural solution of many problems presented by everyday life."

Selye does not use the expression "natural solution" by chance. The word "natural" occurs throughout the discussion, and unifies it and gives it power. For instance, he talks of "our natural craving for variety in everyday life. We must not forget that the more we vary our actions the less any one part suffers from attrition."

If you find yourself becoming obsessed with running in the self-same destructive way that I did, you might try putting this suggestion into practice. It will help you regain a sense of proportion and you'll probably find yourself training less, enjoying it more, and —in the long run—racing faster. A life dominated by a racing obsession can be highly stressful. A varied and balanced range of activities, based on a holistic view of *all* that life has to offer, is much to be preferred.

Perhaps this will be more meaningful once the relationship between stress and aging is made clear. It's common knowledge that our lives are shortened by the burden of wear and tear we experience every day, but few people have more than a vague idea of how the body's adaptive mechanism handles this problem.

Apparently, each of us inherits a limited amount of adaptation energy from our parents. This adaptation energy, or vitality, is like "a special kind of bank account which you can use up by withdrawals but cannot increase by deposits."

Adaptation energy is stored in two forms: "the superficial kind, which is ready to use; and the deeper kind, which acts as a sort of frozen reserve. When superficial adaptation energy is exhausted through exertion, it can slowly be restored from a deeper store during rest. This gives certain plasticity to our resistance. It also protects us from wasting adaptation energy too lavishly in certain foolish moments, because acute fatigue automatically stops us."

The implications of this idea stopped me cold. I had always thought that rest was a complete restorative, even from the exhaustion of a hard marathon. A week or so of easy recovery jogs and the fatigue and soreness would evaporate. I assumed that the race hadn't really taken anything out of me; rather, that it was wholly beneficial, as an insurance against cardiovascular problems. I didn't like the idea that with every hard race I had lost irreplaceable adaptation energy from my limited reserves. I wanted to go on believing that rest really does restore. But Selye wouldn't let me dodge the issue.

"This is false," he writes. "Experiments on animals have clearly shown that each exposure (to excess stress) leaves an indelible scar, in that it uses up reserves of adaptability which cannot be replaced." He continues, "It is the restoration of superficial adaptation energy from the deep reserves that tricks us into believing that the loss has been made good. Actually, it has only been covered from reserves—and at the cost of depleting reserves. We might compare this feeling of having suffered no loss to the careless optimism of a spendthrift who keeps forgetting that whenever he restores the vanishing supply of dollars in his wallet by withdrawing from the invisible stocks of his bank account, the loss has not really been made good. There was merely a transfer of money from a less accessible to a more accessible form."

Reading this, I saw clearly how Selye's theories were used in support of the practice of natural endurance training. I knew why Tom Osler insisted that, contrary to popular belief, "running can indeed cause physical harm when done to excess and without common sense," and that each runner "must learn not to train when the body is really tired."

Acute exhaustion is the body's warning that its stress tolerance has been exceeded. The symptoms in Osler's list are more subtle, but they too are the body's warning of overstress. We should never forget that we are wasting irreplaceable adaptive reserves whenever we allow ourselves to become really fatigued, and whenever we stubbornly continue with the same training load that produced the less obvious warning signs.

This doesn't mean that we should swear off all hard racing and training, but we should definitely observe common sense and mo-

Olympic 5000-meter medalist Ian Stewart grabs a training run on the streets of London. Regular training is the key to adapting to stress. (Tony Duffy photo)

deration. What moderation will mean for you depends on personal factors entirely. Remember, you are "an experiment of one."

If Selye's book converts you from training with "the careless optimism of a spendthrift" to a more natural form of training and a thriftier attitude, then I'm sure you'll be convinced that reading it was one of the best favors you ever did for yourself. Even if you apply the book only to the question of training methods, it will prove itself well worth your while.

But it would be a pity if you limited yourself to adopting natural training, or even to adopting a combination of natural training and natural diet. Selye has so much more to offer. Like a sage or a guru, he can convert you to *natural living*—to a powerful, exciting vision of the breath-taking richness of experience.

Decades of intense research has convinced him that we can
"enormously lengthen the average human life-span by living in better harmony with natural laws." And he has sound physiological
grounds for believing that this harmonious kind of living must be
for each individual, full of variety and guided by high purpose.

Selye believes that, in the final analysis, "gratitude and revenge
are the most important factors governing our actions in everyday
life." These are two factors, "more than any other," account for
"the absence or presence of stress in human relations." They are
both the rewards of our actions—gratitude for good actions and revenge for bad. Obviously, our lives will be far more harmonious
and far less burdened with needless stress, if we consciously work
for the reward of gratitude rather than revenge.

Selye identifies "fights, frustrations, and insecurities" as
"among the most important stressors..—these three and one more,
perhaps the most vitally important stressor: the sense of aimlessness. Unless we have an ultimate aim in our lives, we will be burdened each and every day, with the stress of meaninglessness. Most
of us search for meaning in our lives, but few of us find it. Most
people "just give up and drift from day to day, trying to divert their
attention from the future by some such sedative as compulsive
promiscuity, frantic work, or simply alcohol." (For my own case,
maybe for yours too, I could add "or by an obsession with some
sport, such as long distance running.")

Selye believes man's ultimate aim should be "to express himself fully, according to his own lights." This formulation should
help to correct a common mistake: the tendency to interpret the
stress theory as an excuse for avoiding stress at all costs, for becoming a kind of hypochondriac about stress.

"The goal is certainly not to avoid stress," says Selye, "Stress
is a part of life. It is a natural by-product of all our activities. There
is no more justification for avoiding stress than for shunning cold,
exercise, or love. But in order to express yourself fully, you must
first find your optimum stress level, and then use your adaptation
energy at a rate and in a direction adjusted to the innate structure
of your mind and body. It is not easy... It takes much practice
and almost constant self-analysis."

I am still a beginner in this path. Yet I have already discovered
the truth of this last remark. I agree; it is not easy. However, I
have found the rewards of the effort to be inconceivably abundant.
I feel as if, after spending all my years wobbling and falling, I have

finally learned to ride the bicycle of life. Now I can devote myself
to perfecting that skill.

I can hear voices of resistance saying, "Tell us what's happened
to your running. We've had more than our fill of philosophy." Well,
my running, too, has become far more rewarding on my terms at
least. I'm sure some will consider my new pattern a simple case of
gutless dropping out.

The primary change is that I have returned to the kind of training (if you can call it "training") that I was enjoying while dreaming casually about breaking three hours in the marathon. I no longer take running seriously. Once again it is my most pleasurable form
of recreation. Once again I have an overabundance of robust energy.

This time, however, I'm not wasting my surplus on the racing
obsession. I'm devoting it to honing my skills on the bicycle of
natural life. I no longer see natural training and natural diet as mere
tools for fast racing. They are components of the health and vitality
I need in order to express myself as fully as possible according to
my own lights.

But don't count me out of racing. Right now I want to assure
complete recuperation from my extended bout of overtraining.
And when I do begin racing again, I'm going to be conservative
about it. I'd like to break 2:30 for the marathon some time. But
I'm dreaming casually about it, the same way I did about breaking
three hours. The seriousness and obsession are gone.

Something tells me, though, that if casual dreaming and casual
running can produce a 2:33, then someday, some race, they'll produce something better. If not, no matter. But if so, especially if
I run a lot faster, then I'll probably be in a dangerous state of temptation again, and I'm going to reread this article and Selye's *The
Stress of Life* to keep a firm hold on my sense of proportion.

GUIDING PRINCIPLES

The training summary here is written for this book.

"You get writers who think that there's some kind of magic formula, and they want to be the first to tell the world how to do it. What's the secret? Yogurt? Vitamins? Maybe. I don't know. But I'll tell you one thing. You don't run 26 miles at five minutes a mile on good looks and a secret recipe."
—Frank Shorter

There aren't any secret recipes for success in running. There are recipes alright. Hundreds of them. But no one has a secret one hidden away to put him measurably ahead of all other runners.

For one thing, runners talk too much to keep secrets for very long. When they get together, they argue about and analyze their training methods the way less active people discuss religion and politics.

Everyone has an opinion on which methods are best. Everyone keeps looking for better ones. This keeps the talk among runners lively.

Runners can't agree on a single recipe because there's nothing to agree upon. As long as certain general routes are followed, there are an almost infinite number of ways to reach the same end. Half the fun in running is in mapping out those ways, watching where they lead, and arguing with runners who come at the same place from a different direction.

Rather than get bogged down here in the details of running it's better that we talk in terms of general guidelines. The details change as quickly as the leaders of the running world. The underlying principles of training have always and will always be the same.

Every system worth its sweat incorporates certain established principles. Knowing them and following them insures a quicker, smoother trip to the end you're seeking.

DEFINING TRAINING
The dictionary defines "train" this way: "1. to cause to grow

as desired; 2. to form by instruction, discipline or drill; 3. to make or become prepared (as by exercise) for a test or skill; 4. to aim or point for an object."

The *Runner's Training Guide* puts the word into a running context: "Training, by definition, is practicing to perfect a skill. It is reaching for something better in the future than what you now have, or at least keeping from slipping below self-imposed minimum standards. In running, the object in training is learning to go farther, faster. Standing in the way are distance and time, effort and pain. Training allows runners small but significant victories over these."

Training is a selective, carefully planned courting of stress. Stress, as Ian Jackson wrote in the preceding section, is the root of all training. It makes or breaks a runner, depending on how it's applied. A runner needs some of it but can't stand too much. The trick to training is finding the right edge between effort and exhaustion, and tiptoeing along it.

THE PRINCIPLES

Training, at first glance, might look confusing. It has a language all its own. It takes complex math to figure out the schedule some runners follow.

But if you look beneath the surface details (the "eyewash," New Zealand coach Arthur Lydiard calls it) to the substance, it's really fairly simple. A child can follow it, perhaps because it is rooted in the unconscious play activities of children. The basic methods have been around as long as people—and animals—have run.

Bill Bowerman, the most successful middle-distance coach in US history, says, "Types of *application* differ, but basic principles don't. They're like the Law of Gravity. People talk about the 'new' method of interval training. Interval training—in crude form—is probably as old as running itself. Continuous, steady running is as old as running, too. All that has changed is our use of these methods."

Forbes Carlile, an Australian who once ran long distances and now coaches swimmers (he was Shane Gould's coach), works as an exercise physiologist. He studies the effects of training. In the 1950s, Dr. Carlile produced a list of 10 principles he said applied to all athletics. The principles here are based on his original set.

1. **Stress**—Ian Jackson's article in this chapter discusses stress in detail, defining it as the "wear and tear" on the body. Stress, in

manageable amounts, provokes a positive training response. But if the load is too heavy, it overloads the adaptive system.

2. **Overload**—This isn't to be confused with "overwork." Forbes Carlile says, "The training load must be severe and must be applied frequently enough and with sufficient intensity to cause the body to adapt maximally to a particular activity." But he cautions, "It is at the same time true that sustained all-out efforts in training or in races should be made only sparingly."

3. **Specificity**—The body adapts to the specific exercise it receives. Therefore, training must closely approximate the activity you're preparing for—in both distance and speed. If you're a sprinter, the bulk of the running must be short sprints. If you're a long distance runner, it must be sustained running.

4. **Regularity**—Almost any runner will stay in good form on even a slight amount of running— if only he trains regularly. Physiologists think runners need to train at least 3-4 days a week to gain and maintain minimum acceptable fitness levels. If they want higher levels, they need to train even more regularly. Condition is lost in a matter of weeks without running.

5. **Progression**—Progress is most rapid and apparent at the beginning of training, and slows as maximum potential is approached. The more one improves, the harder it is to keep improving. If further improvement comes, it often comes in fits and starts—with a "plateau effect." But the ground that has been won is relatively easy to hold.

6. **Diminishing Returns**—The first mile yields the most return. Each one after that gives less. Runners work more and more for less and less. Runner-writer Hal Higdon says, "It doesn't take much to get 90% fitness—only a few miles a day. But it takes progressively more training as you get closer to your ultimate potential—until at the highest levels you're putting in a huge investment for a very small (additional) gain."

7. **Recovery**—Work and rest go together. Forbes Carlile writes, "Recuperation periods are essential both during a single training session and throughout the year. Rest, with consequent physical and mental relaxation, must be carefully blended with doses of exercise. A rhythmical cycle of exercise and recuperation should be established. There is a time for strenuous activity and a time for resting. The rigidity of too definite a program of training may easily drive the athlete to exhaustion."

8. **Seasons**—Sub-maximal training has been equated with putting money in the bank. All-out effort is withdrawing it. A runner can't withdraw indefinitely, but must go back and replenish his reserves during an "off-season." World-ranked athletes have been shown over the past several years to "peak" at the end of their second month of racing, in about the third important race. Few of them race well year-round, or attempt it.

9. **Pacing**—This has short-term and long-term connotations— the pace of individual runs and the pace week to week, month to month, year to year. One principle applies to both: the harder and faster a person goes, the shorter distance he'll be able to go. Fast pace gets you there quickly. Slow pace lets you go longer.

10. **Individualizing**—Dr. Carlile: "Always the most important consideration must be how the individual is responding to training ...Training must be tailored to the individual for best results."

WAYS OF TRAINING
Centuries before man trained for prizes and records, he ran for his life. And only in times of dire emergency did he run for all he was worth. While traveling long distances or hunting, he ran one of two ways: at a steady, easy lope, or with short bursts of speed broken by recovery periods.

These two kinds of running—steady and sporadic—are the ancestors of 1970s training. All of our current training comes from one of these "families." Each of the families has two members— a primitive, childlike one, and a modern, mature one.

The steady-running family includes "slow" and "fast distance."

● **Slow Distance**—This is the "LSD" (long slow distance) popularized recently by Ernst van Aaken, Tom Osler, Joe Henderson and others. It is done at a pace that feels "comfortable," with little or no emphasis on time. Van Aaken, a medical doctor, says true LSD is run at a pulse rate of about 130 beats per minute— certainly no higher than 150.

Proponents say this kind of running keeps them free from injuries because of its low stress, and that it allows them to build a great reservoir of endurance. They maintain that occasional fast races give them all the speed they need.

Critics, however, say that slow distance is "non-specific" for racers—that it doesn't relate closely enough to racing effort and speed to have much value.

● **Fast Distance**—"Long slow distance is better than nothing," says *Track Technique* Editor Fred Wilt," but it's not nearly so good as long *fast* distance." The runs Wilt recommends are obviously faster and harder than LSD. Pulse rates are 150 and higher. Times are generally taken. Sometimes these are called "time-trials."

Fast distance runners are a short step removed from racing. The fitness they give is quite specific to the race, and running them is almost as exciting and straightforward as racing. These are the advantages.

The main disadvantage is the work load involved. This can be very hard work. There is always the possibility of escalating from training to *straining*.

The sporadic-running family, the one that evolved from stop-and-go activity, is split into "fartlek" and "interval training."

● **Fartlek**—The Swedes gave it the name. It means "speed-play." Playing with speed is what it is—going through the entire set of gears from jogging through sprinting. Fartlek is moving out and slowing down as the feelings of the moment move you. It is free-form speed training, done without a schedule or stopwatch.

Users say they like it because it is a change-of-pace in more than the speed sense. It allows them to combine the speed of track running with the freedom of cross-country.

Detractors say the method is too easily abused. It can deteriorate either into a too-easy slow distance or a too-exhausting fast one. A related problem is the lack of specific goals and controls, which make results hard to measure.

● **Intervals**—These are the more formalized version of fartlek, alternating effort with recovery. Intervals are usually (though not always) carefully planned and timed, and are run on the track. Several factors can be juggled: *distance* of the fast run; interval of rest or recovery between fast runs; *repetitions* of the fast run; *time* of the fast runs; your *activity* (walking, jogging, resting) between fast runs. The variables are identified by the code word "dirty."

Interval training offers endless possibilities for combinations (ex-Hungarian coach Mihaly Igloi is said to have 40,000 different interval workouts). No other method allows its degree of control. Properly applied, it's said to produce the fastest results.

Runners who don't like interval training say it is needlessly complicated and sterile—that it has a machine-like quality.

TRAINING COMBINATIONS

Seldom will a runner use one method—slow or fast distance, fartlek or intervals—to the exclusion of all others. The elements are combined depending on his aims in the sport, and his racing and training preferences.

The booklet *Runner's Training Guide* summarizes the practice patterns of 20-30 top-level runners in each event. Several generalizations can be made from the chart on page 306).

● Nearly all athletes combine two or more of the methods. Only the percentages vary.

● As racing distances go up, so does running frequency—from 5.8 days per week for sprinters to 6.9 for marathoners, with long distance runners often training twice a day.

● As racing distances go up, the percentage of speed work drops steadily. Only 100-yard dashmen do a majority of fartlek/intervals.

● Longer distance runners seem to prefer fartlek to interval training.

● Runners in none of the events race more than 8% of their total mileage– which is in line with the recommended limits of Arthur Lydiard, Ernst van Aaken and other authorities.

● Ken Young has observed that a long distance runner needs to train at least one-third of his racing distance per day. The long distance runners in this study easily meet this requirement, with the marathoners averaging half a marathon daily.

Two prominent technical writers, Ken Doherty and Fred Wilt, say that training should be planned according to the oxygen demands of a runner's specialty. A bit of physiology: aerobic means with oxygen; anaerobic means without oxygen. In aerobic metabolism, oxygen needs are filled at the same rate they're required. But in anaerobic activity, there is an oxygen "debt" that must be repaid later.

Running is a combination of aerobic and anaerobic. The percentages depend on the running pace. The chart on pages 304-305 lists the approximate proportions Doherty and Wilt have found to be needed. Training, they imply, should prepare a runner to meet these needs. It should be specific to the event.

The essential elements vary event to event. Races 220 yards/200 meters and less rely on what we'll call "short sprint speed."

SUMMARY OF TRAINING NEEDS

Race Distance	Category	Aerobic Needs	Anaerobic Needs	Training Emphasis
100y/100m	Short sprints	less than 5%	more than 95%	"Short sprint speed" gained through sprint intervals (30 seconds or less, all-out) or high-speed fartlek.
220y/200m	Short sprints	5%	95%	Same as 100, but perhaps adding some sub-maximal pace intervals or fartlek because these races border on the long sprints.
440y/400m	Long sprints	25%	75%	"Long sprint speed" gained through pace intervals (close to racing pace, but at shorter distances) or fartlek and fast distance runs.
880y/800m	Middle distances	50%	50%	"Middle distance endurance" gained through pace intervals, fartlek, or fast distance runs (paces related to one's racing ability).

Mile/1500m	Middle distances	70%	30%	Same as 880/800, but with adjustments for racing distance and pace.
2 miles/3000m	Middle distances	85%	15%	Same as 880/800, but with adjustments for racing distance and pace.
3 miles/5000m	Middle distances	90%	10%	Same as 880/800, but with adjustments for racing distance and pace.
6 miles/10,000m	Middle distances	95%	5%	Similar to the other middle distances, but perhaps adding slow distance runs or endurance intervals because these races border on long distances.
Over 10,000m	Long distances	more than 95%	less than 5%	"Long distance endurance" gained through slow distance runs, fast distance runs, or endurance intervals-fartlek.

SURVEY OF TRAINING PATTERNS

Race	Ave. Time	Days/Week	Miles/Day	Types of Running* (% of each)					Training Site (% of each)		
				S.D.	F.D.	Int.	Flk.	Race	Track	Road	C-Country
100 yards	9.8	5.8	4.8	17%	16%	49%	12%	6%	50%	30%	20%
220 yards	21.9	5.9	5.0	35%	12%	39%	10%	4%	37%	37%	26%
440 yards	48.8	5.9	7.5	40%	12%	35%	9%	4%	44%	33%	23%
880 yards	1:52	6.4	9.0	55%	17%	17%	7%	4%	28%	50%	22%
One mile	4:10	6.8	10.5	55%	19%	15%	6%	6%	22%	52%	26%
Two miles	9:00	6.8	11.0	58%	18%	11%	7%	6%	17%	60%	23%
3 miles	13:50	6.8	12.8	53%	26%	9%	8%	4%	18%	50%	32%
6 miles	29:00	6.9	13.0	59%	21%	10%	4%	6%	18%	63%	19%
9-15 miles	——	6.9	13.0	51%	21%	5%	15%	8%	17%	54%	29%
Marathon	2:26	6.9	13.1	51%	25%	5%	13%	6%	13%	63%	24%

*S.D. = slow distance; F.D. = fast distance; Int. = intervals; Flk. = fartlek.

From 220/200 through 880yards/800 meters, "long sprint speed" is at a premium. Then endurance takes over as the main concern. From half-mile through six-miles/10,000 meters, it is "middle distance endurance;" from there up,"long distance endurance."

Slow distance runs are 95% or more aerobic. Their most obvious benefit is long distance endurance. This running must be long enough to stimulate development in that area.

Fast distance runs work according to the distance being run. If it's less than a half-mile, the effect is on speed. If more than a half, endurance results. Length of these runs should relate rather closely to racing distances.

Fartlek can yield anything from short sprint speed to long distance endurance. Run it according to your needs.

Intervals come in several varieties: (1) sprint (all-out, 30 seconds or less, to develop short sprint speed); (2) pace at or near the pace of the race, for long sprint speed or middle distance endurance); (3) endurance (slower than race pace, for middle or long distance endurance). Pick your type with the race in mind.

THE BEST WAY

If you're still wondering, "What's the best way to train?" the advice of two runners from diverse backgrounds may help. They both say don't train at all.

New Zealander Jack Foster ran a 2:11 marathon after age 40. He runs a lot, of course, but he doesn't consider it "training."

"When I was asked about training and schedules last time," he once said, "I told the guy, 'I don't train. I just went for a run each day.' It has to be a pleasure to go for a run. Otherwise, no dice. This fact that I'm not prepared to let running be anything but one of the pleasures of my life, is the reason I fail by just so much. However, this doesn't bother me. Neither does the prospect of running 2:30 or even 2:50 marathons in the future."

Sid Gendin, a philosophy professor who has an article in this book, writes, "I don't believe in training. Any runner who divides his running into two phases—(a) training; (b) competing—is committing the worst error he can make in this sport. Training implies drudgery undergone for the sake of some alleged greater end. This means that 95% of running won't be fun."

Gendin's First and Last Law of Running is "enjoy it." If you enjoy it, you'll keep doing it. If results are meant to come, they'll come. If not, you'll still have the fun of trying. Who can say your way is less than the best?

BASIC TRAINING

Reprinted from the booklet "Beginning Running."

"How you jog is never as important as that you jog. Performance is what counts. It is always more important than technique."

—Bill Bowerman

How do you start? By taking the first step. The first step is the longest and hardest one. Although this is a glib answer to give you when you're looking for hard facts, it's the best possible answer. Don't think about it any more. Go out now, today, and start putting one foot in front of the other. It's that simple, and that difficult.

We intellectualize too much about running. We complicate it too much, and make it sound like too much of a choice. We talk too much of times, schedules and formulas. When, where and why. Form, diet and injuries. Equipment, facilities and formal structures.

You don't really need so much of this. You don't need to get fancy in what you do, where you do it, and what you do it in. You don't need to be a student of the sport or an expert in physiology.

All you need is to know the general direction you want to go and the general route needed to get there. You already know the first. The second is surprisingly simple. We can outline the basic principles of running training in a couple of minutes (and have in this chapter).

The principles are as universal as they are simple. They apply to Olympians, same as beginners. Seventy-year-old and seven-year-olds are bound by the same physical laws. So are men and women. The only differences are in amount and intensity of application.

After overcoming your inertia, the next big job is getting acquainted with yourself as a runner. Learn to evaluate yourself, your motives and your reactions as you go along. The body and mind give off distinct sets of signs. Knowing how to read and interpret them is a major boost towards fitness.

Be realistic about this. You can't fool yourself for long. Do too little running and you won't get fit. Do too much and you'll break down, one way or another. The body's signs will tell you where the happy medium lies.

Keep goals in line with reality. Remember, you are a beginner. As Kenneth Cooper has said, it has taken you years to get unfit. Don't expect to get fit again in a matter of days. If you're goal-oriented, establish a set of intermediate goals that are well within reach. For instance, start by aiming at one mile—even it it's walking. Then gradually work up to running the whole mile. Then add a bit more. It helps to have goals, and it hurts to have goals—depending on what they are.

Plunge into running—cautiously. Stick with it. Give it a fair test. Promise yourself you'll stay with it for at least a month, no matter what. If you seem to be doing everything right by that time but aren't progressing, and worse yet you can't stand doing it, maybe your body is trying to tell you something. If the overall effect of running seems bad, maybe you'd like bicycling or swimming better.

Start with two aims firmly in mind: (1) to establish basic fitness for running, and (2) to make running a habit.

The first, in most cases, will mean shedding excess weight, toning up inefficient respiratory and circulatory systems, and correcting muscle-tendon weakness. All these things take time and patience.

"The average American," Dr. Kenneth Cooper says, "takes 20 years to get out of condition, and he wants to get back in shape in 20 days. You can't do it. If your heart tolerates it, your legs won't."

It is said, in reference to the second aim, that running is an addiction. Committed runners are healthy addicts, who suffer withdrawal symptoms if they go three days without a running fix. It takes time to get addicted. Running takes hold of you slowly, and appreciation of it only builds in tiny steps. The basic training period is where old habits of physical inertia—of *avoiding* exercise—are shaken off, and where running is made as normal a part of the day as getting up and brushing your teeth.

The advice offered here is the meat of the issue. This is basic methodology—the "how" of running. It is the best available guidance, presented in the simplest possible terms. The idea is to get the beginner fit and hooked in the strongest, fastest and above all safest manner.

Bill Bowerman. Kenneth Cooper. Arthur Lydiard. These three men, not necesasrily in this order, are the Big Three of Running for Fitness. Alone and in combination, they have sparked the "jogging revolution" in the United States and elsewhere.

Bowerman was the track coach at the University of Oregon. He traveled to New Zealand in the early 1960s and met Lydiard, a coach from that country. Bowerman started running himself. He came back to Oregon and spread the word. Now his hometown of Eugene claims it is the "jogging capital of the world" with some 5000 converts.

Lydiard, a onetime international marathoner, translated his highly successful endurance training methods into schedules beginning runners could use. A dynamic speaker (one writer has called him "the Billy Graham of fitness"), Lydiard roams the world talking up his methods.

Dr. Cooper is a scientist. His major contribution has been to put endurance training on a sound scientific footing. He has test results from nearly a million subjects to back up his claims.

All three have written books on the subject. If you want to get deeper into the whys and ways of running, read Bowerman's *Jogging,* Cooper's *Aerobics* and *New Aerobics*, or Lydiard's *Jogging the Lydiard Way* (also *Run For Your Life*, which is about the Lydiard method).

The suggestions here are a synthesis of the successful Bowerman-Cooper-Lydiard plans, which share many basic principles. The vital ones:

● **Cover 10-15 minutes.** According to Cooper, it takes between five and 10 minutes of continuous movement before the "training effect" is activated. It takes this long to get the kinks out and to get the strides and juices flowing. So anything much less than 10 continuous minutes won't contribute much to conditioning. The three experts agree that 10-15 minutes, regularly applied, gives an adequate workout. Start at this level on Day One (unless preliminary tests have indicated that condition is so low you can't walk this length of time comfortably; then remedial work at lower levels is advised). If you prefer, a one-mile workout may be substituted. If so, *do not* time the mile. Time and distance should not be combined at this point, because they stimulate competition.

● **Use the "talk test."** This is Bowerman's term. He says if you can talk while you run, you're okay. If you're gasping, you're going too fast. Oxygen intake should be regular and adequate to meet immediate needs. Slow pace insures a full supply of oxygen. The "talk test" insures a slow pace.

● **Train, don't strain.** This is Lydiard's catch-phrase. It is a valuable one to remember, not only as a beginner but throughout the running career. Running should *not* be exhausting, particularly at this stage. Lydiard says runners should not go beyond the limits of "pleasant tiredness" in their training.

● **Employ "intervals" if necessary.** Start the 10-15 minutes (or one-mile) period with the intention of running as much of it as you can, remembering to keep it aerobic and strainless. Set off at an easy shuffle, little faster than a walk. If breathing becomes labored or pains set in, slow to a walk. Keep walking briskly, until you feel recovered. Then run again. Repeat the process, as necessary, until the time (or distance) runs out. Some beginners will run the whole thing. Some will walk most of it. It doesn't matter either way, so long as you do it. Trust your own body signs and reactions.

Running can be done anywhere. That's the beauty of it. Why stay on the track when you can be out on the beach with the birds? (George Beinhorn)

● **Progress at your own rate.** Each runner has to establish his own starting point, his own standards of progress, and his own criteria of success. But no matter what the specifics are, each person needs to feel he's progressing—whether from walking a full 10-15 minutes to running the whole way, or starting with that and working on up. In running, progress is easily measured. Use time (or distance) and your reaction to it as the best guide.

• **Be regular.** Progress won't come unless you practice the new activity at least every other day. Remember, too, that rest is important—particularly at the beginning when the body is going through drastic changes. Every-other-day running is an application of Bowerman's "hard-easy" principle. He says progress comes quickest when you alterante days of effort with easier days (in this case, rest days). Later there will be other variations of this theme, such as increasing the length of certain runs.

• **Allow time.** The experts say it takes deconditioned individuals from one to four months to get "over the hump," to the point where 10-15 minutes of running at least every other day is taken easily and eagerly.

• **Avoid the "Stopwatch-Schedule Syndrome."** There's a thin line separating useful plans and times from those which are dangerous. Goals are good and necessary, but only if you remain in charge. When you become a slave to them, they start hurting.

SPRINTING TRAINING

BY VERNON GAMBETTA

Gambetta was a graduate student and assistant track coach at Stanford University when he wrote this article. He competes in the decathlon.

This program I'm outlining here reflects the evolution of sprint training over the past 20 years. The trend now leans away from the idea that sprinters are born, not made. Sprinters can be "made" through sound all-around training aimed at developing every aspect of the organism needed in a sprint race. The program is based on intelligent work. The effects of it can be compared to putting together a puzzle. When all the pieces are assembled in the right places, the successful sprinter is the end result.

A word of caution: Each athlete will have to evaluate this program in terms of his or her ability and level of development. It is a guideline, not a dogma. The short sprinter should also keep in mind that this program is biased toward the quarter-miler, and centers on pre-season "foundation" training.

The foundation period is the most important part of the sprinter's training year. This is the period for building a base for the work to be done during the racing season. The broader the base of conditioning, the higher the peak of speed work that can be developed during the season. Hard, intelligent work during this period will prevent injury and lead to a higher level of performance.

The most important requirement during this period is patience. It is important that the sprinter take a gradual approach, constantly keeping in mind that the goal is to run fast times during the season. Attempting too much, too fast, too soon will narrow the conditioning base and create subsequent problems during the season.

The sprinter should plan to work five days a week, a sixth day being optional. Whenever possible, the workouts should be on a hard-easy principle—that is, a hard day followed by an easy one. Two hard days in a row could lead to injuries and detract from the building process.

The foundation phase will encompass the fall and early pre-season conditioning period from October to the end of January. This period would consist of two six-week phases and one four-week phase. Each phase will have a slightly different goal and emphasis.

In setting up the program for the foundation phase, the sprinter should thoroughly evaluate past performances, present level of development, and goals for the coming season. When this is done, the sprinter should concentrate on areas of weakness so as to bring

Olympic champion sprinter Valeriy Borzov (right) with Soviet teammate Yevgeniy Arzhanov. (Steve Sutton photo)

all aspects of performance up to a consistent level of development.

In training for absolute speed, according to German technical expert Toni Nett, the aim should be the improvement of neuro-muscular coordination. Form problems and general breakdown during high speed runs are usually caused by the tiring of the nerves rather than the tiring of the muscles. Neuro-muscular coordination depends on the ability of the central nervous system to cut out all the superfluous breaking of those muscles which are not directly involved in sprinting. To maximize the development of neuro-muscu-

Valeriy Borzov winning his 200-meter race at Munich. (Shearman)

lar coordination, the program progresses from slow to fast, from easy to difficult and from quantity to quality.

Another premise of this program is that the short sprinter should be able to run a respectable 440. The long sprinter should be able to run a respectable 660. This is based on the idea that the sprinter must learn to maintain his speed. This is a test of the development of the quality of speed endurance.

The specific areas the sprinter should develop during the foundation phase are: (a) *speed-endurance*—the ability to maintain a specific speed for a given time or distance; (b) *stamina*—the aerobic endurance base; (c) *technique*—running form and rhythm; (d) *strength*—both general strength (overall developed by standard weight training exercises) and special strength (bounding, hopping over hurdles, stair work and harness running); (e) *flexibility*—increasing the range of movement in the joints, especially hip, shoulder and ankle joints; (f) *speed*, and (g) *relaxation.*

Each workout should include some of the above components, blended in a compatible manner. It would not be desirable to work both speed and stamina on the same day because one would detract from the other. It would be more beneficial to work on speed, flexibility and strength together.

FIRST SIX-WEEK PHASE

The primary purpose of this phase is the development of stam-

A winter's training compressed into a few seconds. (Ed Lacey)

ina, general strength, flexibility, relaxation and technique. Speed-endurance work will also be included.

The stamina work will be aerobic, striving for good cardio-vascular development. Cross-country running of the fartlek type is a good way to achieve this. Other workouts emphasizing stamina are long (330-880 yards) repeats with short recoveries and steady-paced half-hour runs, preferably on grass.

Hill work emphasizes speed-endurance. The workout might begin with four long hills 250-300 yards long with a good recovery. Then the runner might go to the flat and run three or four 150s or 220s. He might finish by doing 4 x 100-yard hills all-out. A good recovery should be taken between hills. Going back to the flat will enable the runner to lengthen out his stride, relax and also work the hamstring muscle group which does not come under as much stress on the hills.

The goal in strength training in this phase is the development of overall body strength with all-around weight exercises. The sprinter can profit by lifting every day, with Monday, Wednesday and Friday devoted to upper-body exercises, and Tuesday and Thursday to leg exercises, for instance. The workout should be short and intense with the emphasis on fast, explosive movement. One of the upper-body days should be heavy, 90% of maximum. Another should be medium, 75-80% max, and the other light, 50% max. One leg workout should be heavy, 90% max and one light, 70% max.

The flexibility program does not vary during the foundation phase, nor does it change during the in-season period. The purpose of the flexibility program is two-fold: (1) to increase the range of motion in the joints and (2) to prevent injury. All exercises should be static, because, according to Herbert A. de Vries, "A muscle that is stretched with a jerky motion responds with a contraction whose amount and rate vary directly with the amount and rate of the movement that causes the stretch." Traditional bouncing exercises tighten the muscle and result in muscle soreness.

Herbert de Vries suggests that an athlete should assume a position which allows the greatest possible muscle length and with as little muscle activity as possible. This will result in the smallest possible stimulation of the stretch reflex. Each exercise should be repeated two or three times with the tension maintained for about 10-12 seconds. Each sprinter should choose about eight stretching exercises that work the key areas which need mobility: hip, hamstrings, lower back, ankles and shoulders.

Most coaches include relaxation under running form. I believe it is more than this. It is a mental state that must be constantly worked on by the sprinter. Fred Wilt writes, "Relaxation is achieved by losing one's self-awareness, especially of the negative aspects of effort and fatigue. This may happen best and most completely by accepting them for what they are, without doubt or fear."

The sprinter should constantly strive to achieve this mental state, whether he is running fast or slow. A mental picture of what he wishes to look like would help to achieve it.

SECOND SIX-WEEK PHASE

The primary areas of emphasis in this phase are: speed-endurance, special strength, flexibility, relaxation, technique and stamina.

One workout is devoted to speed-endurance work on the track. For the short sprinter, the workout might be a 440-330-220 breakdown workout. For the long sprinter, the breakdown might be a 660 or 550 and 440-330.

Two days are devoted to hill work. In addition to uphill repeats, some downhill running is done. This enables the sprinter to run with increased stride length and frequency, which should help develop new neuro-muscular patterns of speed.

The strength training during this phase changes over to the development of special strength. The special strength exercises are designed to develop the more explosive type of movements specific to the actions used in sprinting. Research done in Russia has shown the value of special strength training. The researchers, Werschosanski and Semjovov, write, "Ability to produce useful power as fast as possible is by far more important than the capacity to develop maximum strength under conditions which have no limiting time factor, because in sprinting there is not sufficient time available to develop maximum strength."

During this phase, weight training exercises are cut down to three days a week. The emphasis is changed so that only exercises on one day are done to develop maximum strength with weight 90% of max. The other day's exercises are done with 40-50% max. These should be fast initial movements to develop explosive strength.

Two days each week, the athlete should work on the special strength exercieses. These might be 60-yard bounds or two-leg hops over low hurdles. These help increase the efficiency of the leg extensors. Another might be hopping up stairs. This develops the efficiency in the flexors and extensors of the ankle. The more experienced sprinter might add a weight vest to increase resistance.

FINAL FOUR-WEEK PHASE

This phase serves as the transition into the racing season. During this phase, the sprinter will continue to work on speed enduraance, special strength, flexibility, relaxation, technique and stamina. Some speed-work will be introduced into this phase.

The main difference between this and the preceding phase is that hill training is reduced to one day per week and a speed workout is added. This might include repeated 60-yard dashes with full recovery, or 110s-150s at 90% effort.

From this point, the sprinter gradually moves into more technique work, more intense speed training and into competition. The success there depends to a great extent on the foundation laid weeks and months earlier.

REFERENCES
1. Bush, J.—"The 440 Dash and Mile Relay at UCLA," in *United States Track Coaches Association Track & Field Quarterly Review*, Vol. 72, No. 4 (Dec. 1972), pp. 227-233.

2. De Vries, Herbert A.—*Physiology of Exercise for Physical Education and Athletics*, Wm. C. Brown Company Publishers, Dubuque, Iowa, 1966.

3. Kruczalak, E.—"Strength Training for Sprinters," in *Modern Athlete and Coach*, Sept. 1967, pp. 30-33.

4. Le Masurier, John,—*Hurdles, Sprints and Relays*, Stanley Paul, London, 1972.

5. Nett, Toni—"Physiological Basis of Training for Running," in *Run, Run, Run*, Track & Field News, Los Altos, Calif., pp. 214-229.

6. Petrovsky, V.—"Training and Guidance of V. Borzov," in *Leichtathletik*, June 13, 1973.

7. Tennov, V.—"How European Sprint Champion Valeriy Borzov Trains," in *Modern Athlete and Coach*, Vol. 8, No. 6 (Nov. 1970), pp. 27-28.

8. Werschosanski, J., and W. Semjonov, "Strength Training for Sprinters," in *Modern Athlete and Coach*, Vol. 11, No. 4, July 1973, pp. 2-6.

9. Wilt, Fred,—*Run, Run, Run*, Track & Field News, Los Altos, Calif., 1964.

10. *How They Train, Vol. III: Sprinting and Hurdling*, Track & Field News, Los Altos, Calif., 9173.

11. *Guide to Sprinting*, World Publications, Mountain View, Calif., 1973.

12. *Runner's Training Guide*, World Publications, Mountain View, Calif., 1973.

DISTANCE TRAINING

BY PAUL SLOVIC

Paul Slovic, a psychologist at the Oregon Research Institute, had his statistical survey published in the October 1973 Runner's World.

On Feb. 24, 1973, 541 runners started the Trail's End marathon at Seaside, Ore. In the preceding 54 days since the first of the year, this group had run more than 100,000 miles in preparation for the event. The runners' training programs were as varied as their backgrounds and abilities. Whereas some had run close to 900 miles during this time, averaging 17 per day, others had done virtually no training.

The casual, unprepared runner is atypical, however. Most marathon runners are quite concerned, if not obsessed with training. Although only a few of them entertain visions of finishing high in the standings, almost all have personal goals: to achieve a certain time, or perhaps just "finish the distance." Training proceeds with these goals in mind.

The amazing thing about this tremendous expenditure of time and effort is that most of it is fashioned without the benefit of sound factual evidence. Intuition and hearsay, mixed with imitation and eventually modified by personal and sometimes painful experience, serve to shape the runner's program.

This study is a first step in the examination of the relationship between a runner's training program and his performance in the marathon. It reports the results of a survey of runners at Seaside, in which their answers to questions about their training were systematically related to their intermediate and final times in the run.

The Trail's End race is a particularly attractive setting for such a study for several reasons: It draws one of the largest fields of participants in the US, and the runners cover the entire range of experience and ability, from national and international class to novice.

The survey questionnaire was enclosed with the packet of materials distributed to each runner on the morning of the race. Questionnaires were returned at the post-race dinner and by mail. Out of 441 finishers, 178 men and six women returned the question-naires. (There were not enough women respondents to warrant ana-lyzing their replies separately, and their results were combined with those of the men. There were only a few returns from non-finishers and these were not analyzed.)

The survey questions provided over two dozen items of infor-mation about each runner. Table One presents some basic descrip-tive statistics on each of these items for the 184 individuals. Includ-ed are the maximum and minimum values in the group, the average value, the median, and the 25th and 75th percentile values (denoted P-25 and P-75).

Each of the 184 respondents was assigned to one of eight cate-gories, according to his final time at Seaside. Table Two presents the average values of the various physical and training measures for runners in each of the time categories. The implications:

● **Ponderal Index:** Runners who finished under 3½ hours were markedly leaner than those who finished after them. Those who fin-ished above 4¾ hours had particularly low values on the ponderal index. The average heights in each of the eight groups were quite similar (three-fourth-inch range from shortest to tallest average), but average weights varied from 137.4 pounds in the 3:01-3:15 cate-gory to 163.8 pounds in the slowest category.

● **Prior Completed Marathons:** The fastest runners had con-siderably more experience in marathoning than did the slower run-ners. Fewer than 20% of those under three hours had not complet-ed a marathon before, whereas over 90% of those in the slowest ac-tegory had no prior completions. (The high average in the 3:31-3:45 category is primarily due to one runner who had completed 24 mar-athons).

● **Miles Run:** As one would expect, the fastest runners logged considerably more miles than the slower runners, regardless of whe-ther the period under consideration was a month, a week, or a single run. The slower runners ran a higher percentage of their total miles in February and had the maximum-mileage week closer to the mara-thon than did the faster runners. Both of these results are indicative of a relatively late start in the training programs of the slow runners.

● **Training Days Per Week:** There is no surprise here. The faster runners, who were covering much more ground in training, were also taking more training days to do it.

● **High School or College Experience:** Eighty-five percent of the runners who finished under 2:45 had experience on a college or high school track team. The percentages are lower for the other groups, and there is no systematic change from one time category to the next as final time increases. About half of the runners over 2:45 had running experiences in high school or college.

● **Fastest Mile:** It's also no surprise that the fastest marathon-runners had the fastest mile times in the past year. Of interest, however, is the generally fast level of times in all categories, and the fact that the average mile times in the two slowest categories were as fast as those in the 3:46-4:00 group.

● **Illness and Injury:** Of particular interest is the finding that the percentage of runners who reported that their training was interrupted by illness or injury did not differ systematically across the time categories.

TABLE 1: DESCRIPTIVE STATISTICS OF ENTIRE SAMPLE

One-hundred eighty-four runners responded—178 men and six women. Only 148 of them reported a fastest mile time. Note that "ponderal index" is height in inches divided by cube root of weight, and is a measure of leanness (higher the value, leaner the individual). All training information, plus injury/illness statistics, apply to the January/February period.

	Minimum	P-25	Median	Average	P-75	Max.
Final Time	2:20	2:57	3:24	3:28	4:03	5:20
Age	13	20	28	30	40	65
Height	4'10"	5'8"	5'10"	5'10"	6'0"	6'4"
Weight (pounds)	74	140	148	149	160	209
Ponderal Index	12.0	12.9	13.1	13.2	14.1	14.5
Years Running	0	2	4	5	7	24
Prior Completed Marathons	0	0	1.2	2.5	3.0	24
Miles Run (January)	0	100	170	181	237	510
Miles Run (February)	9	100	150	160	200	420
Miles Run (Jan. + Feb.)	9	215	328	340	433	890
Miles Run (week prior to race)	0	24	36	37	48	120
Maximum Miles (one week)	9	45	62	63	77	133
Weeks Since Maximum Week	1	2	2.5	2.7	4	7
Longest Training Run	3	14	20	18	21	40
Runs Over 20 Miles	0	0	.9	1.7	2	10
Days Trained Per Week	0	5	6	6	7	7
Fastest Mile (past year)	7:00	5:40	5:07	5:16	4:48	4:12

Illness or Injury	47%	Having a Coach	8%	
Flu	19%	Self-Coached	74%	
Foot or Leg Injury	24%	Coached & Self-Coached	18%	
First Marathon	35%	On H.S. or College Team	56%	

TABLE 2: AVERAGES BY TIME CATEGORY

FINAL TIME (NO. OF RUNNERS)

	2:20-2:45	2:46 3:00	3:01-3:15	3:16-3:30	3:31-3:45	3:46-4:00	4:01-4:30	over 4:30
	(26)	(33)	(16)	(31)	(19)	(26)	(17)	(16)
Ponderal Index	13.4	13.2	13.5	13.2	13.0	13.0	13.1	12.8
Completed Marathons	4.5	4.3	2.5	1.9	3.1	.8	1.2	.4
First Marathon	16%	12%	38%	29%	32%	65%	35%	81%
Miles Run (January)	300	252	175	147	179	122	96	98
Miles Run (February)	240	192	164	144	158	121	103	115
Miles Run (Jan. + Feb.)	540	444	339	290	337	242	199	212
Miles Run (week prior to race)	50	43	40	35	39	31	28	23
Maximum Miles (one week)	92	80	64	57	62	48	42	42
Weeks Since Maximum	3.2	3.4	2.8	2.2	2.9	2.5	2.0	2.2
Longest Training Run	22	22	20	18	19	16	14	13
Runs 20 Miles & Over	3.0	3.2	2.0	1.1	1.7	.5	.4	.2
Days Trained Per Week	6.5	6.2	6.2	5.5	5.5	5.3	4.4	4.8
Fastest Mile: Past Year	4:39	4:56	5:06	5:13	5:31	5:32	5:45	5:52
Illness or Injury	46%	48%	62%	45%	47%	42%	35%	56%

A statistical technique known as "correlational analysis" was used to generate equations to predict final time in the marathon. The best single predictor was the runner's fastest mile time in the past year. The equation was:

$$FT = .69X - 12.8$$

"FT" is final time in minutes and "X" is fastest mile time in seconds. Thus, for a runner whose fastest mile was 300 seconds (5:00), the equation predicts a marathon time of 194.2 minutes (3:14:12). Another implication of this equation is that predicted final time decreases about 6.9 minutes for every 10 seconds' reduction in fastest mile time.

Correlational analysis was also used to develop equations that included more than one variable. These equations predicted more accurately than any equation having just one variable. Table Three presents the equation found to provide the best predictions of final time.

Part A of the table has equations that include fastest mile as a predictor. In addition to fastest mile, previous marathon experience, mileage in the previous eight weeks, longest training runs, runs 20 miles and longer, and maximum-mileage week were all-important predictors.

Since not all marathon runners have a recent mile time, equations in Part B purposely excluded this variable. When fastest mile is excluded, age and ponderal index also come into play as important factors.

Of particular interest is the finding that having completed a marathon is associated with a 14- (equation one) to 19-minute (equations six and eight) reduction in predicted final time, independent of the runner's training and ability. It may be that runners who have previously finished a marathon are motivated to improve their times rather than simply "getting through." Or perhaps the experience gives them confidence that the escalating discomfort can be endured.

The presence of longest run and runs 20 miles and longer in the equations that also included eight weeks' mileage and maximum-

---

TABLE 3: EQUATIONS TO PREDICT MARATHON TIME

Abbreviations include: Mile—fastest mile time (in seconds) within the last year; Prev—previous completed marathon (if yes, multiply by one; if no, zero; do not multiply by total number of completed marathons); 8 Wks—miles run in previous eight weeks; Long—longest run (miles) in the eight weeks; 20+—number of runs 20 miles and more in the eight weeks; Max—most miles in one week during the eight weeks; PI—ponderal index; Age—age in years.

Note in the calculations of Part B that you're working with minus figures. For instance, -20 and -10 = -30, not -10.

Part A. Equations including Fastest Mile as a predictor variable:

1. $FT = .51$ (Mile) $- 14.3$ (Prev) $- .05$ (8 Wks) $- 1.22$ (Long) $+ 94.0$
2. $FT = .51$ (Mile) $- 15.7$ (Prev) $- .05$ (8 Wks) $- 2.86$ (20+) $+ 75.6$
3. $FT = .51$ (Mile) $- 14.9$ (Prev) $- .27$ (Max) $- 1.34$ (Long) $+ 95.0$
4. $FT = .51$ (Mile) $- 16.0$ (Prev) $- .31$ (Max) $- 3.31$ (20+) $+ 80.2$

Part B. Equations not including Fastest Mile as a predictor:

5. $FT = -19.2$ (PI) $- 18.3$ (Prev) $+ .7$ (Age) $- .07$ (8 Wks) $- 1.7$ (Long) $+ 504$
6. $FT = -21.2$ (PI) $- 19.5$ (Prev) $+ .7$ (Age) $- .07$ (8 Wks) $- 3.8$ (20+) $+ 511$
7. $FT = -19.2$ (PI) $- 18.6$ (Prev) $+ .7$ (Age) $- .5$ (Max) $- 1.4$ (Long) $+ 507$
8. $FT = -20.7$ (PI) $- 19.0$ (Prev) $+ .7$ (Age) $- .5$ (Max) $- 3.7$ (20+) $+ 511$

---

mileage week indicates that the more long runs taken, and the greater the length of the longest run, the faster the final time—independent of the total or maximum weekly mileage. In other words, longer runs would be associated with faster times even if total or weekly mileage were held constant.

Using equation one for runners who finished in less than four hours, predicted times and actual times differed by an average of 15.3 minutes. Runners finishing in more than four hours were less predictable. The average error of prediction for them was 32.2 minutes.

The results of this study indicate that equations can be constructed to predict performance in the marathon from knowledge of personal characteristics and training variables. These equations predict moderately well, but there are nevertheless frequent and large deviations from predicted and actual performances.

Generalizations from these results should be made with caution, for several reasons. First, the results may be specific to the particular sample of respondents to this survey, who tend to be older and faster than the non-respondents. Also, non-finishers were not included in the results. And the results may be somewhat specific to the particular marathon course, and the weather on race day and during the preceding two months.

One way to test the general application of the present results would be to repeat the survey on another group of marathon runners. This should be done. If it is, questions about mood or feelings during and after the race, and about diet would make an interesting addition to the survey.

Author's Note: *I am indebted to Ralph Davis, director of the Trail's End marathon, for his assistance in the collection of data for this study. Thanks also to the runners who took the time and trouble to complete the survey questionnaire.*

TRAINING TOO MUCH

BY DR. GEORGE SHEEHAN

Dr. Sheehan's contention is that most running ailments are the result of "overuse," which simply means working too hard. Here, he tells how to avoid it.

The main worry of the competitive runner is not injury but overtraining. The runner knows the race is as easily lost by training too much as by doing too little, by trying too hard rather than not enough, and by going too far with the Nietzschean wager, "What doesn't destroy me, makes me strong."

The Italians, who have made a science of observing this destructive phenomenon in their beloved bicyclists, call it "sur-man-age." We call it staleness or overtraining or peaking too soon. The causes are many and vary for each athlete, but Nietzche's dictum still holds. A stress is applied and the body reacts. If it adapts, the body is stronger. If it fails to adapt, it is destroyed. To prevent such catastrophies, the process must be caught in the early stages, at which time a cure is still possible.

Unfortunately, the early symptoms are quite vague: lack of enthusiasm, decrease in interest, tiredness and irritability are complaints all too common for most of us from time to time. The runner may also notice a shortened attention span, difficulty in studying, trouble with staying asleep at night, a drop in grades. And during this time, he becomes more liable to develop allergies as well as colds and strep throats and mononucleosis. There is an increased susceptibility to inflammation and infection.

All this may alert the runner that something is amiss. But the first definite sign of staleness he may recognize is a poor performance. If so, it is already too late to do much. The runner will now have to spend weeks and even months getting back to the peak he has just passed.

The best treatment, therefore, is prevention, and the absolute essential for prevention is what horse trainers call (1) *"bottom,"*

Heavy-training Briton Dave Bedford. (Ed Lacey photo)

8-10 weeks of endurance work. And along with that the runner
needs *adequate rest.* This means (2) eight hours' sleep in early
training and nine when the training gets tough. It also means (3)
a nap before the afternoon workout.

Next, the runner enters the dangerous six-week period of
high intensity interval training that will bring him to his maximum
capabilities. These sessions increase his body's ability to use high
energy phosphates and handle lactic acid. They build up his anaerobic capacity which so often is the decisive factor in dividing winners from losers.

He must, however, keep this work within his personal limits.
And no coach can tell the runner his appropriate pace as precisely
as his own body can. (4) *Speed workouts therefore must be individualized.*

But even an experienced runner finds listening to his body can
be deceptive, he needs (5) *more scientific ways of monitoring his
progress* toward this treacherous zenith on his performance charts.
And our Italian friends have provided one.

When you first awaken in the morning, lie quietly in bed for
five minutes, then take your pulse. Rise, go to the bathroom, and
then weigh yourself. Record both pulse and weight. Following
training, shower, weigh and then lie down for 15 minutes (do not
sleep), then check pulse. Again record both pulse and weight.
These figures will show if you are training too little, too much, or
just enough. If your morning pulse is highter than the previous
morning you are not completely rested from the previous day and
should either not train or train lightly. If your weight is also falling,
you are overtraining. Your afternoon pulse and weight should get
closer and closer to the morning figures as you get nearer and nearer to your peak.

Now the runner is finally ready for (6) *his tapering period, 7-10
days* of decreasing work to husband his strength, both physical
and psychological, for the final assault.

It all sounds so easy. But what about the cross-country runner faced with three three-mile races a week almost as soon as he
gets his uniform. Instead of a diet of pure endurance runs, he has
these tri-weekly high intensity equivalents of six interval halves at
2:30-2:35 with no rest in between. And if somehow he escapes
peaking prematurely under this program (and the interval halves his
coach adds on), he is faced with six championship races in a row.
"Sur-manage" is the inevitable result.

12

COMPETITION

RUN WITHOUT "COMPETING"

BY SID GENDIN

Gendin is a philosophy professor at Eastern Michigan University.

It is two decades since my college days and I don't have to race weekly any more. Since then, I have run in about 75 races. My friends ask why I don't compete more often, but the wonder is that I compete as much as I do.

What is competition anyhow, and what is its value? First, competition is the endeavor to gain what someone else is also trying to gain at the same time; it is legalized strife. When someone says that winning isn't important or that he competes only against himself, and when someone else says that he competes only against time, they simply are misusing the term "competition."

They can more accurately express their meaning by saying they are trying to develop their abilities to the fullest. Instead of entering full-fledged competition, they can achieve their sensible goals by getting together with friends and holding their own private time trials. Why travel and pay entry fees? The fees are only used to subsidize someone else's award. But, actually, I doubt that even the successful runner has much to gain by organized competition.

As almost everybody knows, Vince Lombardi announced to the world that winning wasn't important—it was all that mattered! Instead of inviting a flood of condemnation, he was worshipped. For the first time in human history, a football coach was proclaimed as a *genius*. Nowadays, as long as one is excellent people don't ask whether the excellence is in something worthwhile or achieved at reasonable cost. Virtue is winning; the game itself is beyond question.

The competitive urge is often justified in terms of alleged side benefits. For example, some people say it prepares youth for the later competitive battles of life. On the other hand, somewhat opposed to this, it is said to develop a sense of fair play and sportsmanship. All this is nonsense, of course—and insulting, too. It is the usual picture of the athlete as a perennial child; the athlete as youngster, not yet ready to take his place in the world, who readies himself by playing games.

This approach just does not address itself to the older athlete.

Moreover, there isn't the slightest shred of evidence that it applies to young athletes, and there is some evidence against it. For example, the ability to endure is highly specific. A man who can suffer the agonies of marathons may be a poor dental patient, unable to tolerate low degrees of pain. The runner who patiently puts in 200 miles per week may not be patient in everyday tasks.

On the other hand, dedicated athletes are used to letting nothing interfere with their daily running. Accordingly, this tendency to let one's immediate wants always have priority is more likely

A family that runs together... The "Hunky Bunch" from Hawaii, Dr. Hunky Chun (center) and his six children. (Doug Schwab)

to become habitual and carry over to the non-athletic sphere than is the ability to withstand marathon agonies.

Then, too, competition is at least as likely to develop hostilities as love for one's opponents. For myself, I have never noticed that athletes are on the whole nicer persons than non-athletes. The unbridled competitive urge spills over itself in trying to get whatever advantage it can. The fierce competitor is not concerned with idealist goals like "developing his potential to its fullest" or the "achievement of excellence" but with winning. Losing sickens him. There is small satisfaction in having done well if another grabs the prize. So people unashamedly state cliches like "Winning is what it is all about" and "The name of the game is winning." The taking of steroids, blood-doping and other desperado moves are looked upon with growing equanimity.

Organized sports thrive on competition and cannot exist without it. Competition motivates interest because people don't care to take part in most things unless there are some who are better and some who are worse   An activity that does not allow for differences of ability is probably very low level work, but that doesn't mean your interest has to be in proving your level is higher than the next guy's. And it certainly doesn't prove that competition is the way to happiness.

Competition, for example, doesn't figure highly in the pursuit of non-material goals. And I rather think we would all be better off if we could reduce the ratio of our material wants to our non-material wants. Given that we can't eliminate material desires, we can at least try to keep under control the extent to which we sacrifice other things in their pursuit. Hence, we ought to restrict the *intensity* of our competitive urge. Maniacal dedication takes the joy out of running.

The most successful athletes have found success less and less worth it as they have had to put in more and more to attain it. So they are deserting to the professional ranks. They leave amateurism with the sense that some awful period of their lives has ended. We hear complaints like, "I've paid my dues," (Rod Milburn) or, "I'm through with all that hypocrisy" (Bob Seagren). Professionalism may be fine, but what is not so fine is the mounting feeling that running can't be worth doing unless one is paid for it. And as runners feel the need to escalate training so, too, will the feeling grow that amateur running isn't worth it.

Competition is not everywhere self-destructive. It may be the best means of attaining a worthwhile aim. But for this to be true, the aim has to be identifiable apart from the competition. In industry, competition is a selective mechanism for sorting people into jobs they are good at and, hopefully, enjoy. In sports, competition is a selective mechanism with no end in view. It separates the good from the bad with no purpose in sight.

The beaten, but fiercely competitive, athlete redoubles his efforts and for this he is congratulated. Here we should take to heart the philosopher Santayana's remark that a fanatic is one who, having forgotten his aims, redoubles his efforts. But as for goals like self-

Some goals are attainable without competition. (Steve Sutton)

satisfaction, the feeling of well-being, and the pleasure of camaraderie, these are all attainable without competition.

In sports, there is no objective measure of achievement. In baseball, one's success is determined by another's defeat. The same is
true of running. There is no objective standard of what is fast and
what is slow. We know these things only by comparison with others.
The competitive runner wants not only to run fast but wants his opponent to run slowly. He has no other way to evaluate his performance. He may not understand that this is what he wants, but he
wants it just the same.

The runner who says, "I don't care if my opponent does well so long as I do," does not grasp the simple fact that if everyone in the world could run a mile in three minutes then three minutes would not be a respectable time. Such a person is not competitive. But the man who fantasizes running a mile in one minute is by that very fact a man who is fantasizing that everyone else is running very slowly.

Competition in sports thrives on the spectator element. Those athletes who appeal to the rhetoric of "the athlete comes first" don't know what they are talking about. The athlete who competes wants to be appreciated. Without that appreciation, he would not have the incentive to compete. Some athletes, however, are very good at self-deception and so they claim they don't give a damn whether crowds come to watch. They are content to compete in a "lonely" sport.

Decathletes who usually compete before "crowds" of 20 people or so are prone to exaggerate the aim of self-satisfaction. But they refuse to admit that the possibility of idolatry, with them as the object, exists in their sport as elsewhere. Who has not heard of Rafer Johnson, Bob Mathias, C. K. Yang, Bill Toomey?

I know no one would be content to be the champion long distance spitter of the world although nobody knew of his prowess. People wish to excel in things other people take seriously. They wish to be noticed. Not every competitive athletes has illusions of grandeur, but they all seek to carve out a place for themselves in other people's estimations, and they would not be competing were they seeking self-satisfaction only.

The noted anthropologist, Ashley Montagu, has written that it is a mistake to enter a sport in order to win. The reason for this is not hard to figure out. It is a psychological fact that the pain of losing, when you had your heart set on winning, is far more intense and long lasting than the pleasure of winning. Compare the intensity and the after-effects of leaving our finger in a flame for one second with any pleasurable experience of equal duration. Can you think of anything you want to do for one second for which you'd be willing to put your finger into a flame for one second?

Multiply the pain of losing by the number of losers, since there have to be more losers than winners, and you can see that the joy of triumph doesn't compare to the disappointments of defeat. I barely recall any of my basketball triumphs in high school, but the disappointment of losing a city championship game still lingers on as a "highlight" of my athletic career. Montagu's warning seems only the pronouncement of common sense.

So why run in races at all, even if only 75 in almost 20 years? Well, it is one thing for me to recognize intellectually the evils of competition, and quite another thing not to feel the competitive urge. Many a cigarette smoker accepts full well that his is a stupid vice, yet continues it.

Then, too, a steady diet of non-racing gets as monotonous as any other kind of steady diet. But to alleviate the monotony, racing can be done in the form of time trials. Those who claim it isn't possible to run as fast in time trials as in competition are wrong. It doesn't speak well for someone who can only be provoked into running his best by anticipating that others will finish behind him.

THE MEANING OF SPEED

BY BRIAN MITCHELL

Mitchell, a British coach, is the author of "Athletics Through the Looking Glass."

An examination of the speed factor can be made by asking three questions: (1) To what does the word "speed" refer? (2) What relationship is there between the kind of speeds developed in training and racing ability? (3) What arrangement and balance of speed is necessary in training?

Any look at the meaning of "speed" must involve, first, a look at the thing that lies behind the word—trying, as George Orwell put it, to "think things, not words." Speed over what distance? Absolute speed or relative speed? Speed in relation to how much sloth? Speed to what racing end?

Wayne Collett is a picture of controlled speed in the Olympic 400. He finished second to Vince Matthews. (Horst Muller photo)

Picture a man or a woman running once around a track while the watch-hand passes 50 marked sections on the watchface. Such an athlete could be said to be moving at speed (notice the first complication: the woman's speed would be startling, the man's nothing much for Germaine Greer to write home about). Were the athlete to keep on at this pace for another 24 laps and do 10,000 meters in 21 minutes, he would be rounded up by the British Museum of Natural History, and she would be thought to be a cheater.

My point is, lifting and pushing your body at a measured rate over a set distance, grunting and sweating for 400 meters or 400 miles, attracts the label "speed." This lifting and pushing at a measurable rate over a set distance necessarily also implies an infinite number of variations, from strolling to sprinting.

Above 200 meters or so, speed in a race must be *deployed*, spread over a set distance, with very rare use of maximum capacity. Even the world's greatest 400-meter runners get wooden legs if they do the first 200 fractionally too close to their absolute fastest tempo. The race is run in a series of virtually undetectable phases, the speed pulsing, the tap being opened at exactly the right pressure by the athlete who knows himself, so that the contents do not run out before the finish.

This fact about the manipulation of speed must be borne in mind, because the ability to do it in a race is one that is acquired in training. The qualities needed to spread your speed over, say, 800 meters or more, are sought in training. But the speed is *speed*. Bearing in mind that speed is deployed in a race, what proportion of training should be at what speed, and over what distance? What arrangement, or balance, of speed should there be in training, to give an athlete what he needs in a race?

Training demands must be married to racing demands. Imagine a piece of wild polygamy, where 600 training sessions are wedded to one race—a year's work to a single competition. This is the only way to look at training—not at the content of an individual session so much as to the final effect of hundreds of sessions, the composite physical (and mental) outcome of a huge pattern of training.

Unless the runner is a pure sprinter, about 5% of the time should be spent on pure speed, sprinting and short-hill training, to sharpen reflexes, toughen muscles and joints, develop stride, reaching down into the skeletal clothing to get at every fiber.

The rest of a runner's training should be divided among work just above current racing speed (George Young once said, "I rarely run longer than a mile, because I can't go faster than race pace, and I believe that you have to train faster than you race.") and that manageable speed which is called "steady." In general, it is the speed at which an individual is not straining but is setting up some tension in the fibers, effecting chemical changes in the muscles, getting the capillaries open and profitably thumping the whole heart and lung system.

The "racing plus" speed may be 15% of a pattern and the "steady" 80%, though some marathon men have done all of their training at what Derek Clayton called (on his own behalf) "nerve-splitting pace."

So by arranging in training these three speeds, it becomes possible to exert required pressures, to lift and push the body through the whole range and tempo of movement, thereby activating the total mechanism and gradually giving the athlete the kind of efficiency and reserves he needs. The runner who builds his foundations of steady speed, his ground floor of racing speed and his upper floor of absolute speed will be able to open his doors generously in a race and distribute his stored wealth successfully. It is also true that some houses have better attics than others, so that physical preparation is not everything. Artists traditionally live in attics.

THE RACE FOR FIRST

BY BRIAN MITCHELL

Mitchell, a regular contributor to RW publications, wrote this article for the Complete Runner.

"Too many runners are preoccupied with training. A big mileage will give you a slow pulse rate, but you've still got to be able to screw yourself up to run faster than ever, before a race. It doesn't take care of itself."

Brendan Foster

"I wanted to be a winner. It was in my mind to become a winner."

Lyudmila Bragina

Kneeling or standing on the line, waiting for the gun to go, the athlete is a split-second away from an extraordinary situation, one not experienced by many people, clear-cut in its demands and its revelations. Peter Radford, bronze medal sprinter at Rome, said of it that you would never again know so unanswerably that your best was not good enough. Radford did lay down all he had, even if he found that two men had more. Most men and women cannot genuinely pour out every fluid ounce of energy and strength and do not, therefore, know just how good their "best" is. The race frightens them, and they withdraw, however slightly.

The keys to racing-success are: (1) the long-term physical preparation; (2) the deep, acquired familiarity with the race circumstance; (3) the pre-race attitude, and (4) the reaction to the fiercely demanding situation itself.

Whatever else is said, the physical preparation remains the most important part of the athlete's approach to a race. All the will-power in the world will not take a poorly conditioned, sick or old runner to the front of an 800-meter field that is going through in 1:45. All the physical preparation in the world will not take most men through at that pace anyway, but they will at least be producing their "personal best" if they are thoroughly trained. Moreover, knowing that everything possible has been done in training breeds confidence, which in turn is a great provoker of success.

Training that has been meticulous, hard, balanced and specifically directed will, in itself, teach that kind of discipline which is an ingredient of racing. It is not the only ingredient, but the sense of purpose and the self-control which carries an athlete through months of conditioning also holds him or her in good stead when the race is on. It is often clear from the way someone pursues training how he or she will race.

Intelligent preparation, carefully designed to improve a runner's racing ability as well as the level of physical fitness, would also embrace a series of preparatory races, none of them either impossibly beyond his present ability, or so easy as to make no real demand.

You "learn by doing." Peter Snell said, "One learns to push closer to the limits of physiological fatigue." There is plenty of time to learn and plenty of repeated opportunities. They all matter and should be used. Frequency leads to familiarity, which in turn creates the capability. Ron Clarke never went more than three weeks without a race, and Lasse Viren competed 48 times in 1971. Runners who race often do know what racing is all about. In so far as every race is an experiment, those who race a lot will get very near to a solution of the problems inherent in racing. Pekka Vasala goes so far as to say, "The Olympic final is only another race. Even if I don't win, there are more to come."

Not only the nature of the preparation but also the general attitude to racing matters significantly. Vasala's attitude is most healthy. Clarke's belief that the competition matters more than the result is equally sane and should be recommended to all who compete. The Australian said that he probably cared less about defeat than most athletes, and that this attitude was "not inconsistent with my wholehearted effort to win every race." So often we forget that winning is not something that is going to spin the planet right off its axis—forgetting, too, that most of the world is not taking a scrap of notice."

If the athlete fixes his attention upon the competition and relaxes his obsession with the result, he will run more freely. Concentration on the possible result brings in an element of doubt which is a negative force, and competition results are brands which burn the losers while elevating too high the winners. Winning is good, of course. Yet losing was not, until recently, either a crime or a symptom of national degeneracy. It is better to lose while trying to win than to lose having accepted that is what you will do. How often do even the top athletes settle to run in the second group of a middle or long distance race when a few runners have broken away? These athletes are willing to survive the exhaustion of the remaining laps, but will not give the screw another half-turn and thereby give themselves a chance of winning.

The period just before a race is as crucial as any, for then the mind is being "made up." What happens to that second group of runners could well have been settled *before* the race. Marty Liquori said, "An hour before, I concentrate totally on the race." And it

The end of all the work and worry–the 1600-meter relay, final track race of the '72 Olympics. (Mark Shearman photo)

may be that firm, rational, imaginative decisions taken during that hour have their effect during the race. It may also be true that most athletes do not concentrate in that way, do not make up their minds, and do not therefore race successfully.

All of this leads up to the race itself, where there is no total guarantee that the athlete's reaction to the circumstances of competition will be as he or she wants it to be. One thing is observable: that strong competitors are triggered positively by the race. Peter

Snell spoke of his "elation" when the gun went. This is the exact situation long anticipated and now willingly received, a situation that is open-ended and likely to be claimed by the runner who is, in every way, best prepared. Thus, the meticulous craftsman becomes for a while the supreme artist, and takes the opportunity for which he has been waiting. The spectator can only guess at the level of effort required and satisfaction offered here.

FRONT-RUNNER'S ROLE

BY GEOFF FENWICK

Geoff Fenwick of Britain is a frequent contributor to Runner's World.

One of the fascinations of track distance racing is that natural ability has never been an overwhelming factor of success. One cannot become a great sprinter without the gift of natural speed above the ordinary and the same applies, to a lesser degree, to middle distance runners. But beyond 3000 meters, lack of speed can be compensated for by, among other things, stamina.

Emil Zatopeks are made, not born—although, admittedly, they are not made all that often.

It would be an oversimplification to say that speed and stamina are the only factors involved. Clearly the mental approach to running must also be taken into account. The individual's attitude, character, temperament or personality, call it what you wish—in all probability plays some part in running, but to what extent and in what exact way we don't yet know.

Let's suppose we have two runners of equal physical ability who both train exactly the same way. Will their performances be virtually identical? And if not, can we attribute the differences in performance to mental variables? And if we can, is it possible to change an individual's personality in a way which will improve his performance in long distance running? All of this is mere hypothesis at the moment. But that is not to say it will remain so.

Meanwhile, until we know more about personality in relation to running around a track many times, there are plenty of problems of a physical nature to contend with.

There was a time when some of the most enthralling top-class races were between men of great natural ability who trained moderately and those of lesser ability who trained hard and often. The epitome of this type of race was the London meeting of Vladimir Kuts and Chris Chataway over 5000 meters in 1954 in which Chataway never led until the last few strides. Not that this is a judgment of the talented Chataway, for who is to say that sticking behind a

Ron Clarke (right), one of the great front-runners. (M. Shearman)

searing pace and following excruciating bursts of speed is any less courageous than making them? It simply happens that there are some observers who appreciate tactics like these and some who don't.

Those days of contests between highly trained pace-makers and talented sitters are gone for good. Nowadays, everyone in top-class athletics trains hard save possibly African runners in high altitude countries where conditions are exceptional.

Despite this increased training, the same type of contest exists. Now, however, the sitters train harder and for a number of reasons the odds against the pacemaker have increased. The successors to Zatopek and Kuts have been great runners in their own right, but have rarely won gold medals. The last athletes who could remotely claim to be front runners and who won Olympic gold medals at 5000 meters and beyond were Pyotr Bolotnikov and Murray Halberg way back in 1960.

Sports writers and some coaches now claim that the long distance athlete who can't manage a last lap of 54 seconds in 5000-

and 10,000-meter races is never going to make it. They base their claims on the evidence of the 1971 European championships where Juha Vaatainen recorded last laps of 53.2 and 53.9 seconds for these two distances respectively.

Somehow this doesn't seem right. Admittedly the whole marathon is a whole lot longer than the longest track race. Admittedly the competitors are not so bunched together, but the marathon runner who finished with a frenetic sprint is usually thought to have misjudged his race. Even allowing for the excitement encountered in the final stages of an important marathon, most runners in such races usually look pretty tired at the finish.

Is it too naive to apply the same thinking to track distance races? Is an athlete who produces a 54-second last lap really running as well as he can? Or is good running too often sacrificed on the altar of tactics and medals?

One day we may find that the very personality of the sitter prevents him from making the pace. Until then there is plenty of research to do on even-pace running, on racing posture and the way people train. And maybe we would get better races if the field were smaller and we had heats for the 10,000 meters in championship events (as was the case in the '72 Olympics). After all, it's the pace-maker who takes the brunt of running around the stragglers. Maybe we should treat him a little more kindly.

RACING AND PACING

This study first appeared in Racing Techniques, July 1972.

The way you run a race depends on what you want most from it. Competitive runners want one of two things (often both, but usually one more than the other): high placing or fast time.

Simply stated, runners come in one of two types:

- **"Racers"**—whose main goal is to win the man-vs.-man test, or if he can't win it to come as close to winning as he is capable.

- **"Pacers"**—who are most interested in the man-vs.-stopwatch challenge. They want to run faster than they've ever run before, or at least as fast as they're capable under current conditions.

Marty Liquori typifies the "racer." He has said, "You have to hold a gun to my head before I'll go for a fast time." But whether the time is 4:10 or 3:55, Marty usually wins when he races.

John Landy of Australia, the second man to break four minutes, was a "pacer" by nature. Landy said "I'd rather lose a 3:58 mile than win one in 4:10." Landy ran many fast miles, but won few big races.

As we said, though, this is a simplistic view of racing. There are definite types like these. But there are also others: the "tortoises" who plod along at a reliable pace vs. the "hares" who dash out faster but run more erratically; or the "leaders" who compulsively run from the front and must control the pace vs. the "followers" whose style is to wait-and-kick.

However, as competitive stakes go higher, the lines between the different types of racers are blurring. Speed is the reason. Races —all races—are pushing closer to the outer limits of speed, leaving little room for games.

"Tactics can still be used," wrote Arthur Lydiard of New Zealand in his book *Run to the Top*, "but their days are numbered." Lydiard said this in the early 60s, and it's more true with time. He pointed to the 1956 Olympic 1500-meter final, where the entire field was so close together with a half-lap remaining that it could have been covered by a large beach towel. Races like this were rare in the 1960s and appear to be growing rarer.

In today's high-speed racing, with packs of highly-conditioned runners, it's a rare individual who can "steal" a race with tactical bursts—as Vladimir Kuts did so effectively in the 1950s. And it's a rare runner who can spring from the field like a dashman in the last 50 meters to win—as Ron Delany did in the Melbourne Olympic 1500.

Lydiard had a reason for predicting that plotting, jostling, "burn 'em-off" and "sit-and-kick" racing is doomed. When racers are racing at their limit and pacers are pacing at theirs, their "tactics" become very much the same. They are trying to make fullest and most efficient use of energy resources. Whether they're trying to beat another runner or beat the clock, they want to get from Point A to Point B the fastest way possible. And for reasons we'll get to, the best way to do that is to groove in on maximum efficient pace and hold it.

The race against men and against time isn't always—or even frequently—to the swift, but to the smart. Swiftness is important to be sure, but it's wasted if you don't know how to—and how not to—use it.

This may seem to be more a "pacing" than a "racing" article. This is somewhat true. More emphasis is on pacing technique than on racing tactics, but only because the two are becoming more and more alike. The poeple who do the best racing are the ones who do the best pacing, and vice versa.

A number of physiological/psychological/philosophical/practical factors explain this blending of the two types of competitive running.

● **Speed, not distance, is the killer.** High-mileage athletes have no problem going long. They go long every day. But no matter how well prepared they are, they have trouble when they go long *and* fast. The faster the pace, the more it hurts. And the closer one comes to all-out speed, the less room he has for pacing errors.

● **The most efficient pace is even pace.** As the premium is put on faster (i.e., more demanding) racing, there is a leveling of pace and a tendency for each runner to run at his own level. Nearly all the current world recoreds have been set at remarkably even speeds, with only slight variations in the first few and last few yards.

● **The effects of unwise pacing multiply.** A super-fast start isn't "money in the bank." It's a severe drain on limited reserves. Physiologists have estimated that every second faster than level pace in the first half of the race costs a second or two at the end;

A tactical affair—the 5000 final at the Munich Olympics. Lasse Viren came from the back to win. (Mark Shearman photo)

two seconds costs you four or more; three seconds slows you by... Well, they say there's a geometric progression.

• **Pacing problems grow as distance grows.** There's not much

we can say about the sprints—through 440 yards. They're either
all-out all the way, or so close to it that it's unnecessary to analyze
them. But starting with the half-mile, early restraint is increasingly critical. The reason is simple. Running too fast too soon is painful and in longer races you have to endure the pain for a longer
time.

• **"Momentum."** This is something of a physical factor, and
something of a psychological one. Momentum is the feeling of
commitment, progress, and of holding firmly to a pace or place.
It isn't easy to define, except to say when you have it you know it;
you feel power and drive. When you've lost it, you know it too;
you drop out of the race mentally, falling into a resigned "survival
shuffle," if not actually stopping physically.

• **The race is a whole.** This may sound too obvious to mention. But runners still have a hard time remembering this when
they're racing. Too many run the race as if it were fragmented—
as if prizes were given on the basis of how they ranked at the end
of the first quarter, how long they stayed with the leader before
dying, or how fast they sprinted the last hundred yards. Pace and/
or place for the whole distance are all that count.

"Survival of the fittest" is the best way to describe most middle and long distance racers. The classic pattern runs as follows.

Say it's a mile. At the end of the first quarter, all 15 runners
are bunched within a few yards. At the half, five have dropped off
and are slipping back. At three-quarters, five more have fallen
away from the front runners. Three more slip away on the back-
stretch. Now, coming off the final turn, two men are left. The
strongest and fastest of the two wins the race for the tape.

A good race, you might say. Sure it was—for the leaders who
could hack the pace. But what about the other 10 who tried to
stay up and couldn't? They started too fast for their abilities. They
lost "contact"—and probably momentum with it—and ended up
shuffling home slower than if they'd let the leaders get away at the
start.

Dreams of glory are fine, front running is fine—if you have the
ability to carry through on them. In any race, however, only a few
runners are capable of handling front-running pace. The majority
will be hurt by it. The beginner gets hurt most by his dreams and
his impatience.

Arthur Lydiard advises: "(The novice) should firmly resist

the temptation to try to go with the local champion for the first half-mile. Let him go. The ideal starting pace is the pace he knows he can maintain all the way.

"Only among top athletes who are fighting for championship honors should it be necessary for tactics to enter into it. Between them, fast takeoffs in an attempt to break up the field are expected and warranted, but we take good care to warn our learner not to get tangled up in this sort of cut-throat running. He is the one whose throat will be cut first."

"Contact" is a concept still applied in racing to some degree. The reasoning goes, "You have to go out with the leaders. Once you lose contact with them, you're dead." However, from what Lydiard has said and from what you've read already, "contact" may have cut far more throats than it has saved.

There's no reason whatsoever why only the fastest and fittest runners should survive races and be satisfied with them, and that the slower ones should always be the victims.

Lydiard says that by running intelligently, the slow man may even be able to do a little innocent victimizing of his own. "If he bats along at his best comfortable pace, and finds towards the finish that he has a useful reserve of energy left, by all means uncork it. A flying finish might bring him back within sight of the fast-starting bunch of champions."

This beats the "survival shuffle," anyway.

You never need to lose a race. And you never need to keep anyone else from winning, because everyone can win. The way to win all the time is to concern yourself mostly with yourself. This is the one factor you can control. Let other people worry about themselves. They are uncontrollable as far as you are concerned. Thinking this way, any runner can maximize himself without reducing anyone's else chances to do the same.

Two nice features about running make this possible.

● **It has objective standards.** Times offer a measure of success and a comparison that transcends the immediate competitive setting.

● **Races are personal.** The longer ones particularly are more a struggle with the man inside than the men outside.

Comparative times give every runner meaningful and personal standards. He doesn't have to beat anyone to reach them; only to control himself. No matter how many other runners finish before him, he has won if he has met his own standards.

Using the Principles

Every race is really two races. The parts are about the same size, but they're drastically different in content.

The first half seems easy—too easy. You know you should be saving something for later, but your body is crying "faster." It's hard to hold back.

Then comes the second half, which is a different problem altogether—almost a different race. This is where you begin to hurt. Where did all that speed and energy go? Your body now cries "slower," and you know you should be going faster. It's hard to hold on.

Bad races are the result of a common human failing: running fast when we feel speed in our legs, and slowing when they start to hurt. Good races, on the contrary, are largely the result of ignoring instincts of freshness and pain—holding back when we feel best, and saving energy to spend when we feel worst.

The difference between a good and bad race is the way the last part is run. The first half merely sets the stage; the last half is where the main performance takes place. The strength of the final performance rests on the groundwork that was laid down at the start.

The race and the racer both have to take on split personalities in pacing. The race has two distinct halves, demanding separate responses. Ideally, a racer treats the stage-setting half with coolness, care and restraint of a technician. There's a definite job to do here, within certain time limits, but this is the businesslike part of racing.

Going into the second half, the race shifts in character, and the racer changes roles. Now he's an artist, an actor in full view of others and himself. He has to live on and with the stage that has been set. He has to throw off inhibition and race with all he has left. If the technician has done his job, the artist can run his good race. If not, the mistakes of the first half will spoil the second.

Enough analogies. Let's get down to some hard facts about this concept of split-personality pacing. Pacing starts to become a key consideration at about a half-mile (or 800 meters). As distance gets longer, early restraint becomes more important.

Arthur Lydiard described mile pacing like this: "In my opinion, the best way to get the full benefit of ability in the mile is to go out with the attitude that it is a half-mile race and, as far as you are concerned, the time to start putting on the pressure is when the first half-mile is behind you."

Lydiard wasn't talking so much about a slow start as about a *cautious* one. "The ideal starting pace," he says, "is the pace (the runner) knows he can maintain all the way." At first it will seem easy; later, not so easy.

The New Zealand coach, whose athletes have held world records from 800 through 5000 meters, adds, "The three and six miles are far more exacting than the mile, and the athlete has to exercise more caution. It is far easier to go too fast too soon in the six-mile than in the mile. The average speed of the six-mile is not what you would call 'fast running.' "

And the longer distance man obviously has to have even more self-control. Pacing mistakes that would mean a low finish on the track will be more likely to produce a non-finish on the road.

"Undoubtedly," Lydiard says, "even pace running is the best way to get the best out of yourself." The reasons for this are explained in detail in other parts of this booklet. Here, we're simplifying the even-pace concept into a first-half/second-half comparison.

"Even-pace" means that the times for the two halves are very close to equal. But this doesn't mean that effort is equal. Running this way, there is holding back early and pushing late.

In theory, the closer the two halves are to equality, the more efficient the pacing has been. If you start faster than you finish, you lose considerably more speed in the last half than you gained in the first. However, it's possible, too, to drop so far behind even pace in the early stages that the lost time is impossible to make up.

The "safety range" is apparently about five seconds *per mile* on either side of even pace. For instance, a 9:00 two-miler can run between 4:25 and 4:35 on his first mile and still reach his goal. With anything faster or slower than that, however, he'll have trouble.

These figures haven't just been pulled from the sky. Take a look at the chart of 1972 men's world records. Nearly all of them fall within—or quite close—to this "safety range."

● One man—Kerry O'Brien—in the steeplechase—ran exactly equal splits.

● The majority—13 of 25 records—were run with the second half slower than the first, but well within acceptable tolerances. Six were within a second of being equal.

● Another four times were run with the second half faster than the first, but within the five-seconds-per-mile limit.

● Both Jim Ryun's 1500-meter and mile records were run

with the second half considerably faster than the first: in per-mile terms, 5.4 and 6.7 seconds faster, or slightly outside the theoretical limit.

• Five records had a finish five seconds or more slower (per mile) than the start, though all but one of them was within a second. (The 50-mile was far outside the limit, but complications of pit-stops and heat arise towards the end of such ultra-marathons.)

We of course can second-guess the world record setters and can ask "Would so-and-so have finished even faster if he had started a bit "slower?" or "Would such-and-such have had a better time yet if he had gone out at a stronger pace?" These are fair questions, but the fact remains that almost all of the world records have been run at very nearly even pace.

If this method applies to the fastest and finest conditioned runners in the world, it should apply to the little man, too. Perhaps attention to pacing is even more crucial to the runner with less basic speed, less training background and far less to gain from bold tactical gambles.

Runners in all classes can profit by timing at least the half-way split of races, and analyzing pace. Find the five-seconds-per-mile tolerances by using this simple formula:

Slow half minus fast half; divide the difference by the distance of the race (in miles).

For example, if a runner goes 2:20 for the second half of a mile, and 2:10 for the first, he has slowed down by 10 seconds. The slowdown factor of 10 seconds is quite high. Next time, for the sake of more economical pacing, he might consider an easier start

This is an oversimplified view. There are other factors to consider when analyzing and planning races, such as responses to competition, terrain and weather changes, and sudden changes in condition. Statistics can't account for everything, nor would we want them to. Every race has a personality of its own—a *split* personality. And the racer needs some schizoid characteristics of his own to cope.

Plan the first half, then let the second half happen. Run slower when you feel like going fast, and faster when you feel like slowing. Run the first half with the caution of a scientist, and the last half with the creative abandon of an artist.

Page 354: Neil Cusack after winning the 1974 Boston marathon. (Jeff Johnson photo)

13

TEAMWORK

RUNNING'S TEAM SPIRIT

The series was published in the December 1973 Runner's World. Arnd Kruger's article first appeared in the West German magazine Leichtathletik, and was translated by George Beinhorn.

The balanced pscyhic diet for a runner has at least two—better yet three—courses.

An article in *Guide to Distance Running* looking into the relevance of running says, "running's real values are its aloneness and togetherness," and goes on to explain that this isn't as contradictory as it sounds.

A runner wants to feel apart from the mass, to be a distinct individual. But without the opportunity to share this feeling with like-minded individuals, the personal experience is meaningless. Running offers some of both—being alone and getting together.

George Sheehan sees a further splitting. The doctor thinks a well-rounded running program is a blend of three ingredients—two "alones" and one "together":

● **Solo runs**—The chance to think and to see, to open up to the surrounding scene and to the images floating through one's head.

● **Speed runs**—No matter who else or how many others are around, hard runs are alone. The runner turns on speed, turns inside himself and to an extent turns *against* himself. Concentration is totally on running and on ignoring his senses that scream in protest.

● **Social runs**—The chance to talk and to share the results of the other types of runs, and of other essential trivialities.

Dr. Sheehan wrote in the April 1973 *RW*, "For me, no time passes faster than when running with a companion. An hour of conversation on the run is one of the quickest and most satisfying hours ever spent. It is rivaled only by those solitary hours when I've been able to withdraw from the world and be inside myself. Such moments can open doors impervious to force or guile."

Running is an individual sport. That side of it gets most of the attention—and rightly so. But even the most independent of runners sometimes needs someone he can lean on—for praise or sympathy, for advice or simply company. The best support comes from other runners.

"The loneliness of the long distance runner," as Arnd Kruger notes in the article that follows, is as overworked and misunderstood a phrase as exists in the athletic language. Few runners are lonely. They run alone, of course, but mostly because they prefer it that way. When they want to get together with other runners—as they often do—others aren't far away.

"Many factors go into the togetherness we feel," says the "Relevance" article. "Mainly there's an unspoken understanding of how fellow runners feel and think. We have common bonds that don't allow any other runner to really be a stranger..."

Tribal instincts urge the banding together of small groups with common interests and goals. This results in team relationships even in a sport as individual as running. It isn't the same kind of relationship found, say, in football, where individual players submerge themselves totally into the team machine on game day.

In running, runners pull strength from the group so they can race better than they could if they'd gone in alone. But on race day, they must run alone again.

Team scores mean everything in football. In running, they mean very little except to the participant in that place on thay day. Individual times and places are the measure of success and failure.

The worth of a running team can't be reduced to a set of scores. In a sport like this, team scores are less important than team spirit—the spirit which comes of working together and which translates into stronger personal performances for each member of the group.

This is a spirit that needs promoting, whether in informal training groups, closely organized club teams or structured school programs.

Workings of One Group

BY ARND KRUGER

The cliche of the "loneliness of the long distance runner" is too strong in the mind of sociological researchers, and running training groups haven't caught their attention. As far as I know, no serious study has been made of such groups. Yet it has been my ex-

The Florida Track Club's men are in good position to win the
1973 AAU cross-country title. (Penny Crowell photo)

perience that it is precisely these middle and long distance runners
who seek group contact and do their training in small "teams."

The style of training that many runners now do may contribute
to this tendency. The long, steady runs that most athletes include
in their programs for at least part of the year are especially suited to
group effort. With others, this kind of training is more pleasant
psychically and runners cover more miles more comfortably than
they might do alone.

This study centers on the distance runners of ASC Darmstadt,
a successful West German club which has repeatedly won the national forest-running and marathon championships. The success is
largely due to a high number of runners (more than 40). Few clubs
in the country have so many middle and long distance athletes.

These runners train chiefly in groups. Although distance runners are usually characterized as "introverted," most of the athletes
in this club named "group solidarity" as their most important training motivation.

We observed the club members through an entire winter of
training. The runners broke into two distinct groups: (1) the
"Walter Weba Group" (WWG), and (2) the "Six-O'Clock Group"
(6-G).

It is easy to see by the names that one group has a leader respected by all—a fellow runner who holds the group together—while only a common starting time binds the other group.

The group leader determines running direction and pace. This includes the procedure that when individuals run ahead and take the "wrong" direction, they recognize the authority of the leader to the extent that they turn back and follow him. This is the case in the WWG.

In the 6-G, however, the group often splits up on the way since no generally accepted leader is present to give direction and pace in cases of doubt.

Walter Weba is neither the best runner, nor the one with the highest education, nor does he have the best athletic background, nor is he an important social figure in the group. He is the oldest and the most regular trainer. He is also the most strongly group-oriented.

Such is Weba's influence that other exceptionally strong personalities, who were centers of training groups in other clubs, have accepted his leadership, thus insuring the solidarity of the group.

The presence of men like Weba is essential to a group of high-performance athletes such as this one. Another club in Germany attempted to bring together the strongest middle distance runners in its region. The fact that no sovereign group leader emerged led to a situation where training often took the form of competition. Inner regulation was lacking. The same thing has happened at national training camps when groups lacked accepted pace-regulators.

Even though the composition of the WWG varies slightly from day to day, this is its general membership. All are "performance athletes" (as opposed to "health runners"), striving for the best possible competitive results:

Name	Event (time)	Age
WW	marathon (2:30)	45
KW	marathon (2:30)	26
WR	5000m (15:00)	25
FW	10,000m (29:30)	24
WS	Steeple (8:40)	22
OE	Steeple (8:40)	23
CR*	1500m (4:20)	21
AK	1500m (3:40)	28
RF	800m (1:40)	23
TL	5000m (13:40)	28
LP	marathon (2:13)	32

*woman

It is striking that only two pairs compete at the same level in the same event. With KW and WW, this has no effect, since Walter Weba is not measured by his athletic performance in his role as group leader.

The cases of OE and WS, however, had considerable consequences for the group because of performance rivalry. Both had a chance to qualify for the German Olympic team, but most likely it would be one at the expense of the other. (They actually finished fifth and seventh in the trial race, and neither made the team.) During the winter of the study, they provoked each other in training distance and speed, and thus put considerable strain on the group's work. It required decisive efforts by the group leader and other older participants to channel and neutralize the rivalry.

A participating group leader has special significance as a neutralizer of rivalries. In groups without such a leader, there is always the danger of overstressing. Best results come from *cooperation* in these runs rather than from competitive training.

Group members have profound respect for a leader like Weba. Our questionnaire asked, "Who has the greatest influence on the structuring of your training?" The expected answer might be the coach. Yet he was the greatest influence on less than 50% of the club members. Among health runners and young performance athletes, 75% listed the coach as the main helper. But among older and more successful runners, the figure drops to 25%. Here the group leader and the group itself step into the key role.

The Walter Weba Group's training run starts each afternoon at four. The set starting time allows runners to leave the group and re-enter as they please. The group takes a standard "pick-up lap" at the start, coming back to the starting point by 4:30 to collect late-comers.

Weba's group has run this way for nearly 10 years, through varying membership. The group norms are the standard times, route of the pick-up lap and the understanding that there is no further waiting for runners to start.

The group goals are to lay a basis for reaching optimum individual performance level, and to win team championships at the German forest-running, European club cross-country and German marathon races. No one questions these goals.

Strains on the group membership come during periods of specialized training. The long, steady runs of the group don't, for instance, satisfy the needs of the track racers. It is hard for a person who has trained all winter with the group to start running alone or at most with one partner.

Evidence in this study indicates that the group bond among runners is indeed strong, and that the formation of such groups is to be encouraged. Some practical hints based on the Darmstadt groups:

● Little consideration need be given to individual sympathies or antipathies. Only 32% of the Darmstadt runners found their training partners "sympathetic." Members seldom meet outside of athletics, and talk about little else that is not connected with their sport.

● Take care to concentrate runners of similar events or of related performance levels and goals.

● Find a generally accepted group leader. An older participant is especially suited, one who no longer has great individual ambitions but who can inspire younger athletes.

● Coordination between coach (if any) and group leader must be free of rivalry, since otherwise both lose respect and leadership capacity.

● Determine group size. There are an average of seven runners a day in the WWG. The 6-G has six. The Darmstadt runners questioned considered seven the ideal number.

● Outsiders will always have a harder time falling in with a stable group than with one that features continually changing membership.

COACH-ATHLETE TEAM

This article originally appeared in Coaching Distance Runners, September 1971.

Distance runners aren't football players. Or basketball or baseball players either, for that matter. Distance runners, of course, look different, being built on smaller and skinnier lines than team jocks. They also think differently, in the independent, introspective manner that suits their activity. And most of all they play differently, apart rather than together.

When applied to distance runners, the concept of "team" is little more than an abstraction. Uniforms and scores loosely tie the runner to his school or club, but that fact can't change the basic thrust of the sport—lone runner vs. lone runner, and runner vs. himself.

A football player can't play without his team surrounding him. And a football team can't bring order out of chaos without a coach in charge. Runners, though, can run as they please without either a team or a coach. This isn't to say they'll do their *best* running without team support and coaching counsel. But they can run.

The point is, the distance runner—by his nature and the nature of his sport—is different than the team-sport man. He requires a different kind of coaching. Coaching these independent guys can become one heck of a headache if a football set of values is forced into their unwilling heads.

Football's values and running's values conflict. Football demands the surrendering of individuality for the good of a smoothly functioning team unit. A football coach can't have his centers, backs and ends all planning their own plays and executing them on their own. However, the runner *does* run on his own. His maximum individual development is the number one concern, and the coach's main job is to nourish this carefully.

The really meaningful "team" in the individual runner's life is not the group of athletes who wear the same colored shirt (though they offer certain social and motivational boosts). The key team is the one composed of the runner and his coach. This relationship, more than any other, establishes how the runner views his sport, and how far he goes in it.

In their book *Problem Athletes and How to Handle Them,* Drs. Bruce Ogilvie and Thomas Tutko wrote: "The social interaction of the coach and athlete should lead to the enrichment of both their lives. Success should be gained in terms of the athlete's realization of his true potential and the realization of the coach's personal needs for achievement. By the coach's need to achieve, we mean the coach's personal pride in having successfully handled his athletes."

A strong and productive coach-athlete relationship, they suggest, relies on *both* the coach and the athlete understanding realistically the needs and roles of the other. The athlete, for his part, has an understandable desire for both personal success and freedom. The coach desires realistic quantities of achievement through his runners and control of them.

"We tend to reject the blanket assumption of the altruistic concept that 'builder of men' is the role of the physical educator," say Ogilvie and Tutko. "Our view suggests that there must be a wholesome selfish interest on the part of the coach and that he is willing to admit to himself that his ego needs are being satisfied."

If the coach-athlete relationship is going to last and thrive to the satisfaction of both parties, each has to give a little. As with members of any team, they must strike a mutually acceptable balance among selfish interests—a balance based on mutual understanding and trust. At best it's a delicate balance.

The booklet in which this article appeared wasn't intended to tell coaches how to train runners. It is an examination of coaching, and what makes some coaches better at it than others. In other chapters, there are discussions of specific coaches and what makes them so special. Their approaches vary to the extreme, but they share one common trait. A solid faith in themselves and their methods, which is in turn passed on to their runners.

When writing about Arthur Lydiard, the dynamic coach from New Zealand, running observer A. M. La Sorsa commented, "He reveals almost classically the *sine qua non* of nearly all such individuals (or "prime movers,' as they are sometimes called)—an unswerving, unquestioned, indomitable faith in himself and belief that he is right. It is also the secret of their success because this profound faith is transmitted to and acquired by their followers. In biblical terms,

this kind of absolute faith, once incorporated in a person's life, can move mountains.

"In the case of a coach, as long as he and his athletes have this absolute faith in their method of training, the actual method is of little real significance. Hence, the observable: coaches with widely differing approaches to training have all produced champions. Scientifically, we have barely scratched the surface in our understanding of the physiology of conditioning, and witchcraft (or whatever you want to call it) continues to play a very prominent role. The Witchcraft Factor is extremely high with Mr. Lydiard and all those of his genre (e.g., Vince Lombardi), and is the key difference often between average success and greatness."

It should be added here that the coach must also acquire faith in the runner. The hold a coach has over a runner is never more than tentative. And as the runner gains knowledge and experience, the coach's grip can naturally be expected to slip. As it slips, the coach's faith in the runners and what he has taught is tested.

Distance runners are perhaps the most committed, self-motivated individuals found in sport. They have to be to voluntarily cover the distances they do. In coaching, it would be wise to take these personality traits into account. A coach may not be seeing much of his distance runners. Typically, they don't lean heavily on their coaches for counsel. They disappear into the countryside on their daily treks.

Recognizing the basic nature of the coach-distance runner relationship goes a long way towards solving any problems that might come up between the two. Coaches are recognizing it. They're seeing that strong independent streaks in distance men aren't to be feared or resisted, but guided and nurtured instead.

The British Commonwealth coaches are ahead of the Americans in this attitude. Largely this is because the English, Australian and New Zealanders generally aren't paid for their work, and don't have the same "pressure to produce" that hangs over the US school coach. On the other hand, the Commonwealth athletes aren't tied to their coaches as rigidly as many Americans. In Com-

A coach and an athlete who've shared the ups and downs of training for a big race now share the triumph—Steve Prefontaine and Bill Dellinger at the 1973 NCAA cross-country. (Jeff Johnson)

monwealth countries, both athletes and coaches can move about and experiment a bit more freely.

Mick Hamlin, a Briton who lived for more than a year in the US, has written, "Thankfully, a lot of US coaches are catching on, and thankfully a lot of runners are managing to exist without being babied by 'coach.' Thankfully, not so many runners nowadays think that the coach makes the sun rise and set."

Once an athlete learns distance running and accepts the commitment it demands, he no longer has to be driven. Only guided and encouraged. Not every runner needs a mimeographed schedule handed to him every Monday, to be followed to the letter (or number). Every runner—regardless of his stage of development—needs an advisor and a friend to get him past the rough spots. There'll always be a crying need for this kind of coach.

All things considered, this is a healthy, mature view of the sport, wherein coach and athlete view each other less as master and servant and more as teacher and student...or parent and child. The latter attitude is taken by Lionel Pugh, a British subject who now serves as a Canadian national coach. He says, "I believe a coach's role, like a parent's, should be to kick the fledging out of the nest as soon as possible. A coach should never be a crutch."

But Arthur Lydiard suggests that the "driver" type of coach is disappearing from the scene. "The days of the sarcastic type of coach who spurs his pupils on with sneers and jibes, designed to whip him to greater effort, are gone." Lydiard says, "It is the wrong kind of mental stimulus in the modern world. Practical psychology gets the results twice as easily and usually much more effectively. The results are also generally more lasting. From the beginning, when you start getting a boy fit and set him to training assiduously, let him know when you consider he has done well. Give him full credit for what he puts into his work, and he will respond by putting more in. A pat on the back these days works much better than a kick in the pants."

Naturally, every coach must pick up the tools of his occupation. He has to know theory and know how to apply it. But this is the mechanics of coaching. All coaches have free access to these tools. But like running itself, coaching runners depends on how artistically and humanely the coach uses his technical tools.

When Arthur Lydiard is asked about the "secret" of his distance coaching methods, he doesn't immediately launch into talk about 100-mile weeks, hill training and sharpening. He gives other coaches a simple piece of advice:

"Know your job and make sure your athlete *knows* you know it, and you have established a mutual understanding that is worth more than a bookful of high-flown technical theory."

Page 368: The classic race in the United States—Boston. (Johnson)

14

PROMOTION

RACE ORGANIZING

BY RICHARD RAYMOND

Ric Raymond has carried most of the burden of road racing programs in Portland, Ore. His articles appeared originally in Runner's World, August 1973 and November 1973.

Stripped-Down Model

In the New Testament is a verse about wherever two or three Christians are gathered constitutes a potential worship service and church. A similar thing could be said of distance runners. Wherever two or three are gathered constitutes a potential race. This fact makes it very simple to promote road racing. All you have to do is get a minimum of two runners, tell them which way to go, and shoot a starting gun.

With this in mind, let us suppose that you want, for whatever reason, to organize a road race. What should you do?

First, find a suitable course. This is not as difficult as it may seem. You may rest assured that 90% of all runners will not agree with what you think is a suitable course, so just choose something *you* like. At least one person will be happy.

Second, find some other runners. The easiest way to do this is to get hold of a ditto machine and make a race announcement to pass out at other races. If there are no other races you could try mailing your announcements. Good sources of addresses are race directors of big races nearby (e.g., Seaside, Boston).

Third, show up on the appointed day and run the race.

Let us now suppose that you wish to provide more than the basic model road race. You want to give times, places, perhaps even awards, keep people from becoming lost, run in the race yourself, and have some time left in the day to spade the garden. This may sound like an entirely different endeavor, but it is not. What follows is a detailed plan of action and equipment lists that will allow you to handle any race up to about 70 runners.

Assuming you have chosen the course and publicized your race
(at least three weeks in advance), you must measure it. Now, contrary to what some would have you believe, accurate measurement
is not always important. It is only critical when you advertise
your course to be a certain length. If you do that you had better
be *sure* it is that length. What I suggest is not specifying the length,
or specifying it within "confidence limits." For example, "about
six miles," "more than nine miles," "between 1.9 and 3.4 miles,"
and so on. This way people can excuse a bad time by saying the
course if off; you needn't worry.

Now the course is chosen, publicized and measured. Race day
has arrived. Since you have scheduled the race for 9:30 a.m. (or
perhaps 10:00) to avoid the summer heat, and leave your afternoon
free, you and your two officials must arrive at the starting line about
8:30 (or 9:00). Some of the things you should bring with you are
a folding table and chair, one or two stopwatches, a starting gun
or whistle, some athletic field marking compound, a two-pound coffee tin with a plastic cover that has a silver-dollar sized hole near
the edge, four clipboards, with paper, notices of your next race,
some sort of legal release for people to sign, a pack of heavy paper

**Boston marathon organizer John (Jock) Semple (left) with 1968
winner Amby Burfoot. (Jeff Johnson photo)**

tickets about two inches square numbered from one through 75 or 100, and whatever awards you plan to give out.

Upon arrival unfold the table and chair, place the awards on the table to one side, and place one official on the chair with a clipboard. This official will register entrants, collect entry fees (if any), hand out shirt numbers and pins if used (these are really only necessary in short races with very large fields), and direct people to read and sign the release form.

Meanwhile, you have gone off in your car (or bike) with the marking compound and the coffee can to mark the course. By drawing arrows on the street only at corners and points of confusion you can save considerably on marking materials and time. The coffee can and lid with the hole serves to make a very functional dispenser, and with practice you may be able to mark and drive at the same time, thus considerably speeding the process.

When you return to the start you will find a group of worried looking runners milling about. You should find a child of one runner and ask him or her if they would mind helping out. You will never be refused. You then look for an obvious spectator, be it wife, mother, father, whatever, and ask if she or he would mind helping at the finish. You will always be successful at this, although you may have to put it off for one of your officials to do after the race begins.

You now shoot the gun or blow the whistle and announce that the race will start in five minutes. Then give the pack of cards to the child and tell her to give them, in order, to the runners as they finish. Impress upon her how important this is. Then call your second official and the volunteer. Give one of them two watches, the other a clipboard. One will call times at the finish, the other record. The extra watch will be stopped when the winner finishes. Five minutes will now be gone.

Assemble the runners on the line for instruction. You tell them how the course is marked and that at the finish they will receive a small card with their place of finish on it. They must then turn this card in to the person who registered them. Explain that this is the only record of their finish. Then remove your sweats, hand the gun or whistle to the nearest bystander, remind the officials to start their watches, join the group of runners and run the race.

When the last runner finishes, take the list of times to the registration table, where the list of finishers will be. Transfer the times to the finish list, and distribute the awards. Stand around a few minutes to receive the congratulations and thanks of your fellow runners for such a well-organized race. When it seems proper, pick up your equipment and drive home.

Depending on the length of the race, you should be home in time for lunch, and have the rest of the day to work in the garden.

You may be thinking that this is a rather ineffective way to run a race, but it works! My wife and I have run a 14-17 race schedule for three years with fields of from 5-75 runners precisely the way I have described. The whole point is to get people to realize that the biggest races with the fantastic organization and huge fields are not the norm, that by far the majority of races are small, informal and minimally organized.

So, don't complain that your area has no races. There are races to be had wherever there are runners. All you have to do is get the runners together. And race!

Races with the Extras

In 1972 the Island marathon was the ninth largest in the United States. A year before that the Island marathon was just an idea in the minds of a few runners. What was done to bring the idea into reality?

Two outstanding things we learned were that big marathons mean lots of work, and lots of money. The amount of work required can be reduced by good organization. But short of having a rich sponsor, I can see no way to reduce the amount of money required. What you must do is draw enough entrants to pay the bills. We reduced the work load by finding sponsors to do specific jobs. We almost covered our expenses by drawing 400 entrants at $2.00 each.

Our race was scheduled for late November. Our major organizational effort started in mid-August. We had already established the course and the date (this had been done a year earlier to be listed in the *Marathon Handbook*), obtained an AAU sanction, and established the awards and entry fee. Our first act was to list our planning needs:

1. Manpower for promotion, registration, officiating, measurement, refreshments, awards.

2. Facilities for dressing, parking, toilets, awards ceremony.

3. Logistics for road permit, traffic control, runner transportation.

4. Money for everything above.

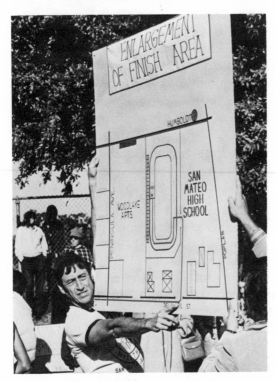

An official points the way in the first AAU national women's marathon—San Mateo, Calif., February 1974. (George Beinhorn)

The three biggest challenges arising from these needs were getting the right sponsors to deal with the needs, avoiding the traffic congestion of the road to maintain good public relations, and getting adequate entrants to defray expenses.

Each of the sponsors for this race was selected for the ability to handle a particular need in a most efficient manner. The sponsors were (a) the Oregon Road Runners Club, an organization with experienced personnel able to lay out and measure the course, and anticipate and describe solutions for problems that might arise; (b) the Portland Junior Chamber of Commerce, a respected organization with young manpower and a "get-it-done" reputation to handle registration details and provide manpower to assist with parking problems; and (c) the Portland Park Bureau, able to provide manpower, equipment and supplies to handle all phases of the seven refreshment stands.

Not only did we ask for something from our sponsors, we also offered them something. We offered an event sure to draw much favorable publicity that each sponsor could capitalize on in its dealings with the community. In order to be able to promise publicity and exposure we had to work at it. This aspect was handled by the race director personally.

In mid-September, a publicity flyer suitable for posting was mailed in multiple copies to group assembly areas. A list of the places might be instructive. It included the Portland YMCAs, running shoe stores in Portland and Eugene, Multnomah Athletic Club, Elks Club, Park Bureau, Jaycees, all high schools and intermediate schools, community colleges and colleges in Oregon and Washington, the County Medical Society, the Oregon Medical School, running clubs in Oregon, Washington and Vancouver, B.C., all members of the ORRC, and all participants on Oct. 1 marathon at Eugene.

Special interest articles were prepared and taken, in person, to the Portland daily papers. The day before the race each daily was provided, in person, with a master registration list so that picture captions and news stories would be accurate and convenient to obtain.

Finally, a pre-registration mailing including a course map, two-page information sheet and two full-page application forms was sent to all the places already mentioned plus all entrants in the 1972 Trail's End marathon. This package also was sent immediately to all who inquired about the race. In all, 1400 packets were distributed.

All the work paid off. We had 400 entrants, two days of full-page spreads in the local dailies, TV coverage on race day, and ended up with a inch-thick file of newspaper clippings.

Our successful publicity created some problems. The large number of entrants required that we have dressing rooms. We were able to rent a school two miles from the course. This necessitated a shuttle bus to transport runners to and from the school since there was no parking area at the course. It also required rental of chemical toilets for the race site to take care of last-minute emergencies.

We made arrangements with the County Sheriff to have several cars on hand to handle traffic and control the runners, and got a permit from the County Public Works Department to use the road. We also felt it necessary to obtain insurance and coverage for the race just in case of an accident. Most of this was necessary only because of the size of the field.

We could have run a race of 20 or 10 runners with no preparation and no one would even have noticed. That is just the point: we wanted to be noticed. We wanted to get people to try running. The Road Runners Club wanted to expand membership. The Jaycees wanted a public service project. We wanted to give distance running a bit higher profile in our area, and we succeeded.

In order to ensure a good race next year, and also to make things a bit easier, we continued our efforts after race day. We want runners to feel eager to run our marathon again so we did some things to promote this. Results—with splits at 10, 15 and 20 miles—were mailed to all registrants. Any finishers who were written about in the papers also received copies of the news clippings.

Results were also sent, with a personal letter of thanks or appreciation, to about 40 individuals who had helped or had an interest in the marathon. These people included coaches, sports editors, broadcasters, school principals, doctors, parks personnel and others. These efforts resulted in offers of assistance and support for our next effort. This groundwork should ensure that future races will be even better than the first one.

COMPUTERIZED SCORING

BY ALAN JONES

Jones is a senior engineer with IBM in Endicott, N.Y.

Anyone who has run cross-country knows how disconcerting it is to sit around after a large meet while the officials try to figure out the team score. Also, unless his coach has been manning the finish line, the runner may not know his time for days—until the official results are printed. Even then, the results may include the times of only the top finishers. It would seem that in this day of rapid data processing, a runner should know his place, time and team position shortly after finishing a race.

To fill this gap, I began working on such a system in 1970 with Bob Osborne, who coaches a local high school team. Bob runs a large meet every fall which consists of three races (varsity, junior varsity and junior high). In the fall of 1973 the New York State High School cross-country championships was held at Binghampton, and the meet director, Ron White, asked us to score it.

Data processing in cross-country scoring is nothing new. The NCAA meet was scored with IBM card equipment in the 1930s. Also, the last few years the NCAA and National AAU meets have been scored by computer (see "Computerized Cross-Country," by Jack Daniels and Jimmy Gilbert, *Runner's World*, Aug. 1973).

We timed our meet in real-time (while the race was happening) as well as scored it. We did this through a computer terminal which is connected via an ordinary phone line to the computer (which may be miles away). The terminal looks like an ordinary typewriter. The difference is that what a person types is transmitted over the phone line to the computer. The computer, if programmed properly, can transmit messages which are typed out automatically by the terminal. The computer we used was on the campus of the State University of New York at Binghampton, while the terminal was in a building only about 200 yards from the finish line.

The computer was programmed to allow easy data entry. Several days before the meet, we typed in the names of all of the entrants, including alternates, their competition numbers and school affiliations. Any entry in the list could be easily altered up to the time of the race.

On the day of the race, we set up two terminals near the finish. A friend of mine, Andy Lavin, was stationed at the finish line with a walkie-talkie. The other end of this communication link was at one terminal, where I was stationed. A similar link was established from the end of the chute to the other terminal, where another friend, Steve Bespalko, was stationed. It was the job of my terminal to record the timing information and Steve's to record the finish order. This actually can be done with one terminal, but the use of two speeded things up since we could be doing both jobs at the same time.

This is the way the timing worked. As the first runner approached the finish line, Andy alerted me over the walkie-talkie. When the winner crossed the line Andy said, "one," and I depressed the carriage return key on the terminal. This signal was passed over the line and recorded by the "time-of-day" clock built into the computer. Also, a finish judge recorded the winner's time in the normal fashion. When the next runner crossed the line, Andy again said, "one," and I again hit the carriage return.

As the race progressed, the runners would be closer together. In fact, they started crossing the line so fast that there wasn't time for Andy to say "one," have me hit the key and be ready for the next "one." In this case, Andy would group the runners as they crossed the line and say, for example, "three" as a group of three crossed. Then I would depress the "three" key and the carriage return. This told the computer that three runners crossed at about the same time. We kept this going up until the last runner crossed the line.

While this was going on, another helper was reading out the competitors' numbers as they emerged from the chute. This list was being recorded on paper and also being sent over the other set of walkie-talkies so that Steve could enter this list of numbers into his terminal. Since there was the chance of error by sending the numbers over the walkie-talkie, we proofread them against the written list sent up from the finish line. As back-up for both the timing information and the finish order information, both Andy and the helper at the finish line recorded what they said on a cassette tape recorder.

After all of this information was stored in the computer memory, we entered the winner's time. Then, since the computer knew all of the finishers' time-of-day finish, the program was able to adjust each time based on the winner's time. The program checked to make sure that a number was not entered twice, that there was an entrant for each number and that the number of finishers was the same as the number of times.

The result sheet was then typed at the terminal onto a stencil. After typing all of the finishers with their place, school and time, the program did the team scoring. To do this, it has to cull out all individual runners and all runners on a team with fewer than five finishers. Also, if a team had more than seven finishers, extra runners were culled. After this culling, the positions of the first five runners were added to obtain the team scores. The teams were sorted using this information and the final team scores printed by the terminal.

We scored three races (classes A, B, and C) at the state meet and three at the sectional meet the week before, using this system. In most cases, we were handing out results within 35 minutes of the time the last runner crossed the line. At the state meet, we recorded exactly the same number of runners crossing the finish line as emerged from the chute in all three races. The only error that caused a problem in scoring was a human one. As I entered the auditorium where the awards were being handed out, Bob Osborne ran up to me and said, "The computer messed up!" It seems that a coach had a boy finish in 22nd spot but the computer listing had another boy in that spot who hadn't run. There was no mention of the fellow who had finished 22nd. After studying the final result sheet, we found the error. The person writing down the finish order had written the competitition number "3" so it looked exactly like a "20." If we had used our tape recording of the finish judge calling out the numbers instead of the written version, this would not have occurred.

The advantage of this system is the rapidity with which the results can be entered into the system and the fact that the computer is aiding in recording a time for each finisher. All of the sorting of entrants into the order of finish is done automatically, thus reducing the chance of human error. Also, it may be a small point, but a system of this sort virtually eliminates misspelled names since the names are typed in ahead of time and can be carefully proofread.

It has always been my opinion that a runner should be able to leave a race with a copy of the results including a time for each finisher and the team scores. Systems such as this allow this to happen with more accuracy and speed than possible before.

To use our system, the meet director would have to have available a computer which runs the APL system and a person who understands the system well. Since APL is being run currently on many campuses, it should not be hard to find such a system. Also, it should be recalled that the computer can be many miles away. All one needs at the race site is a terminal and a phone.

REWARDING CONSISTENCY

BY EDWARD KOZLOFF

Kozloff is an educator, distance runner and running promoter from the Detroit area.

Having participated in, officiated and organized long distance races over the years, I have noted that races generally are dominated by the top runners in a given area. During the years they compete, most of the awards go home with them. While most runners are in the sport for the physiological benefits, the psychological effect of never winning or receiving an award can be discouraging.

One of the motivational devices that the Motor City Striders of Detroit have used to perpetuate interest and add to participation in the program is the designation of a club champion based on the club's total program for the year. Each race contributes points towards the award, and this depends upon three factors: (1) the distance of the race; (2) the total number of runners in the race; (3) the position the runner finished.

By using a relatively simple mathematical formula, accurate scores can be determined for races of various distances with different numbers of contestants. First place receives 10% of the distance run, times the number of finishers in the race.

Formula: *First Place = 10% (distance run) times finishers. Each place after first subtracts 10% of the distance from the place above him. Subsequent Places = Place above points minus 10% (distance run).*

It is more easily understood if you look at the following examples:

- Ten-mile race with 10 finishers. 10% of distance = 1 times 10 finishers = 10. First place receives 10 points. Taking 10% of the distance for each succeeding place would give these results: (1) 10 points; (2) 9 points; (3) 8 points; (4) 7 points, etc.

- 10-mile race with 56 finishers. 10% of distance = 1 times 56 finishers = 56. First place receives 56 points. Taking 10% of the distance for each succeeding place would give these results: (1) 56 points; (2) 55 points; (3) 54 points; (4) 53 points, etc.

Naturally, the 10-mile distance is the easiest figure to work with due to the nature of that number. However, other distances can be as easily computed:

• Six-mile race with 15 finishers. 10% of distance = 0.6 times 15 finishers = 9.0. First place receives 9 points. Taking 10% of the distance for each succeeding place would give these results: (1) 9 points; (2) 9.4 points; (3) 7.8 points; (4) 7.2 points, etc.

• Marathon race with 100 finishers. 10% of distance = 2.6 times 100 finishers = 260. First place receives 260 points. Taking 10% of the distance for each succeeding place would give these results: (1) 260 points; (2) 257.4 points; (3) 254.8 points; (4) 252.2 points, etc.

As you can see, the longer the race and the larger the number of participants, the greater the number of points a high-placing runner can receive. Thus, the scoring system has a built-in regulating device for important races, which usually are the ones that have large fields.

Races at metric distances can be rounded off to the nearest mile. So 5000 meters becomes three miles and 10,000 meters would be six miles. Since all the runner would have the same factor added to their scores, the additional fraction of a mile represents a constant that may be moved without costing any significant points.

At the conclusion of the season, points from all the races are added together and the club can designate the high scorer as its club champion. In addition to the individual winner, other categories may be established. Some of these might include a 17 and under group, 18-29 years of age, 30-39 years of age, 40 and over, highest scoring women, etc.

An added dimension may be provided for any area's running program with the inclusion of this award system. Competitive interest of runners of all abilities is stimulated, and the nature of the program reinforces the basis of our sport which is consistency...in this case consistency of participation.

RACE HANDICAPPING

BY ROBERT WELLCK

Wellck works closely with the long distance running program in the Denver area.

For several years, the Rocky Mountain Road Runners Club (RMRR) has run a program of handicap races of from 2-10 miles as part of the yearly race schedule. Judging by the participation, these races have been quite successful. These races account for 16 of the 22 races put on each year.

In order to be able to handicap runners, one must have some standard which the runners can be compared against; thus, the concept of a handicap "table." (I use quotation marks since we use a fairly simple equation from which tables for any distance can be generated.) Having a handicap table for whatever distance is run, a runner can then determine his or her handicap and use the handicap to predict potential for other distances. Our handicaps take the form of numbers from 15-100 with the lower numbers denoting the faster runners. (The range 15-100 is for purely historical reasons.) As an example, a handicap of 15 corresponds to 9:33 for two miles and 52:35 for 10 miles, and a handicap of 100 corresponds to 17:19 for two miles and 95:24 for 10 miles. This range of times obviously includes runners of quite varied abilities.

Before describing the details of how a RMRR handicap race is organized, let's look at the handicap "tables." One way of presenting this data is in the form of curves where the running rate in minutes per mile is plotted as a function of handicap for three different distances. As one can see on the graph, the rates range from less than five minutes per mile to more than nine minutes per mile. Also shown is the handicap equation. The distance dependence is a simple power law with $2 = 0.06$, and the handicap dependence is quadratic.

Another way of presenting the times predicted by the handicap tables is to give examples for an average runner with a handicap of 55, a faster runner with a handicap of 40 and a slower runner with a handicap of 75. The predicted running times for these runners is given in the table below for distances of two, three, five, seven and 10 miles.

Hcp.	2 mi.	3 mi.	5 mi.	7 mi.	10 mi.
40	11:08	17:08	29:26	42:04	61:24
55	12:23	19:02	32:42	46:43	68:12
75	14:21	27:03	37:54	54:08	79:01

When staging a handicap race, we stagger the runners in time. That is, everyone runs the same distance, but the slowest runner starts first and the fastest runner starts last at what we call the "scratch" position. This time is zero, or when the clock starts, for the slowest runner with a handicap of 100 and is simply the difference between the slowest runner's predicted running time and the faster runners' predicted times. For a two-mile race, our fastest runner with a handicap of 15 would start 7:46 after the clock

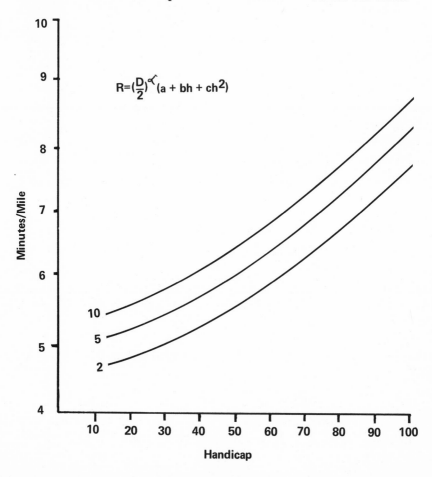

starts (17:19 - 9:33 = 7:46). The handicap race positions are then the actual order in which the runners finish the race.

An obvious question at this point is, does this handicapping work? The answer is, yes, quite well. Theoretically, all runners entered in a handicap race should approach the finish line at the same time. Due to the variation in an individual's performances from day to day, weather conditions and the fact that the handicap tables are not perfect, this does not quite happen. However, one comes close to this goal with 90% of the runners finishing within a few minutes of each other in, say, a five-mile race. Another, perhaps more important, indication that this handicapping system

All classes of runners, all abilities, compete together in Oregon's annual Seaside Beach Run.

works is that everyone seems to enjoy themselves—the fast and slow runners, male and female, and young and old. There is nothing quite like the sight of a runner proudly collecting a first place ribbon for running a 38 minute five-mile race when the fast time that day was 27 minutes.

The actual logistics of staging a handicap race consists first of signing in the runners and assigning numbers to them. Then, using the computer printout of the starting order for this race, the race clock can be started and the runners set off in their correct positions. New runners start with the fastest runner of the day, the "scratch" runner. Following the new runner's initial race, a handicap will be computed based on our handicap tables. This handicap will

then determine when the runner starts in the next race. A returning runner's handicap is adjusted after every race. If you run faster
than your handicap predicted, then your new handicap will reflect
the improvement in your performance. If you run slower than your
predicted handicap then your handicap will be adjusted upward
by averaging your most recent performance with your previous handicap. This averaging is limited to an increase of five in the handicap to discourage "sandbagging," or intentionally running slowly
in one race in order to place high in a later race.

A master card deck is maintained for all runners who currently have a handicap. At the end of 1973, this deck contained handicaps for about 500 runners. The cards contain the runners' name,
birthday, whether or not the runner is a RMRR member, current
handicap and current number of handicap points. Before a race, this
deck along with the length and date of the race is used as input to
a computer program to produce a card deck containing the runner's name, age, club, member designation, handicap, handicap
points, birthday and his handicap starting time.

The program also produces a listing of the runners in the order that they will start the race with their starting times and predicted running times, which is used by the officials to start the
runners. The cards are pulled as runners sign in, the number assigned
to the runner is written on the card, and the runner's name is under-
lined on the starting time listing. The race clock can now be started and the race gotten underway. The officials record the finish time
of each runner along with his number and, using the sign-in cards,
the runner can be identified and his actual running time computed.

After the race, the actual running time of the runner is punched,
onto the sign-in card, and this card along with the race distance is
used as input to a computer program which produces a listing of the
race results including name, age, order of finish, handicap finish
time, actual running time and fast time ranking. The program also
produces new master cards for the runners with an updated handicap and number of handicap points. These cards are then inserted
into the master deck and we are ready for the next race. While this
procedure may sound terribly complicated and time consuming, it
really is not. Each race requires about two hours of keypunching,
card sorting, etc., by the handicapper and a very small amount of
computer time.

We feel that this handicap race series offers a form of competition and a fitness program unlike any other running program. The

runner can compete with himself, with the clock and with every other runner in the race regardless of ability. In this way, a beginning runner can compete successfully against a fine long distance runner.

INDEX